around the global church, makes a start in answering that question. Since the intention of the book is to identify gaps and needs, it is a start that will certainly need ongoing reflection and action, for which we trust Lausanne will provide a catalytic and holistic impetus.

Christopher J. H. Wright, PhD
Global Ambassador, Langham Partnership

It is refreshing to read a book on leadership that focuses on fulfilling the mission God has given the church, rather than primarily on what we learn about leadership from "leadership experts." The book starts with a vibrant retelling, from active players in the Lausanne movement, of the progress of mission leadership and the thinking around mission in the recent past. It then looks at the key issues of developing missional leaders who can meet contemporary challenges with faithfulness to God and his many-faceted call. Throughout this book the passion to be biblical, bold, and faithful is evident. This is a much-needed and different perspective on leadership by those whose lives and ministries testify to their authenticity as God's effective ambassadors for this age.

Ajith Fernando
Teaching Director,
Youth for Christ, Sri Lanka

Dive into a treasure trove of global wisdom with *Leading Well in Times of Disruption*! This invaluable resource brings together astute voices from around the world, offering profound insights on fostering flourishing churches and confronting pivotal challenges in discipleship and leadership on a global canvas. Responsively guiding on resilient and collaborative kingdom-impacting initiatives, this book not only charts a historic course but also offers a prophetic contribution to propel the mission of the church forward. A must-read for disciples and leaders navigating the complexities of our ever-changing world.

Jessy Jaison, PhD
Theological Education Consultant and Regional Training Hub Leader,
United World Mission and Overseas Council, South Asia

Grounded in the rich history of the Lausanne Movement, *Leading Well in Times of Disruption* masterfully weaves together a tapestry of diverse, global voices that speak to the collaboration required to reach the world for Christ. The testimonies are inspiring and the in-depth analysis is convicting. This book is an essential guide for any leader wanting to engage the most critical issues related to fulfilling the Great Commission in the coming decades.

Tom Lin
President/CEO,
InterVarsity Christian Fellowship

The crisis of the church and its global mission is *leadership* – both in terms of the quantity and quality of leaders. Churches, mission organizations, and theological institutions must intentionally and strategically work together to address this crisis. This insightful book serves as a helpful roadmap in developing the kind of leaders needed in times of conflict, chaos, and catastrophes in today's world. It is a must for all aspiring to effectively prepare God's people for gospel witness and transformational impact in their place of service.

Theresa Roco Lua, PhD
General Secretary, Asia Theological Association
Director of Global Theology, World Evangelical Alliance

The nineteenth century is called the century of world missions and brought forth great leaders. In the middle of it, in 1846, evangelical leaders gathered together as World Evangelical Alliance to assure unity around the globe when Jesus is preached. But after two world wars, the momentum was gone. It was the Lausanne Movement rekindling the fire and the vision in 1974 on a large scale, which also finally rekindled the World Evangelical Alliance, made up of churches emerging from evangelism, discipleship, and leadership with a vision. This story has never been told better than in this book, not as a history but in taking the vision forward in the development of leadership for church and mission in the next generation. A must-read for all concerned about leadership in the footsteps of Jesus Christ.

Thomas Paul Schirrmacher, PhD
Secretary General,
World Evangelical Alliance

Obeying the Great Commission, as our humble participation in the whole-Bible breadth of the *missio Dei* for all history and all creation, is a self-replicating summons for all disciples of the risen Lord in the power of the Spirit until the day when God the Father announces his Son's return. For all disciples to be disciple-makers, however, also calls for discipled leaders, leading all God's people in evangelism (baptising), teaching, and comprehensive whole-life obedience to all that Christ commanded. What kind of leaders are needed to equip the saints for every kind of ministry and mission to which God calls us in every sphere of his creation? This extensive collection of thoughtful essays around the four key areas of Lausanne's own vision and mission, and from

Leading Well in Times of Disruption

GLOBAL LIBRARY

Leading Well in Times of Disruption

Leadership Development for Global Mission

Edited by
Joseph W. Handley, Gideon Para-Mallam, and
Asia Williamson

© 2024 Joseph W. Handley, Gideon Para-Mallam, and Asia Williamson

Published 2024 by Langham Global Library
An imprint of Langham Publishing
www.langhampublishing.org

Langham Publishing and its imprints are a ministry of Langham Partnership

Langham Partnership
PO Box 296, Carlisle, Cumbria, CA3 9WZ, UK
www.langham.org

ISBNs:
978-1-83973-985-9 Print
978-1-78641-061-0 ePub
978-1-78641-062-7 PDF

Joseph W. Handley, Gideon Para-Mallam, and Asia Williamson have asserted their moral right to be identified as the Author of the General Editor's part in the Work in accordance with sections 77 and 78 of the Copyright, Designs and Patents Act 1988.

All rights reserved. No part of this publication may be reproduced, stored in a retrieval system or transmitted, in any form or by any means, electronic, mechanical, photocopying, recording or otherwise, without the prior written permission of the publisher or the Copyright Licensing Agency.

Requests to reuse content from Langham Publishing are processed through PLSclear. Please visit www.plsclear.com to complete your request.

All Scripture quotations, unless otherwise indicated, are taken from the Holy Bible, New International Version®, Anglicised, NIV®. Copyright © 1979, 1984, 2011 by Biblica, Inc®. Used by permission. All rights reserved worldwide.

Scripture quotations marked (ESV) are from The Holy Bible, English Standard Version® (ESV®), copyright © 2001 by Crossway, a publishing ministry of Good News Publishers. Used by permission. All rights reserved.

Scripture quotations marked (NKJV) are taken from the New King James Version (NKJV). Copyright © 1982 by Thomas Nelson, Inc. Used by permission. All rights reserved.

Scripture quotations marked (NASB 1995) taken from the New American Standard Bible® 1995, Copyright © 1960, 1962, 1963, 1968, 1971, 1972, 1973, 1975, 1977, 1995 by The Lockman Foundation. Used by permission.

Scripture quotations marked (NASB) taken from the New American Standard Bible®. Copyright © 1960, 1962, 1963, 1968, 1971, 1972, 1973, 1975, 1977, 1995, 2020 by The Lockman Foundation. Used by permission.

Scripture quotations marked (NLT) are taken from the Holy Bible, New Living Translation, copyright © 1996, 2004, 2007, 2013, 2015 by Tyndale House Foundation. Used by permission of Tyndale House Publishers, Inc., Carol Stream, Illinois 60188. All rights reserved.

British Library Cataloguing-in-Publication Data
A catalogue record for this book is available from the British Library

ISBN: 978-1-83973-985-9

Cover & Book Design: projectluz.com

Langham Partnership actively supports theological dialogue and an author's right to publish but does not necessarily endorse the views and opinions set forth here or in works referenced within this publication, nor can we guarantee technical and grammatical correctness. Langham Partnership does not accept any responsibility or liability to persons or property as a consequence of the reading, use or interpretation of its published content.

Contents

Foreword... xiii

Introduction.. 1
    Joseph W. Handley, Gideon Para-Mallam, and Asia Williamson

Section I: The Lausanne Movement

1   Evangelical Leaders Cooperating in World Evangelization 15
    Ramez Atallah

2   The Early Beginnings... 25
    Allen Yeh

3   The 1974, 1989, and 2010 Lausanne Global Congresses on World Evangelization... 35
    Doug Birdsall

4   *The Lausanne Covenant* (1974), *The Manila Manifesto* (1989), *The Cape Town Commitment* (2010): The Foundation and Fruit of the Movement... 49
    Kiichi "Paul" Ariga and Kohei Takeda

5   Leadership Development in the Lausanne Movement 59
    Nana Yaw Offei Awuku, Rudolf Kabutz, and Lars Dahle

Section II: The Gospel for Every Person

6   Leadership Development for Unreached People and Places 73
    Joshua Bogunjoko

7   Learning from New Believers 83
    Abigail Abok and Sarah Breuel

8   Developing Outward-Looking Leaders........................... 93
    Kavitha and Jeyakaran Emmanuel

9   Digital Technology to Accelerate Capacity for Leaders Worldwide... 103
    Andrew Feng, Jonah Jala, and Nick Wu

Section III: Disciple-Making Churches for Every People and Place

10 Collaboration for Disciple-Making and Church Planting 115
   Ken Katayama and Idris Mammadov

11 Moving beyond Silos: Energizing Partnerships in Leader
   Development... 127
   Peter Tarantal, with help from Evi Rodemann and Michael Kaspar

12 Platforming Fresh Expressions of Ekklesia..................... 137
   Mark Williamson

13 Elevating Women in Ministry and Leadership................... 149
   Funmi J. Para-Mallam

14 Going Deeper in Disciple-Making.............................. 161
   Johnson Asare

15 Mentoring Next-Generation Leaders 167
   Asia Williamson

Section IV: Christlike Leaders for Every Church and Sector

16 Collaboration in Theological Education: The Church
   Strengthened for Mission 177
   Michael A. Ortiz

17 Platforming Women in Missions 189
   Pearl Ganta

18 Magnifying Unheard Voices.................................... 199
   Darío López, Jocabed Soliano Miselis, Jose L. Cruz, Laura B. Macias, Paul Turner, and Brenda Darke

19 The Christian Response to Persecution: An Integrated
   Examination of Faithfulness amid Trial 209
   Patrick Fung and Hwa Yung

Section V: Kingdom Impact in Every Sphere of Society

20 Peacebuilding as Christian Mission............................ 223
   Gideon Para-Mallam

21 Leading with Love: Jesus's Incarnational Ministry.............. 237
   Eraston Kighoma and C. J. Davison

22	Developing Leaders for Every Sphere 245
Francis Tsui	
23	Public Leadership 255
Femi B. Adeleye, with an addendum by Prashan De Visser	
24	Accelerating Leadership Development for Missions 269
Mary Ho and Janelle Stoops	
25	Developing Leaders in Unknown Movements 281
Eurico Buanaissa and Esther Chengo	
26	Resilience: Longevity and Preventing Burnout 293
John and Denise Lewis	
27	Building Organizational Capacity 307
Nadim Costa and Sam Metcalf	
28	Looking to the Future: Lausanne 4/Seoul 2024 317
Joseph W. Handley and David W. Bennett	

Conclusion: A Pathway Forward. 325
   Joseph W. Handley, Gideon Para-Mallam, and Asia Williamson

Contributor Biographies 331

Foreword

As we approach the monumental gathering at Seoul 2024, it is with a profound sense of purpose and anticipation that I pen this foreword for *Leading Well in Times of Disruption*. This book is not just a collection of insights; it is a clarion call for transformative leadership in an era marked by profound changes and challenges.

Reflecting on the Lausanne Movement's journey, I am reminded of the power of unity and the beauty of collaborative effort. Our mission, much like the direction of this book, has always been to foster connections that transcend geographical, cultural, and denominational boundaries. This endeavour resonates deeply with the heart of Seoul 2024, where we aim to ignite a renewed commitment to the Great Commission amid the complexities of our time.

Each chapter in this book – from discussing the Lausanne Movement's history to exploring strategies for disciple-making and leadership development – echoes our collective call to be Christ's hands and feet in every corner of society. In times of disruption, our response must be grounded in resilience, innovation, and an unshakeable faith.

As you journey through these pages, I invite you to embrace the vision laid out for Seoul 2024. Let this book serve as both a roadmap and an inspiration, guiding your steps as we together declare and display Christ in every sphere of society. The task before us is immense, but together, with God's guidance, we can lead well and make a lasting impact for his kingdom.

In unity and hope,
Michael Oh
CEO, Lausanne Movement

Introduction

Joseph W. Handley, Gideon Para-Mallam, and Asia Williamson

The Lausanne Movement has had a profound impact on how Christians answer the call of God to reach all nations. As is clear in the first section below, its history is rich and its influence significant. Since its inception, the Lausanne Movement has been at the forefront of facilitating collaboration, dialogue, and strategic thinking among Christian leaders from around the world. This year marks its fourth gathering, which will be more than merely a one-off event, rather it is a dynamic process that began a few years ago.

Lausanne has also made some important contributions to the task of developing leaders. The Lausanne Occasional Paper on Future Leadership, from its Pattaya meeting, set the tone:

> Imagine a worldwide church:
>
> where every leader is mentoring younger leaders, where leadership is both Christ-like and contextual, where leaders partner together across boundaries, where millions of future leaders are emerging – bringing the whole gospel to the whole world.[1]

Beyond this, there are a number of sources that catalyze and foster the development of leaders.[2] Following the last congress in Cape Town, a paper entitled "We Have A Problem! – But There Is Hope! – Results of a Survey of 1,000 Christian Leaders from Across the Globe" was published, showing the challenges facing the global church going forward.[3] And, the latest Issue of the Lausanne Leadership Development Issue Network has a developing site to access materials and resources in the future.[4]

---

1. "Future Leadership," https://lausanne.org/occasional-paper/future-leadership-lop-41.
2. See sources found at https://lausanne.org/?sfid=27242&_sf_s=leadership%20development. For the Lausanne Global Classroom on Leadership Development, see https://www.youtube.com/playlist?list=PLYGxDL2dvuo7PbVIoDuQ5wk4lNvzKG2FJ.
3. For the paper compiled by Jane Overstreet, see https://lausanne.org/content/we-have-a-problem-but-there-is-hope-results-of-a-survey-of-1000-christian-leaders-from-across-the-globe.
4. https://lausanne.org/networks/issues/leadership-development.

This book marks the beginnings of the next chapter in Lausanne's rich history. The pages that follow outline the background, process, and overall scope of the Lausanne contribution, and then set forth a call to action heading into and following Seoul 2024.

Leadership Development

Leadership development plays a pivotal role in shaping individuals who will lead spiritual and societal transformations across the world. It encompasses the task of engaging people to effect changes in systems, structures, and individuals. It is imperative to recognize that leadership development extends beyond the confines of church walls and penetrates the marketplace and every sector of society. To achieve success in global evangelism, it is essential to delve deeply into strategies for reaching out to professionals and influential groups who can impact countless lives with the gospel of Jesus Christ.

The purpose of global mission transcends ushering people into heaven; it also entails transforming them with the power of the gospel while they reside on earth. This transformation equips individuals to exert a positive influence on the world, promoting moral values such as justice, peace, fairness, and love. The proclamation of the gospel, while it remains a pivotal and primary endeavour, represents only one aspect of the whole mission. It is equally imperative to demonstrate the gospel through action – through lives lived in accordance with its teachings.

Unfortunately, some leadership training programmes tend to focus predominantly on disseminating packaged knowledge, techniques, and skills while inadvertently neglecting the development of godly character. In stark contrast, genuine Christlike leaders are called to exemplify qualities akin to those of Christ, including a servant's heart, humility, integrity, purity, freedom from greed, devotion to prayer, dependence on the Holy Spirit, and a profound love for people. As articulated in *The Cape Town Commitment* IID-3,[5] the emphasis should not rest solely on the acquisition of knowledge and skills but also on the cultivation of godly character.

Leadership development assumes a pivotal role in the task of discipleship and transformation. It necessitates an evaluation of the impact of activities undertaken, rather than their sheer magnitude. Leadership development

---

5. Lausanne Movement. (2010). *The Cape Town Commitment: A Confession of Faith and a Call to Action* (2nd ed.). Langham Global Library. https://www.lausanne.org/content/ctc/ctcommitment.

empowers a select few individuals who, in turn, have the capacity to influence and inspire the masses. This approach mirrors the strategy employed by Jesus to reach out to the entire world with the assistance of a small group of individuals known as disciples. In light of the world's pressing needs, there is an urgent requirement for leaders capable of spearheading transformations across all domains. It is essential to recognize that the impetus for transformation derives from the gospel itself. World evangelization hinges on the development of leaders who can effectively fulfil the Great Commission of Jesus Christ, as articulated in Matthew 28:18–20.

Global mission should not be confined solely to the objective of guiding individuals to heavenly salvation; it must encompass the broader aspiration of transforming lives with the potent message of the gospel during their earthly existence. This transformation extends beyond spiritual renewal and also entails instilling moral values such as justice, peace, fairness, and love, thereby facilitating positive impacts on the world at large. While the proclamation of the gospel remains an indispensable facet of global mission, it is imperative to demonstrate its teachings through tangible actions. This is what discipleship is all about. We are to "make disciples of all nations" (Matt 28:19).

Lausanne 4

As we prepare for the Lausanne 4 Global Consultation in 2024, we find ourselves at a pivotal moment in history, faced not only with extraordinary challenges but also with amazing opportunities for fulfilling the Great Commission. Lausanne 4 is a multiyear, polycentric process that includes catalytic events, listening calls, webinars, and a dynamic digital platform. The hope is to foster catalytic collaboration within the global church for world evangelization. This collaboration is centred on the discipling of all nations as we look forward to the year 2050.

Polycentric DNA

At its core, Lausanne embodies the idea of the whole church bringing the whole gospel to the whole world. It operates on the principle of "from everywhere to everywhere." Lausanne 4 is inclusive, seeking wisdom from every corner of the planet to discern the remaining critical gaps in global mission today. Lausanne 4 is not limited by a single direction or leader but encompasses a multidirectional and polycentric approach. It welcomes a multitude of voices, cultures, generations, and perspectives, embracing a polyvocal, polycultural, polygenerational, and polyperspectival approach.

"Listening and Learning"

Central to Lausanne 4 is a polycentric process of "listening and learning." Through this process we seek to discern what the Holy Spirit is communicating to and through the global church. It emphasizes the importance of hearing and understanding the myriad voices and perspectives within the body of Christ.

Preparations for Lausanne 4

The Lausanne Movement – an international network of Christian leaders, scholars, and practitioners – embarked on the monumental task of preparing for the Lausanne 4 Global Consultation, scheduled for 2024. This event holds great significance as it seeks to bring together voices from around the world to address the critical issues facing the global church today.

Global "Listening Calls"

The Lausanne Movement's global listening calls have been instrumental in shaping the agenda for Seoul 2024. On the 25 August 2021, the Leadership Development Issue Network – led by Joseph Handley, Gideon Para-Mallam, and Asia Williamson – hosted the first listening call, which was followed by another call with the regional directors of Lausanne to gain their perspectives as well. These calls included over forty participants, representing different churches and ministries around the world, with a good balance of Western and Majority World voices, men and women, and younger and older leaders. They shared invaluable insights on five strategic questions that are pivotal to understanding the challenges and opportunities in fulfilling the Great Commission:

1. What are the most significant gaps or remaining opportunities toward the fulfilment of the Great Commission?
2. What promising breakthroughs or innovations do you see that can accelerate the fulfilment of the Great Commission?
3. In what areas is greater collaboration most critical in order to see the fulfilment of the Great Commission?
4. Where is further research needed?
5. To whom else should we be listening as part of this process?

The insights gathered from these global influencers provided a comprehensive view of the current realities surrounding mission leadership, setting the stage for a deeper collaboration throughout the Lausanne 4 process. Here are the gleanings from our listening calls:

After a welcome and opening prayer, the conversations focused on five questions.

1. What are the most significant gaps remaining or opportunities to be grasped as we move towards the fulfilment of the Great Commission to make disciples of all nations (Matt 28:18–20)?

Many participants responded by observing that the work of evangelism is far from over. They remarked that, in some places, the impact of evangelism has not been as great as one might hope and that there still exists an urgent need for the evangelization of the whole world with the whole gospel. "The harvest is indeed plentiful, but the workers (labourers) are few." The few workers who are available need further equipping. Around the world, the call to engage in and fulfil the Great Commission continues to offer many opportunities as well as challenges. Some of these challenges present themselves through the rising tide of local and global persecution of Christians, terrorism and insecurity, intense ethnonationalism, issues of climate change, and the long-lasting impact of the COVID-19 pandemic.

The following areas were also highlighted in the discussions in response to this first question:

- Younger generations: reaching Gen Z without neglecting older generations. Gen Z is interconnected across the world, and this interconnectivity can be leveraged for the benefit of the kingdom. Since many Gen Z people have no experience of the church, they have neither rejected it nor been disillusioned by it. This reality presents us with a real opportunity to share the gospel more intentionally with Gen Z. Young people need to be allowed and encouraged to take on some leadership roles. However, they also need more role models who will mentor them.
- An urgent need for evangelism exists among the Unengaged Unreached People Groups (UUPGs) and those of the persecuted nations and churches, many of which are hard to access (Afghanistan, militant political Islamists in Muslim countries such as Pakistan and Somalia, Communist North Korea, Buddhist Burma, and Islamic-dominated countries such as Sudan and others). The need for evangelism is great in Western Europe as well. To be more effective

in reaching the West, incoming missionaries must understand the postmodern, post-Christendom context of the West. There is also an advantage now in that Europe has become postdenominational and is, therefore, more open to partnerships and collaborations. However, there continues to be a need to learn and unlearn many models of what it means to do and be a church.
- All groups have recognized that evangelism and deeper discipleship should go hand in hand as originally intended and practised in the early church.
- In addition, our collective efforts in evangelism and discipleship should not neglect the need for social justice engagement, addressing issues of poverty, hunger, sex trafficking, and so on. However, engaging in such issues and areas of need in today's world needs to be done without compromising the evangelistic message of the gospel.
- In countries where evangelism is possible, there is a greater need for mobilization of pioneering chaplaincy initiatives, which include addressing not only those in hospitals and prisons but also those in places such as homeless shelters and "third spaces" (cafes and sports venues).
- Evangelism and discipleship should also create and leverage opportunities within Business as Mission (BAM) models, seeking to work alongside entrepreneurs, and finding creative models for funding ministry.
- There exists a need for a clear and confident articulation of the Christian world view. This needs to be complemented by expanding lay training and nonformal theological education among the laity. Such training should be made available to the fast-growing but under-resourced leadership networks in church-planting contexts.

The gaps highlighted can only be adequately addressed when church leaders have godly characters and are able to lead based on their deep sense of personal relationship and a close walk with Jesus.

2. What promising breakthroughs or innovations do you see that can accelerate the fulfilment of the Great Commission?

Innovation was described not only as the practice of looking forward to new models and new ideas but also as a reflective practice of looking back and learning from past as well as current models.

The following areas were discussed and highlighted across all groups:

- A definite shift of mindset towards digital technologies should take place in churches around the world. Many who might have been reluctant in the past now see the opportunities technology provides as a tool to advance the fulfilment of the Great Commission. For example, previously, where there might have been twenty people attending a meeting in China, now, thousands can be present on a virtual Zoom call. In North India, there are groups attending online services who would not have been able to do so in person due to fear or shame. In villages, people often gather in clusters around a phone to listen together to the message of the gospel.
- Technology can be utilized not only for training but also for the translation of biblical resources. Some of those belonging to older generations may need some training in how to use these fast-growing and changing technologies.
- International student networks, now scattered around the world, must be equipped and utilized. Business as Mission is also a great innovative field that can be positively exploited.
- Innovation is also needed in engaging rural-based ministries. Presently, most efforts focus on urban ministries.
- Innovation is also needed in figuring out how these technologies can be utilized in what could be termed "whole life discipleship outside of church buildings."

3. In what areas is greater collaboration most critical in order to see the fulfilment of the Great Commission?

True collaboration needs to replace what could be described as a "cut and paste" approach, where too many models have simply been transplanted from Western contexts. Collaboration for a common purpose is essential, as opposed to collaboration that merely serves duplication purposes.

During the listening calls, many participants acknowledged that crisis times could be opportunities for greater collaboration. COVID-19 has generated and accelerated anti-missional and anti-colonial sentiments. We need to seek wisdom from every people group; and while equipping and releasing the young, we must not neglect the older generation as they continue to make a significant contribution to and impact on the global evangelization effort.

Pastors need to work with business leaders in finding creative ways to engage in missions. Theological education needs to be redefined for current missions. For example, seminaries need to offer business strategy classes.

Publishing, too, needs more collaboration to address the gap in resources and scholarship that comes from the Majority World.

The following possible areas for collaborations were suggested:

- Collaboration between nonformal theological training institutions to provide consistent, affordable, and quality biblical and pastoral training
- Collaboration between church and mission leadership and on-the-ground mission practitioners
- Collaboration between those focused on initiatives leading to greater spiritual depth (discipleship) and those focusing on greater spiritual growth (church planting)
- Collaboration between mission practitioners and digital technology experts
- Collaboration between traditional Western mission enterprises and non-Western mission endeavours
- Collaboration between major church denominations (especially in Africa), where the larger the church, the more independent they tend to become from other churches
- Collaboration between mission-minded business ventures and ministry ventures to bridge the economic gap of grassroots mission effort
- Collaboration between old-school, traditional mission leadership and the emerging generation of young mission leaders, many of whom still feel excluded due to their age and lack of leadership experience.

4. Where is further research needed?

During the listening call, participants identified a wide range of research needs. Some of these needs pertain to the expansion of currently available resources, while others relate to gaps in knowledge that require further exploration. Although everyone acknowledged the necessity and inevitability of change, it was also recognized that we lack a clear understanding of how to navigate and manage change. Therefore, further research is imperative to assist individuals in effectively managing change.

Participants of the listening calls unanimously agreed that there is a pressing need for continued research into how to reach difficult-to-access countries – such as China, North Korea, Afghanistan, and Somalia – and how to identify the most effective ministry models for these regions.

Additionally, it is crucial to glean insights from existing models and experiences within the global underground movement. This should encompass comprehensive case studies of both successes and failures.

The need for further research has been emphasized in various areas:

- Chinese theological and missionary training institutions
- The creation and utilization of global networks of Christ-centred business and banking resources, specifically designed to economically empower mission endeavours
- Maximizing the potential of Christian international university students deployed worldwide
- Encouraging the global Christian community to have a more impactful and united voice in addressing negative cultural trends such as abortion and human trafficking
- Identifying the best approaches to educate and influence the burgeoning global youth population, particularly in Africa, who are greatly influenced by social media

One of the primary areas requiring extensive research is understanding and harnessing the potential of digital technologies.

5. To whom else should we be listening as part of this process?

The participants in the listening calls provided recommendations regarding individuals and groups whom the Lausanne Movement should actively engage with. These voices – which should not merely be heard once but should be continually involved in ongoing conversations – include the following:

- Young people from Generation Z
- Refugees
- Internally Displaced Persons (IDPs) and marginalized communities
- New believers (converts) and non-Christians
- Those who are effectively spreading the gospel despite not holding official leadership positions
- Christians and other voices from hard-to-reach countries
- Individuals directly experiencing the grassroots realities of mission mobilization
- Church-planting groups and networks – to identify which strategies are working and which are not
- Data analysts capable of comprehending broader trends
- Visionaries on the cutting edge of new technological breakthroughs in areas such as AI, medicine, aviation, communication, and

cryptocurrency since these areas are poised to reshape the world in the coming years, potentially impacting mission endeavours significantly
- Theological educators, Bible colleges, and other institutions involved in training the next generation of church leaders
- Christian professionals with expertise from the marketplace and Christians engaged in public life, particularly those working in politics and public spheres, who can offer insights based on their experiences
- More voices from Latin America, where greater representation is especially needed
- Unchurched individuals and those who have become disillusioned with traditional church settings
- Christian ministries that are primarily focused on young people and universities

Strategic Plan for Leadership Development

Based on the insights gathered from the listening calls, along with feedback from the regional directors of Lausanne, the following strategic plan was formulated in alignment with Lausanne's fourfold vision:

The Gospel for Every Person:
- Champion leader development for unreached people and places, including UPG/UUPG regions, Western and secular societies, marginalized communities – such as the poor, women, and children – and persecuted populations.
- Focus on the next generations and younger leaders, particularly in the Muslim world.
- Prioritize leadership development for children and women who are in leadership.
- Promote collaboration among those involved in peacebuilding/Shalom Ministries.
- Advocate for learning from new believers and emphasize the significance of incarnational and holistic mission.
- Address issues related to mercy ministries, trauma, insecurity, spiritual poverty, pandemic engagement, and the refugee crisis.
- Pay special attention to individuals with disabilities.

Disciple-Making Churches for Every People and Place:
- Foster collaboration among groups dedicated to disciple-making and church multiplication.
- Encourage partnerships rather than siloed approaches in leader development.
- Highlight and support fresh expressions of disciple-making and church multiplication.
- Elevate the role of women in ministry and leadership.
- Deepen the focus on disciple-making and mentorship.

Christlike Leaders for Every Church and Sector:
- Support the development of leaders for all contexts, including Business as Mission (BAM) networks, workplace ministry networks, and public leadership.
- Emphasize the importance of theological depth and character formation.
- Accelerate initiatives for formal and nonformal theological training.
- Champion the development of women as leaders in the global church.
- Amplify the voices of underrepresented individuals and regions in the global church.

Kingdom Impact in Every Sphere of Society:
- Catalyze initiatives aimed at engaging every sphere of society, including public leadership, servant-leadership, and cross-cultural and intercultural engagement.
- Build capacity for leaders worldwide, particularly in the areas of digital evangelism, financial wisdom and integrity, resilience, and addressing issues related to power and control.
- Identify and promote movements that deserve recognition and platforming.

The chapters that follow include the initial effort to address these critical gaps. Each chapter was carefully selected based on Lausanne's strategic plan and emerged directly from the ideas generated from the listening calls that noted the critical gaps we face in developing leaders for global mission. The authors were chosen because of their expertise in these matters, and we intentionally sought to model the collaborative, polycentric approach in selecting them.

As you read these chapters, we believe that you will be as impressed as we are by the substance and quality of the analysis as well as with the suggestions outlined for action. The Lausanne Movement includes reflective practitioners so some of us are more academically inclined and others less so. You'll sense that as you read through these reflections. They all come from wise, discerning people of God only some of whom are contributing at academic levels. All have critical insights to share which we trust will help us navigate the future. We invite you to join us on this transformative journey (Lausanne 4) as we explore the vital role of leadership development to fulfil the Great Commission. Together, we will discover how to lead well in a disruptive era and boldly declare and display Christ to the world.

Bibliography

"Future Leadership." Lausanne Occasional Paper No. 41, presented by the Leadership Development Issue Group at the 2004 Forum for World Evangelization hosted by the Lausanne Committee for World Evangelization, Pattaya, Thailand, 29 September to 5 October 2004. *Lausanne Movement.* https://lausanne.org/occasional-paper/future-leadership-lop-41.

Lausanne Movement. (2010). *The Cape Town Commitment: A Confession of Faith and a Call to Action.* https://www.lausanne.org/content/ctc/ctcommitment.

Overstreet, Jane. "We Have A Problem! – But There Is Hope! – Results of a Survey of 1,000 Christian Leaders from Across the Globe." Cape Town 2010 Advance Paper. *Lausanne Movement.* https://lausanne.org/content/we-have-a-problem-but-there-is-hope-results-of-a-survey-of-1000-christian-leaders-from-across-the-globe.

Section I

The Lausanne Movement

1

Evangelical Leaders Cooperating in World Evangelization

Ramez Atallah

In 1971, John Gatu, an African Christian leader visiting the USA, gave a speech entitled "Missionary, Go Home." In his introduction, he said this:

> In this address I am going to argue that the time has come for the withdrawal of foreign missionaries from many parts of the Third World, that the Churches of the Third World must be allowed to find their own identity, and that the continuation of the present missionary movement is a hindrance to the selfhood of the church.[1]

The only way Gatu envisioned the church in the Third World finding itself was through a moratorium on the presence of missionaries and money from the West.

It was partially in response to this call for a "Moratorium on Missions" – which had been endorsed by the World Council of Churches – that, in 1974, Billy Graham convened the International Congress on World Evangelization in Lausanne, Switzerland, to reaffirm the imperative of world evangelization.

Of course, humanly speaking, nothing could have happened without Billy Graham. It was his vision that the task of world evangelization could only be accomplished by church and parachurch leaders worldwide cooperating with one another. That first Lausanne Congress included a very broad mix of evangelical leaders from countries, churches, and parachurch ministries. Many came because Billy Graham had invited them. His worldwide reach,

---

1. M. E. Uka, Missionaries Go Home? (New York: Peter Lang, 1987), 191.

personal integrity, and credibility contributed enormously to the success of that historic gathering. The name "Lausanne" came about because this movement was birthed at the congress held in the city of Lausanne in Switzerland.

The Programme Committee was chaired by Leighton Ford, Billy Graham's trusted brother-in-law. Ford was in his early forties and, along with Paul Little (from Inter-Varsity) as programme director, the Committee designed and executed an extremely creative and progressive programme representing the best of evangelicalism worldwide. Never before had evangelicals been exposed to such a broad spectrum of topics from all over the world. It was daring of them, for example, to invite Malcolm Muggeridge – the former editor of *Punch* magazine in the UK and a new convert to Christianity as a Roman Catholic. Muggeridge's powerful speech entitled "Living through an Apocalypse" – a pivotal analysis of the world through the eyes of a very intelligent and insightful new believer (and his analysis of the world is still very relevant fifty years after he gave it!) – will never be forgotten by the participants. Muggeridge had been converted through Mother Teresa, and it was through him that evangelicals heard, for the first time, of her remarkable ministry in India!

The two thousand seven hundred Christian leaders from 150 countries consisted of evangelical leaders *from* evangelical churches and evangelicals *in* mainline Protestant churches. In addition, there were around one thousand three hundred staff and volunteers. The total cost of this initiative was 3.5 million USD which was a very large amount at that time.

At the age of twenty-eight, I had the privilege of being the youngest "speaker" at that Congress, where I led a three-day seminar that was supposed to be about how evangelicals should evangelize Roman Catholics. I did not like that title, which had been included in the same category as several seminars on evangelizing Hindus, Muslims, and atheists. So, without consulting anyone, I changed the title to "Some Trends in the Roman Catholic Church Today," in which I challenged participants to come alongside Roman Catholics and take advantage of their new openness – following Vatican II – to many matters dear to evangelicals such as the study of the Bible and personal piety.

It was a difficult seminar because many evangelicals at that time did not believe that any Catholics were true believers! However, I was fortunate to have, as chairman of the sessions, a wise Anglican pastor who was able to navigate through the minefield of concerns expressed and direct the discussion in constructive ways. The first challenge he faced was defending my unilateral changing of the title of the seminar!

Having a "speaker" badge was a real advantage as I was invited to all the speakers' meetings. Since some meetings also included the 150 "conveners" or "council of reference," members it felt like a "Who's Who" of the evangelical world of that day. This gave me the incredible privilege of getting to know, over ten days, many of the well-known evangelical leaders who were at the Congress.

My Impressions of the Congress

I still have the daily letters I wrote to my wife, Rebecca, during the Congress. Here are some quotations from these letters:

> At dinner, after the prayer meeting, I sat beside Robert Thompson (former Canadian MP), Sam Escobar and Leighton Ford. At the table beside us, were Bill and Vonette Bright. John Stott and Harold Ockenga were a few tables down . . . The exciting thing is that no one made a fuss over anyone else – no "oohs" and "aahs!" I was the only one out of my league!

> Billy Graham is now introducing Corrie Ten Boom, she is an old woman with a heavy accent. She is saying that the key commandment of the Bible is: "Be filled with the Spirit." "I do not ask you if you have the Holy Spirit, but rather, does the Holy Spirit have you?" "We are not called to be burden bearers, only cross bearers and fruit bearers."

> After listening to Fouad Accad (General Secretary of Lebanon Bible Society) this morning, I was challenged! . . . O to be able to get the Bible into the hands of Muslim people of all ages, backgrounds and classes in a format that suits them and can be accepted and read!

> Yesterday morning, John Stott gave an *excellent* presentation "The Biblical Basis for Evangelism" – it was one of the best talks I have heard!

> Mrs. Shoemaker is in my seminar, her husband, Sam Shoemaker (known as one of the best preachers of his day) was influential in starting Alcoholics Anonymous.

> Don McGavran (founder of the Church Growth movement) answered questions sent in about his paper. He was humble and very warm. I appreciated his approach, but still disagree with what he says.

It was interesting to be in on the "behind-the-scenes" of the Congress. I am learning much! It is a real privilege to watch these world-famous leaders from close up. Here you see a man without the external "props" he has in his context. Most wear a plain green (participant) badge, and all look alike. I feel thoroughly embarrassed with my red "speaker" badge! . . . the men who really elicit my admiration are those who work behind the scenes and who shine with love and humility.

What has Lausanne '74 meant for me? What remains with me are not the excellent talks and the mass of new information I accumulated. This was very good and of a high quality. But what I take back with me is the memory of meeting many committed Church leaders from around the world. What impressed me most was the life and actions of these men (no women leaders here to speak of). I saw great men without the "props" which usually support their greatness, and yet many of them demonstrated that their greatness was more than skin-deep. The joy of the Lord radiated from their faces. They did not try to impress by their knowledge or position. I was encouraged to see the strength of the Church and to know that these men really love the Lord. The superficiality of some came out so clearly that it was in stark contrast to the depth of others.

I leave Lausanne with a desire to become closer to God and to reflect His love and warmth in humility. But I also leave with an evangelistic vision to reach others for Christ and not to just "perfect the saints."

Defining the Movement

The Lausanne Covenant, which resulted from that historic gathering, succinctly reflected the major issues presented at the Congress. What it did not reflect, however, were the many deep and difficult differences and divisions in the evangelical world at that time. But because it was the official "statement" of the Congress, people who subsequently read this statement – even though they had not been at the Congress –assumed that this was the "consensus" of the Congress! *The Lausanne Covenant* is widely regarded as one of the most significant and influential documents in modern church history. Its stance on many issues is far more progressive and radical than the stance adopted by many of the participants of the Lausanne congress.

The Lausanne Covenant was used by God to encourage, challenge, and unite a younger generation of evangelicals who were yearning for a more balanced and practical evangelicalism than they had experienced to date. *The Lausanne Covenant* defines the "theology" and "praxis" promoted by the Lausanne Movement. It has also become the foundational statement of hundreds of organizations, movements, and institutions within evangelicalism, which has allowed many who had not previously engaged with one another to find common ground for fellowship.

The Lausanne Continuation Committee

Following that remarkable Congress, I was invited to be the "youth" representative on the fifty-person Lausanne Continuation Committee that first met in Mexico City in January 1975. My twenty years on that committee shaped me in more ways than I can describe. I tell people that I was "discipled through Lausanne committee meetings"!

The first challenge was to define our mission. Eventually, we reached a consensus on two matters: first, that we were focusing on "evangelization" rather than "evangelism" and, second, that we were defining the former as including other aspects of the mission of God apart from simple evangelism. The second challenge, in those early days, was convincing strong-minded evangelical leaders to cooperate with one another. Finally, there was a considerable struggle to define for ourselves a complementary role in relation to the World Evangelical Alliance (WEA). The WEA was the main umbrella organization for a worldwide alliance of evangelical churches and organizations, while Lausanne encompassed evangelicals in both evangelical *and* mainline churches and was uniquely focused on "evangelization."

Defining Our Mission

During the first meeting of the Continuation Committee in Mexico in January of 1975, there was strong disagreement on what should be the focus of this new movement. Things came to a head, with Billy Graham and John Stott disagreeing publicly on the matter. Committee members began taking sides. The tension was partially diffused by Billy Graham's clear statement, the next morning, that he and John were good friends and that their different views in no way affected the deep bond between them.

But later that week, Bishop Jack Dain from Australia – who had been the chairman of the Congress and was chairing this committee – was so frustrated by the disagreements between those present that he walked out of the meeting! Some wise folks were able to convince him to continue chairing the meetings with the promise that a new chairman would be elected at the next meeting.

The fact that I was invited to lead one of the devotions at that meeting – even though I was only twenty-eight years old – was a clear indication that the leadership of Lausanne at that time was keen to include younger leaders in an active way.

By the end of the next meeting in Atlanta, Georgia, there was consensus that Lausanne upheld a broad view of evangelization, a view that included both the Great Commission (sharing the gospel message worldwide) and the Great Commandment (loving our neighbour by demonstrating practical concern for people's well-being).

Persuading Leaders to Cooperate

It was not easy to convince visionaries – who led large, successful, and significant movements worldwide – to agree to work together. At the 1974 Congress, the Canadian delegates met together to consider if they could do a joint outreach at the 1976 World Olympics, which was to be held in Montreal, Canada. They agreed to set up a Lausanne "umbrella" organization called Aide Olympique (AO) that would coordinate the efforts of all the evangelical outreach efforts planned for the Montreal Olympics.

Fifty organizations agreed to join in this endeavour and promised that every piece of literature would carry the Aide Olympique logo alongside their organization's logo. This gave the impression that there was one big organization rather than dozens of smaller ones. We provided discounted sandwiches for tourists, had a 24-hour call centre, printed and distributed large numbers of a small booklet entitled "A guide to all you need to know about Montreal during the Olympics" – which was a unique source of helpful information for Montreal visitors – and planned large rallies each night, featuring well-known speakers. This was in addition to all the many activities planned by each of the fifty groups partnering with AO. I happened to represent AO on the Montreal municipality's Olympics Coordination Committee, which met in City Hall regularly during the event. On the last day, the chairperson of the Committee made this statement: "We all need to thank Mr. Atallah for the remarkable contribution of Aide Olympique to the success of the Olympic event in our city, their group did more than any other group to serve our visitors"! To me, this typified the goal of Lausanne: to mobilize evangelical leaders to cooperate in evangelization.

To me, Aide Olympique represented what we had dreamed of at Lausanne '74 but did not believe could happen. Many of the fifty agencies, ministries, and churches had never cooperated with one another and, in some cases, were even seen as "competitors"! That summer of 1976 in Montreal proved that Billy Graham's dream of evangelicals cooperating with one another could be – and had already begun to be – realized.

The World Evangelical Alliance (WEA)

It took many years for the Lausanne Committee for World Evangelization (LCWE) and the World Evangelical Alliance (WEA) to agree on a mutually acceptable understanding of their distinctives. Before the LCWE, evangelical alliances in many countries of the world had been the only forum that united a broad range of evangelicals. But, at that time, this did not include evangelicals in mainline churches or evangelical charismatic groups. So, Lausanne was the only way for these two groups to fellowship with like-minded evangelicals.

A New Chairman

At the second LCWE meeting held in Atlanta in January 1976, the first item on the agenda was to elect a chairman to replace Jack Dain. Armin Hoppler from Switzerland, who headed up the nomination committee, divided the members of the LCWE into regional groups and asked each group to nominate their candidate for chairman.

When I met Armin before lunch that day, he was very worried. "We made a terrible mistake," he said. "What will we do if each region nominates a different person?"

When he met me after lunch, he was beaming. "You won't believe what happened," he said excitedly, "the top name on every list was that of Leighton Ford!"

And so it was that Leighton Ford led the LCWE from that point on until 1992. He was obviously God's man for the task. Having led the programme of the Congress, he knew all the issues discussed there and was in the best possible position to lead the new movement. Billy Graham had resigned at the end of the first meeting, stating that he felt his presence could polarize the Committee: "It seems to me," he said, "that every time we come to vote on an issue people look at me before voting wondering how I will vote!" But with his trusted brother-in-law at the helm, Lausanne was assured of Billy's continuing full support. So, Leighton's election and leadership was seen as a continuation of Billy's leadership.

With Leighton as its chairman and Gottfried Osie-Mensah from Kenya as its international director, Lausanne was in good hands. But there were no other staff at that time, and Leighton asked me if I would be his assistant. We finally agreed that I would continue my ministry with Inter-Varsity in Quebec but set apart one day a week for Lausanne. It helped that my boss at the time, Samuel Escobar, fully supported that decision.

Consultations on Issues Raised by The Lausanne Covenant

During the 1970s and 1980s, Lausanne convened a host of small consultations (30–40 people) on many of the issues listed in *The Lausanne Covenant*. The results or consensus of each gathering were published in a Lausanne Occasional Paper and widely read worldwide. These papers were especially encouraging to a new generation of evangelicals who had been inspired by *The Lausanne Covenant*.

Because I was Leighton's assistant, I had the privilege of travelling with him to many of these consultations and also attending all executive committee meetings. This forced me to grapple with many issues I had never thought about and gave me the opportunity to rub shoulders with Lausanne leaders in a variety of contexts.

Founders of Lausanne

Here are my personal reflections on a few of the founding fathers of Lausanne whom I got to know closely through twenty years on the Continuation Committee.

Billy Graham

Since Billy Graham left the committee after the first meeting, I never worked closely with him. But on the few occasions I wrote to him for advice on some Lausanne issue, he responded graciously, humbly, and wisely. His greatest contribution, in my opinion, was his ability to elicit the support and admiration of Christian leaders and others from churches and ministries that, at the time, were not comfortable having fellowship with one another. Their respect and admiration for Billy Graham drew them closer to one another.

Leighton Ford

During my many years as Leighton's "assistant" – I did everything from carrying heavy file boxes to reserving accommodation for meetings to being a sounding board for him on many theological and "people" related issues – I was really his "mentee." When I realized that Leighton worked from home and had only one secretary who worked from her home, I wrote to Rebecca: "I can't believe that Leighton Ford – one of the key evangelical leaders in the world – can manage to be so efficient (and I know he is) and yet have so little overhead. I admire the man a hundred times more!"

Leighton's gift of personal friendship and genuine caring helped unite Christians who otherwise would have gone their own way. He was a true peacemaker! When a disagreement between two strong-minded leaders happened during a meeting, he would call for a coffee break. Coffee in hand, he would take the two men (or the angry party) on a walk. The thornier the issue, the longer the coffee break! But by the time the meeting restarted, there had either been a truce or, better still, a reconciliation, and the meeting would proceed smoothly. We often talked about his proverbial "walks"!

Lausanne would not be what it is today if it were not for Leighton Ford.

But Leighton Ford would have not been able to accomplish all he did without three very wise senior mentors.

Jack Dain

Bishop Dain was the chairman of the 1974 Congress and the first chairman of the Continuation Committee. Even though he relinquished the chair to Leighton, Dain continued as his mentor. Many times, he helped Leighton work through a complex issue or figure out how to handle a difficult person. Because I was close to Leighton, I got close to Jack. One of the things I remember was him telling me that when he went on a trip, he wrote to his wife every night. I have never forgotten this.

Tom Zimmerman

Tom always wore a three-piece suit and used a watch on a gold chain that lay nestled in the pocket of his vest. He looked like the manager of a great bank! When Tom confirmed his attendance at a meeting, he always reminded me not to forget to reserve a room for his pilot. He came to most meetings in the US in his private jet! No one meeting Tom would have imagined that he was the general superintendent of the Assemblies of God, supervising more than nine thousand Pentecostal pastors in the US, and also the chairman of the Pentecostal World Alliance.

Once, a Baptist pastor on the Lausanne Committee was boasting to others about his local church's budget, saying, "Last week we passed a million-dollar budget of our church!" Tom, obviously irritated, responded in a quiet voice, "That's very interesting, last week we passed the Assemblies of God's budget of one hundred million dollars!" That Baptist pastor never boasted again!

Tom once showed me the log of sermons he had preached that year – the number was 229!

It was Tom who brought Pentecostals and charismatics into Lausanne. His wise and experienced leadership made many in Lausanne who looked down on Pentecostals and charismatics change their minds.

Leighton depended on him for "procedural" guidance. Tom was an expert on "protocol" and "Roberts Rules of Order" that governed synods and councils.

John Stott

John – a chaplain to Queen Elizabeth – was Leighton's close friend and theological adviser. John was a humble, no-nonsense person, who had the incredible gift of knowing how to express truth in a clear yet non-controversial way. Without him, we would not have had either *The Lausanne Covenant* or the 1989 *Manila Manifesto*. I remember that on the last night of the Manila Congress, John had the task of drafting the Congress statement. He had one serious problem – he could not type, and though there were many typists available in the office, they were all women. "I expect to work all night," he told me, "but I can't have a woman with me in my hotel room!"

So, I ended up being his typist, and we finished the statement by sunrise.

You can imagine what a privilege it was for me to work side by side with these great men of God (there were not enough women in Lausanne in those days). Much of what I learned about being a Christian leader comes because of their influence.

For me, Lausanne has been an inspiration for world evangelization, an unfailing vision for Christians to impact their world, and a broad-based international evangelical fellowship. But most of all, the shoulder-to-shoulder interaction with great Christian leaders has had an incalculable impact on my life.

2

The Early Beginnings

Allen Yeh

Although the Lausanne Movement takes its name from that city in Switzerland where it had its first meeting in 1974, the converging streams that came together to birth this movement have a long history – going back to long before that first Lausanne Congress on World Evangelization. This chapter will explore these converging streams, which are listed chronologically here: William Carey; American Revivalism; Edinburgh 1910; the World Council of Churches; and Berlin 1966. Many of these missionary impulses were transatlantic.

William Carey

William Carey (1761–1834) is commonly dubbed the "Father of Modern Missions"[1] because of the influence he wielded in launching the modern missions movement rather than for any chronological priority he may have had. Though the Moravian Brethren (*Unitas Fratrum*) – led by Count Nicolaus (sometimes spelled Nikolaus) Ludwig von Zinzendorf – preceded Carey by half a century, they were precursors of the larger wave that was to come, much like John Wycliffe (sometimes spelled Wyclif) was nicknamed the "Morning Star of the Reformation"[2] even though Martin Luther – some 150 years later – was credited as being the "Father of the Protestant Reformation." Similarly, the first Latin American liberation theologian was actually Rubem Alves, with the

---

1. Tucker, *Jerusalem to Irian Jaya*, 122.
2. George, *Theology of the Reformers*, 35. Another forerunner of the Protestant Reformation was Bohemian reformer Jan Hus (sometimes spelled John Huss) from the Czech Republic (as it is now known).

publication of his *Theology of Human Hope* (1969) a few years before Gustavo Gutiérrez's *A Theology of Liberation* (1971), even though the latter was called the "Father of Liberation Theology." It is important to note that chronology does not connote importance.

Carey's magnum opus was his book *An Enquiry into the Obligations of Christians to Use Means for the Conversion of the Heathens* (1792), which advocated for three significant changes that led to the "Great Century of Missions" (the nineteenth century): (1) a reframing of the Great Commission as binding on all Christians, not just the original eleven disciples; (2) the establishment of mission societies as apparatuses for the launching of missions to parallel Catholic monastic orders; and (3) the employment of social sciences (demography and statistics).[3]

Though these three did come to fruition, there was a fourth area in which Carey was perhaps too far ahead of his contemporaries: the call for an ecumenical missions conference. In 1806, Carey made this suggestion to his friend, the theologian Andrew Fuller:

> The Cape of Good Hope is now in the hands of the English; should it continue so, would it be possible to have a general association of all denominations of Christians, from the four corners of the world, kept there once in about ten years? I earnestly recommend this plan, let the first meeting be in the Year 1810, or 1812 at furthest. I have no doubt but it would be attended with very important effects; we could understand one another better, and more entirely enter into one another's views by two hour conversation than by two or three years epistolary correspondence.[4]

Andrew Fuller dismissed this idea:

> I consider this as one of bro'r Carey's pleasing dreams. Seriously I see no important object to be obtained by such a meeting, which might not be quite as well attained without it. And in a meeting of all denominations, there would be no unity, without which we had better stay at home.[5]

---

3. George, "Let It Go," 6, 9.

4. William Carey to Andrew Fuller, Calcutta, 15 May 1806, cited by Latourette, "Ecumenical Bearings," 355, note 2.

5. Andrew Fuller to William Ward, Serampore, 2 December 1806, cited by Rouse, "Pleasing Dream," 181.

At the time, "conferences of any kind, missionary or otherwise, national or local, were practically unknown!"[6] But Carey's suggestion sowed within the hearts of many the seed of the idea that mission requires an ecumenically coordinated effort for the purposes of strategizing, fellowship, and cooperation. A century later, this would take the form of the Edinburgh 1910 World Missionary Conference. And two centuries later, the third Lausanne Congress would fulfil Carey's vision at Cape Town 2010.

American Revivalism

Missiologist Andrew Walls writes, "The modern missionary movement is an autumnal child of the Evangelical Revival."[7] A half-century before Carey, the missionary David Brainerd (1718–1747) made a significant impact on the American "frontier" with his work among the Delaware Indians. Brainerd became an inspiration for later luminaries such as Jonathan Edwards (America's greatest theologian), missiologist Henry Martyn, and missionary Jim Elliot, not to mention William Carey himself, who brought Brainerd's book with him to the mission field and used it as fuel for his zeal. Edwards was the person who compiled, edited, and published *An Account of the Life of the Late Reverend Mr. David Brainerd* in 1749, and this singular book, along with Carey's *An Enquiry*, fired the imaginations of Western missionaries everywhere. In addition, Edwards, along with George Whitefield and Gilbert Tennent, helped to initiate the first Great Awakening in the United States. On the other side of the Atlantic, John and Charles Wesley were inspired by what they saw in their American counterparts.

Despite the inroads made by Brainerd – or even much earlier on by John Eliot, the "apostle to the Indians" – the true beginning of the American missionary movement was the Haystack Prayer Movement of 1806. Five students from Williams College in Western Massachusetts – Samuel Mills, James Richards, Francis LeBaron Robbins, Harvey Loomis, and Byram Green – took shelter from a rainstorm under a haystack and decided to wait out the storm by praying together for an American overseas missionary movement. This led, in 1810, to the establishment of the ABCFM (American Board of Commissioners for Foreign Missions), which sent out its first missionaries in 1812.

---

6. Rouse, "Pleasing Dream," 181.
7. Walls, "Evangelical Revival," 310.

Due to the impetus of the Haystack movement, Adoniram Judson (1788–1850) – a product of Brown University and Andover Theological Seminary – along with his wife, Ann, became the first intercontinental missionaries sent out from the United States (thirty years prior to the Judsons, a freed black slave named George Liele had set off as a missionary to Jamaica, making him the first overseas missionary from the United States). The Judsons were commissioned alongside Samuel Newell and his wife (Harriet), Samuel Nott, Gordon Hall, and Luther Rice, and this group became known as the "Immortal Seven." The Judsons set sail from Salem, Massachusetts, stopping in India along the way to rendezvous with William Carey before eventually settling down in their final destination of Burma (modern-day Myanmar). They inspired other collegiate missionaries such as "Borden of Yale" (William Whiting Borden). On the other side of the Atlantic, the famous cricketer C. T. Studd and the "Cambridge Seven" joined Hudson Taylor's China Inland Mission and, later, the Student Volunteer Movement, where he would meet and influence John Mott.

The through line of the modern missionary movement – if there was one – was students. Students drove overseas missions through their prayer and organizational efforts, and this would be seen in stark detail at the Edinburgh World Missionary Conference of 1910.

Edinburgh 1910

Many may not realize that Edinburgh 1910 was actually the *third* in a series of ecumenical missions conferences, following London 1888 and New York 1900.[8] The year 1888 was chosen for London's "Centenary Missionary Conference" that commemorated a century since the beginnings of Anglo-American missions.

The conference would not have had as big an impact as it would eventually be known for if not for the efforts of the American John R. Mott (1865–1955) and J. H. Oldham from Britain (1874–1969). These men filled different roles: the former was the prophet and the latter was the organizer. Though Mott often gets most of the credit – especially for coining the watchword "The Evangelization of the World in This Generation" – it was Oldham who worked behind the scenes and without whom the conference would not have hung together.

Mott explains the point of his watchword:

> If the Gospel is to be preached to all men it obviously must be done while they are living. The evangelization of the world in

---

8. Stanley, *World Missionary Conference*, 18.

this generation, therefore, means the preaching of the Gospel to those who are now living . . . It does not mean the conversion of the world within the generation.[9]

It was Oldham who brought the Student Christian Movement[10] into the picture and decided that the format of Edinburgh 1910 should be based on two preceding Asian ecumenical missions conferences – Madras 1902 and Shanghai 1907 (scholars and experts) – rather than on London 1888 or New York 1900 (enthusiasts). Although it is often assumed that Edinburgh 1910 later impacted Asia and that the influence only went in that direction, it is notable that Asia impacted the Western missionary movement first. In addition, V. S. Azariah of India – one of only seventeen Asians present at Edinburgh 1910 – gave a memorable and impactful speech, imploring Western missionaries, "Too often you promise us thrones in heaven, but will not offer us chairs in your drawing rooms . . . You have given your goods to feed the poor. You have given your bodies to be burned. We also ask for *love*. Give us FRIENDS!"[11] Since Mott himself had connections with the World Student Christian Federation, Student Volunteer Movement, and the YMCA, this magnified the influence of students on the modern missions movement.

The Edinburgh conference is known as the birthplace of the modern ecumenical movement, despite the fact that it was overwhelmingly white, male, Western, Anglophone, and evangelical Protestant. The only way it can be considered ecumenical (unity of all the churches) is if it is evaluated by the standard of what it led to. The conference itself was less important than its burgeoning results.

The World Council of Churches

Out of Edinburgh 1910 came two "children," who, unfortunately, are sometimes deemed to be at odds with each other. Scottish theologian Kenneth Ross writes:

> Though in strictly institutional terms it is the World Council of Churches that is the heir of Edinburgh 1910, in terms of promoting the agenda of world evangelization, the Lausanne movement might be seen as standing in direct continuity. . . . As Andrew Walls suggests: "Both 'ecumenical' and 'evangelical' today

---

9. Mott, *Evangelization of the World*, 6–7.
10. Stanley, *World Missionary Conference*, 24.
11. Stanley, *World Missionary Conference*, 125.

have their roots in Edinburgh 1910. If each will go back to the pit whence both were dug, each may understand both themselves and the other better.[12]

Perhaps it may be a case of "sibling rivalry" – such as Abraham's two sons being the forefathers of Arabs and Jews – but certainly the "ecumenical" World Council of Churches and the "evangelical" Lausanne Movement, while divergent, do have a common ancestry and thus share some critical DNA. However, the way they view the word "ecumenical" differs greatly. At London 1888 and New York 1900, "ecumenical" meant "global."[13] By 1910, the word had taken on the meaning of "denominational." This is why Edinburgh 1910 dropped "ecumenical" from its title and, instead, called itself a "world" missionary conference to retain the sense of "global." Today, while the WCC holds on to the sense of ecumenical as denominationalism, Lausanne sees itself as ecumenical in the global sense, furthering the case that it stands "in direct continuity" with Edinburgh 1910. In fact, John Stott himself writes, "Having read both John Mott's and Temple Gairdner's accounts of Edinburgh 1910, I would guess that something of the excitement and euphoria of Edinburgh were recaptured at Lausanne."[14]

As Ross mentions above, the WCC is the older of the two movements. Out of Edinburgh 1910's Continuation Committee came the establishment of the International Missionary Council (IMC) in 1921, and the world conferences on Faith and Order (Lausanne 1927 and Edinburgh 1937) and on Life and Work (Stockholm 1925 and Oxford 1937). In 1948, Faith and Order merged with Life and Work to form the World Council of Churches at Amsterdam for its first General Assembly. However, it was not until 1961 that the IMC merged with the World Council of Churches at its third General Assembly in New Delhi.[15]

For half a century after Edinburgh 1910, evangelicalism did not have a formal platform similar to that which ecumenism had with the WCC. The "Great Reversal"[16] following the early twentieth-century Fundamentalist-Modernist Controversy meant that missions became bifurcated between the "social action" of the ecumenists and the "evangelism" of the evangelicals. But when evangelicals finally organized themselves, they had to decide between evangelism only or a more holistic mission.

---

12. Ross, "Centenary of Edinburgh," 178.
13. Stanley, *World Missionary Conference*, 19.
14. Stott, "Significance of Lausanne," 288.
15. VanElderen, *World Council of Churches*, 17.
16. Moberg, *Great Reversal*.

Berlin 1966

Billy Graham (1918–2018) came into the national spotlight in 1949 at the Los Angeles "Canvas Crusades" – so named because they were held in giant tents. By the 1960s, he had become an international statesman of evangelism. He was self-consciously a neo-evangelical – or simply evangelical – meaning that he was aiming for a "more irenic title" than fundamentalist.[17] He would even conduct evangelistic crusades with black preachers like Martin Luther King Jr. or cooperate with non-fundamentalists, much to the consternation of his fundamentalist brethren. However, due to his stature, from the mid-twentieth century onwards, he defined what it meant to be an evangelical – it did not entail the rigidity of the fundamentalists and was certainly not liberal but something in between: maintaining the scriptural fidelity of the former while not entirely rejecting the modern world of the latter.[18]

Graham's foray into the international ecumenical missions realm came with his convening of the World Congress of Evangelism, organized by the Billy Graham Evangelistic Association, in Berlin in 1966. The occasion was to mark the tenth anniversary of the founding of the neo-evangelical flagship magazine *Christianity Today*, and it was, therefore, conceived as a one-off rather than a repeated series of conferences and congresses like Lausanne. There were 1,262 people in attendance and fifty-seven of the two hundred speakers were from the Majority World – a commendable representation for that time, although not by today's standards. However, due to the presence of varied political factions and the views of donors, the speakers were asked to keep any talk of social action to a minimum and focus mainly on evangelism.[19] Despite its hopeful theme "One Race, One Gospel, One Task" – the first element following on the heels of the Civil Rights Movement – the gathering did not deal adequately with social issues. Graham also invoked Edinburgh 1910 and John Mott as his inspiration for why he did not want to veer from evangelism alone.[20] However, there was still more evangelical evolution that had to take place before the form of Lausanne would be reached; hence – as pointed out earlier – chronology does not necessarily indicate importance.

Later, at Lausanne 1974, John Stott (1921–2011) would call for even greater reforms. As the chief architect of *The Lausanne Covenant*, he would restore equal status to social action, alongside evangelism, in missions – reversing

---

17. Collins, *Evangelical Moment*, 37.
18. Stanley, *Global Diffusion*, 37.
19. Stanley, 69.
20. Graham, "Why the Berlin Congress?," 22.

the Great Reversal in favour of integral mission. He would invite even more Majority World speakers onto the platform, especially those from the Global South – for example, Latino *evangélicos* like C. René Padilla, Samuel Escobar, and Orlando Costas,[21] who were champions of *misión integral*. However, some of these issues would lead him into direct conflict with Billy Graham. Alister Chapman unpacks it like this:

> By the time of Lausanne, Stott had come to the conclusion that God called his people to care about society and politics as well as evangelism. Many at Lausanne agreed with him, especially people from churches associated with the WCC (World Council of Churches), where social and political issues were high priorities. However, the belief that preaching the gospel was all that really mattered was still common, especially in the United States. Talk of social action brought to mind the dreaded social gospel, which many saw as a chief culprit in the theological drift of America's historic denominations . . . at Lausanne, Stott wanted evangelicals to take social action more seriously. The twist in Stott's message to the congress was his argument that the Great Commission itself demanded that Christians pay attention to people's physical and social needs, as well as their spiritual ones. He did this by focusing not on the standard version of the commission, namely Jesus' command to go and make disciples of all nations as recorded in Matthew's gospel, but rather on John's account of Jesus telling his disciples that as his Father had sent him, so he was sending them. And just as Jesus' mission had involved caring for people's bodies, as well as their souls, so should that of the church.[22]

However, despite their differing views, Graham and Stott enjoyed a strong transatlantic friendship.

Conclusion

The Lausanne Movement was not created *ex nihilo* but – like every good missions movement – is a product of its culture, context, and time. It owes much to the "great cloud of witnesses" who came before it in its early years.

---

21. Douglas, *Let the Earth*, 116, 303, 675.
22. Chapman, *Godly Ambition*, 138–140.

One thread that stands out is the importance of documents. From Carey's *An Enquiry* (which set him apart from Zinzendorf), to Brainerd's diary, to *The Lausanne Covenant*, writings leave a legacy that remains extant long after the people themselves pass.

A second important trend is the transatlantic Anglo-American cooperation seen between towering figures like Jonathan Edwards and George Whitefield, Borden of Yale and the Cambridge Seven, John Mott and J. H. Oldham, Dwight L. Moody and Charles Spurgeon, and even as far back as nineteenth-century missiologists Rufus Anderson and Henry Venn – founders of the concept of the "three-self church." With the Lausanne Movement, of course, the dynamic duo was Billy Graham and John Stott. However, the influences of the Majority World must not be minimized: everyone from V. S. Azariah of India – who literally said, in his plenary address to the white Western delegates at Edinburgh 1910, "Give us friends!" – to Billy Graham's friendship with MLK, to the Latin American influencers of John Stott – "Stott's own position was close to that of Escobar and Padilla"[23] – the Lausanne Movement and its predecessors truly spawned multiethnic and international cooperation.

A third significant factor is the importance of formal movements, organizations, and conferences. William Carey's call to mission societies and his not-realized-in-his-lifetime ecumenical missions conference saw the formation of Edinburgh 1910, the WCC, and the Lausanne Movement.

Finally, there are the students. So much of the great century of missions could not have been accomplished without student leaders and missionaries. Many conferences beyond Edinburgh 1910 have reflected this, including Lausanne's Younger Leaders Gatherings (the first in Singapore in 1987, then Malaysia 2006, Indonesia 2016, and an upcoming gathering in 2026).

Lausanne took all these early elements and combined them into an international, ecumenical, and evangelical missions movement that has produced major conferences and documents and takes seriously the place of youth as the present and future of missions.

Bibliography

Chapman, Alister. *Godly Ambition: John Stott and the Evangelical Movement*. Oxford: Oxford University Press, 2012.

Collins, Kenneth J. *The Evangelical Moment: The Promise of an American Religion*. Grand Rapids: Baker, 2005.

---

23. Chapman, 139.

Douglas, J. D., ed. *Let the Earth Hear His Voice: International Congress on World Evangelization, Lausanne, Switzerland*. Minneapolis: World Wide Publications, 1975.

George, Timothy. "Let It Go: Lessons from the Life of William Carey." In *Expect Great Things, Attempt Great Things: William Carey and Adoniram Judson, Missionary Pioneers*, edited by Allen Yeh and Chris Chun, 3–14. Eugene: Wipf & Stock, 2013.

———. *Theology of the Reformers*. Nashville: Broadman & Holman, 1988.

Graham, Billy. "Why the Berlin Congress?" In *One Race, One Gospel, One Task*, vol. 1, edited by Carl F. H. Henry and W. Stanley Mooneyham, 22–34. Minneapolis; World Wide Publications, 1967.

Latourette, Kenneth Scott. "Ecumenical Bearings of the Missionary Movement and the International Missionary Council." In *A History of the Ecumenical Movement, vol. 1*, edited by Ruth Rouse and Stephen C. Neill, 353–404. Geneva: World Council of Churches, 1954.

Moberg, David O. *The Great Reversal: Reconciling Evangelism and Social Concern*. Philadelphia: J. B. Lippincott, 1972.

Mott, John R. *The Evangelization of the World in This Generation*. New York: Student Volunteer Movement for Foreign Missions, 1904.

Ross, Kenneth R. "The Centenary of Edinburgh 1910: Its Possibilities." *International Bulletin of Missionary Research* 30, no. 4 (October 2006): 177–79.

Rouse, Ruth. "William Carey's 'Pleasing Dream.'" *International Review of Mission* 38 (April 1949): 181–92.

Stanley, Brian. *The Global Diffusion of Evangelicalism: The Age of Billy Graham and John Stott*. Downers Grove: IVP Academic, 2013.

———. *The World Missionary Conference, Edinburgh 1910*. Grand Rapids: Eerdmans, 2009.

Stott, John. "The Significance of Lausanne." *International Review of Mission* 64 (1975): 288–94.

Tucker, Ruth A. *From Jerusalem to Irian Jaya: A Biographical History of Christian Missions*. Grand Rapids: Zondervan, 2004.

VanElderen, Marlin. *Introducing the World Council of Churches*. Geneva: WCC Publications, 1990.

Walls, Andrew. "The Evangelical Revival, the Missionary Movement, and Africa." In *Evangelicalism: Comparative Studies of Popular Protestantism in North America, the British Isles, and Beyond 1700–1900*, edited by Mark Noll, 310–30. New York: Oxford University Press, 1994.

3

The 1974, 1989, and 2010 Lausanne Global Congresses on World Evangelization

Doug Birdsall

Billy Graham was the towering evangelical leader of the twentieth century. When interviewed for *Newsweek* magazine in 2006, he was asked what he thought was the most enduring impact of his remarkable sixty-year global ministry.[1] To the surprise of the interviewer, he responded by saying that perhaps his most significant contribution was the 1974 Lausanne Congress on World Evangelization and the ensuing Lausanne Movement.

In 2024, we commemorate the fiftieth anniversary of that epoch-making congress, which is certainly one of the most impactful world mission gatherings in the Protestant era. In this chapter, we will explore the legacy of Lausanne '74 by identifying factors that contributed to its global impact and the founding of a movement. We will then look at the contributions and significance of Lausanne II in Manila in 1989, which was followed by "quiet years" and a time of uncertainty. We will then turn our attention to the revitalization of the Lausanne Movement and the impact and legacy of the Third Lausanne Congress on World Evangelization: Cape Town 2010.

---

1. Telephone conversation with David Bruce, special assistant to Billy Graham.

The International Congress on World Evangelization (ICOWE): Lausanne '74
Historical Context

In July 1974, two thousand seven hundred Christian leaders from nearly 150 countries met under the theme "Let the Earth Hear His Voice" to consider the challenges and opportunities of world evangelization. *Time* magazine referred to Lausanne '74 as "a formidable forum, possibly the widest ranging meeting of Christians ever held."[2]

The only other missions gathering in the twentieth century comparable to Lausanne '74 was the historic Edinburgh World Missionary Conference in 1910, convened by John R. Mott. "Edinburgh 1910" brought together some one thousand two hundred mission leaders, 90 percent of whom were from Europe and North America. This reflected the reality that the vast majority of Christians at that time were in the Northern Hemisphere. Mission was understood largely in terms of "from the West to the Rest."

However, by 1974, thanks in no small part to the impulses and missionary initiatives of Edinburgh 1910, the church had experienced tremendous growth in Africa, Latin America, and Asia. Furthermore, by 1974, new political, economic, and ideological realities had created the global context in which a congress like Lausanne '74 was possible – and essential. Lausanne '74 thus took place during a time of monumental shifts in global Christianity.

A Leader of Global Stature

Graham was the visionary catalyst for Lausanne '74. Without his convening power, the Congress would not have happened. Graham was able to enlist a team of leaders with exceptional abilities, including Bishop Jack Dain as congress chair, Dr. Donald Hoke as congress director, Dr. Leighton Ford as programme chair, and Dr. John Stott, who would serve as Bible expositor and chief architect of the congress document – *The Lausanne Covenant*.

Though John Stott is often mistakenly identified as co-convener of the Lausanne Congress and co-founder of the Lausanne Movement, he was initially disinclined to even attend. He had to be persuaded by both Billy Graham and Bishop Jack Dain to participate. In God's providence, Stott and Graham emerged as the two greatest figures of both the Lausanne Congress and the Lausanne Movement. Together, they articulated the vision of Lausanne: "The

---

2. "Religion: A Challenge from Evangelicals," *Time* magazine, 5 August 1974. https://content.time.com/time/subscriber/article/0,33009,879423,00.html.

Whole Church to take the Whole Gospel to the Whole World." Together, they also embodied the spirit of Lausanne: "Humility, Friendship, Study, Prayer, Partnership, and Hope."[3]

Whereas the participants at the historic Edinburgh Missionary Conference in 1910 had been almost exclusively missionary leaders, participation at Lausanne '74 was broadened to include pastors, church leaders, and scholars, as well as leaders from business, government, and the media.

Contributions of the Lausanne Congress

Three great contributions of global significance emanated from the first Lausanne Congress: *The Lausanne Covenant*, holistic mission, and an new missiological paradigm in relation to unreached people groups. We will consider each of these in turn. The greatest of these contributions was *The Lausanne Covenant*. *The Lausanne Covenant* – whose primary architect was Stott – is widely regarded as the most significant missions document produced in the Protestant era. A concise and commanding expression of evangelicalism, it has served as a uniting force and mobilizing impetus for world evangelization after the Congress.

The second contribution from Lausanne was an expanded understanding of mission. In response to the prominence given to the "social gospel" in the early and mid-twentieth century by the World Council of Churches (WCC), evangelicals increasingly reacted by neglecting their historic commitment to the social implications of the gospel. Thanks to the work of Latin American theologians Samuel Escobar and Rene Padilla – both brilliant young Latin American theologians and student workers – this trend changed dramatically at Lausanne and in the years that followed.

The third great contribution of Lausanne '74 was the introduction of a new missiological paradigm. Prior to 1974, mission and church leaders commonly thought in terms of sending missionaries to all countries. Because it was believed that churches had been established in nearly every country, some Christian leaders – primarily those in the World Council of Churches – were calling for a moratorium on missions. However, Dr. Ralph Winter challenged this understanding by introducing the concept of nations as ethnolinguistic people

---

3. In a meeting with Billy Graham in his home in October 2005, I told him that I had often heard people speak of "the spirit of Lausanne" but had never heard anyone explain what they meant by that. Billy Graham smiled and said, "The spirit of Lausanne? It's a spirit of humility and friendship, study and prayer, partnership and hope."

groups. He estimated that there were some sixteen thousand *ethnolinguistic people groups*, representing over 2.3 billion people, who had no access to the witness of the gospel.[4] This new paradigm would come to impact virtually every evangelical mission society, seminary, and mission-sending church in the world.

The Lausanne Movement

Perhaps the most unexpected result of the Congress was the birth of the Lausanne Movement itself, an outcome that Billy Graham had not envisioned.

The seed of this idea was first sown early in 1973 on the campus of Trinity Evangelical Divinity School (TEDS) in Deerfield, Illinois, during a discussion between faculty members Paul Little – a professor of evangelism who also served with InterVarsity as the director of the Urbana Missionary Conferences – and Dr. David Wells – a young professor of Theology and Church History at TEDS.

After returning to Trinity following a Lausanne '74 planning meeting, Little, who had been asked by Billy Graham to direct the Programme Team, asked Wells why the Edinburgh 1910 World Missionary Conference had such a powerful ongoing impact. David Wells responded with a rather simple answer: "They formed a *continuation committee*."[5]

With that simple statement, an idea was born. A decision was made to constitute a fifty-person "Lausanne Continuation Committee" to carry forward the work of the Congress.

In 1975, a few months after the congress in Lausanne, Switzerland, the Continuation Committee met in Mexico, and there the "Lausanne Committee for World Evangelization" (LCWE) was born. Leighton Ford was selected as its chairman, Gottfried Osei-Mensah was appointed the first international director, John Stott was selected to chair the Theology Working Group, and Peter Wagner was appointed to chair the Strategy Working Group.

Commenting on Lausanne '74 and the ensuing Lausanne Movement, Stott wrote, "Many a conference has resembled a fireworks display. It has made a loud noise and illuminated the night sky for a few brief brilliant seconds. What

---

4. Ralph Winter's plenary address at Lausanne 1974, "The Highest Priority: Cross-Cultural Evangelism." https://lausanne.org/wp-content/uploads/2007/06/0213.pdf.

5. Interview with Dr. David Wells in his office at Gordon-Conwell Theological Seminary. David Wells was a protégé of Dr. John Stott with whom he served on the Lausanne Theology Working group from 1982 to 1991.

is exciting about Lausanne is that its fire continues to spark off other fires that continue to light up the skies."[6]

Those "fires" were ignited primarily by the Theology Working Group and the Strategy Working Group as they wrestled with issues such as *Christianity and Culture*, *The Homogeneous Unit Principle*, *The Simple Lifestyle*, *The Role of the Holy Spirit and Evangelism*, and *The Nature of Conversion*. Each of these consultations produced a report that was published by the Lausanne Movement and known as "Lausanne Occasional Papers."

Between Lausanne '74 and Lausanne II in Manila in 1989, the Lausanne Movement also convened two global gatherings that were of particular significance to the movement. The first was the "Consultation on World Evangelization," held in Pattaya, Thailand, in June 1980 with almost nine hundred participants. The primary focus of this gathering was on reaching unreached people groups. The second global gathering was the Younger Leaders Gathering, convened by Lausanne chairman Leighton Ford and held in Singapore in 1987. This conference brought together three hundred younger leaders from nearly eighty countries.

Lausanne II in Manila

By the time Lausanne convened the Younger Leaders Gathering (Singapore '87), the Committee had announced plans to convene a second Lausanne Congress in Singapore in 1989. Dr. Thomas Wang – a Hong Kong Chinese leader who possessed formidable skills as a visionary and mobilizer – was appointed to serve as the new international director for Lausanne. He replaced Gottfried Osei-Mensah, from Ghana, who had served with remarkable effectiveness as the first international director for many years.

Wang, who had been a Lausanne stalwart as a leader in the Chinese Coordination Centre of World Evangelization (CCCOWE), was captivated by the discovery of an abundance of global plans that were being developed with a focus on the approaching millennial change in the year 2000. He was eager that the second Lausanne congress should focus on completing the task of world evangelization by AD 2000. However, some Lausanne leaders expressed caution about focusing Lausanne II on overly ambitious plans to complete the task of world evangelization within a ten-year period. Tensions began to develop between Wang and key members of the Lausanne Committee.

---

6. John Stott, *Making Christ Known: Historic Documents from the Lausanne Movement, 1974–1989*.

By the middle of 1988, just one year before the Congress was due to be held, two major crises arose. The first was financial in nature. Singapore was proving to be far too expensive. Second, Wang proceeded to convene a consultation of three hundred global leaders, scheduled to meet in Singapore in January 1989, with a singular focus on AD 2000.

By the end of that meeting, a plan was in place to begin the AD 2000 Movement, with Wang as its chair. This development heightened the tensions within the Lausanne Movement. The Congress needed to be moved to Manila, and its international director was moving in a different direction.

Despite the tensions, and despite the logistical challenges of moving to a congress venue in a predominantly Catholic country that was suspicious of evangelicals, Wang and the leaders of the Lausanne Committee successfully convened "Lausanne II" in Manila in July 1989. Over four thousand leaders from every part of the world were in attendance. Lausanne II was characterized by four great contributions: a convergence of evangelicals, Pentecostals, and charismatics; a sizeable delegation from the Soviet Union; *The Manila Manifesto*; and hundreds of new missions partnerships.

The first contribution was the joyous coming together of mainstream evangelicals with charismatics and Pentecostals. This had been made possible, in large part, because of the trusting friendship that had been nurtured between Leighton Ford, the Lausanne chair, and Thomas Zimmerman, the general superintendent of the Assemblies of God. Plenary addresses were given by Jack Hayford, president of the Foursquare Church, John Stott, chair of the Lausanne Theology Working Group, and theologian J. I. Packer. Each of these addresses provided a biblical and missional foundation for unity and partnership in world evangelization.

The second significant impact of the Congress in Manila was the participation of two hundred pastors from Russia and the Soviet Union. Their arrival, which had been in jeopardy, was met with thunderous applause when they finally entered the congress hall after a two-day delay. At the time of the Congress, in July 1989, no one could have predicted or imagined that in just four months, the Berlin Wall would fall, sparking the collapse of the Soviet Union. The presence of the leaders from Russia and the Soviet Union led to the formation of new friendships that would lead to new mission partnerships that, in turn, fostered Protestant growth in Eastern Europe and Central Asia in the decade that followed.

The third contribution was the production of *The Manila Manifesto*, another congress document that was developed by John Stott. This document built upon *The Lausanne Covenant* by elaborating on issues that needed to be developed further and by addressing new challenges and opportunities for world evangelization that had emerged in the fifteen years since the first Lausanne Congress in 1974.

A fourth contribution of Lausanne II – one of the fruits of the Lausanne Congress that was realized nearly ten years later – was the development of some three hundred new partnerships and world evangelization initiatives.[7] One of the most significant of these was the formation of the Forum of Bible Agencies International, which dramatically increased cooperation among Bible agencies, as well as increasing the rate of Bible translation and distribution. This last development in particular underscores a distinctive value of the Lausanne Movement – "Collaboration," which is made possible by the spirit of Lausanne and by the joyful recognition that "the fruit of Lausanne grows on other people's trees!"[8]

"The Quiet Years": 1990–2000

Though God had blessed the second Lausanne Congress in many ways, following the conclusion of that congress, the Lausanne Movement experienced challenges. There was understandable disappointment that two hundred Chinese participants were not allowed to attend because of the unrest in China following the "Tiananmen Square" incident. There was also disappointment over the absence of Billy Graham from the Congress.[9] More significantly, the Lausanne Movement faced leadership fatigue and turnover.

When it was birthed in 1974, no one knew whether the Lausanne Movement would continue for even five years, let alone ten or fifteen years. Many of

---

7. Roger Parrott, Program Chair, The Lausanne Global Forum, Pattaya, 2004, Opening Address. Roger had served on the Leadership Team of Lausanne II in Manila with Leighton Ford, Chair, and Thomas Wang, International Director. Dr. Parrott first shared this discovery in 1999 at Lausanne Leadership Meetings in Atlanta, Georgia during a time of assessment and reflection on Lausanne II from a distance of 10 years.

8. This statement is not original with the author, however I often used this quote as an expression of the spirit of collaboration, and the spirit of generosity that characterizes the Lausanne Movement.

9. I served as the Assistant to the Congress Director, Paul MaKaughan, at Lausanne II in Manila. I was present when Mr. Hank Holley, a long time associate of Billy Graham, came to meet with Leighton Ford, Paul McKaughan, and Ed Dayton, Program Director for Lausanne II. Hank Holley shared the news that Billy Graham would not be present – as had been planned and eagerly anticipated. The official reason that was given was that Billy Graham felt he must continue his preaching mission in London. However, there was speculation that his interest in the Lausanne Movement was waning. Billy Graham was scheduled to give the opening address in Manila.

the leaders, including Leighton Ford, John Stott, and Don Hoke, had served effectively and continuously from the beginning. There was neither precedent nor an established procedure for a changing of the guard. In addition to the toll exacted by financial, logistical, and philosophical challenges in organizing the Congress, there was also the recognition that the new AD 2000 Movement had co-opted many of the people who had been part of the Lausanne Movement. Thomas Wang stepped down as Lausanne's international director at the end of Lausanne II to become chairman of the AD 2000 Movement, along with his colleague Luis Bush, who served as AD 2000's international director.

In 1992, Leighton Ford – after leading and shaping the Lausanne Movement for seventeen years – stepped down from the role of chairman. Whereas Graham and Stott had played key roles in helping to launch and give global visibility to Lausanne, Ford translated the Lausanne '74 moment into an enduring movement, for which he was properly honoured as Honorary Lifetime Executive Chair.

In the ten years following Lausanne II in Manila, the Lausanne Movement experienced three changes in senior leadership as chairmanship passed from Ford to Bishop John Reid from Australia, then to Fergus Macdonald, a leader of the United Bible Societies, and then to Paul Cedar, who served as president of the Evangelical Free Church and chairman of Mission America – the American counterpart of the Lausanne Movement. Even though all these people were of international stature and exceptional ability, within the Lausanne Movement, these years came to be known as the "quiet years." Although Lausanne was still highly regarded, as was *The Lausanne Covenant*, many national committees ceased to be active, few consultations were held, and funding dried up.

In 1999, on the tenth anniversary of Lausanne II, when the remnant of Lausanne leaders met for a meeting, the primary matter under discussion was whether to continue or discontinue the Lausanne Movement. There were many who thought that although Lausanne had served a useful and powerful purpose for a period of time, that time had now come to an end. But there were others who felt, just as strongly, that the Lausanne Movement was needed more than ever before and that a new season was about to begin. There was a lack of consensus.

Cape Town 2010: Revitalization of the Lausanne Movement

If Lausanne '74 represented the *naissance* of the Lausanne Movement and Lausanne II represented its ongoing global *significance* as a convener and nerve centre for world evangelization, Cape Town 2010 symbolized its *renaissance*.

By 1999, the global Lausanne Movement had no office, no full-time staff, no funds, and no planned regional or global consultations. The only source of income for this "global movement" was a monthly gift of US$1,000 given by World Vision to cover the cost of a monthly sixty-minute conference call between the chairman and the members of Lausanne Committee, which consisted of about fifteen people.

In 2002, one highly respected Christian leader commented, "Lausanne was a select group of people dealing with significant issues at a unique time in history. Those people are gone; the issues are from the past, and that time is now behind us." He went on to add, "Lausanne is a history to be celebrated, but not a movement to be continued."

However, Paul Cedar and those still on the Committee felt differently. There were still national committees that continued to maintain relationships and partnerships. This was particularly the case in the Nordic countries, as well as in England, Germany, Australia, and the US. There was also a biennial gathering in Asia, which was known as the Asia Lausanne Consultation on World Evangelization (ALCOWE).

When the Lausanne Committee met in Lausanne, Switzerland, for their annual meeting in 2001, the decision was made to convene a Global Forum on World Evangelization in 2004. This Forum would consist primarily of twenty-four Issue Groups or "Mini-Consultations." Each Issue Group leader would be encouraged to invite between twenty-five and fifty people to join their group.

This was a risk. Given the fact that Lausanne had not held a major global gathering in many years, it was understood that if this Global Forum generated little interest the Lausanne Movement would have had run its course.

Three years later, when we met in Pattaya, Thailand, in October 2004, all expectations had been exceeded. The issue groups had grown in number from twenty-four to thirty-one. The number of projected participants had doubled, increasing from 750 to a total of more than 1,500 registered participants, over 40 percent of whom were participating in a Lausanne event for the first time.

There was fresh wind in the sails of the Lausanne Movement.

New Leadership

Eight months prior to the 2004 Global Forum, Cedar called me to ask if I was willing to be nominated to serve as the new chair of the Lausanne Movement. I felt that the new leader should be from the Majority World. Paul said that he agreed with me in principle. However, he went on to say that when he had prayed about the matter, my name had come to mind clearly and repeatedly.

I agreed to have my name included as part of the process but said that I would advocate for a non-Western leader. As it turned out, the process eventuated in my appointment in June 2004. I was installed as Lausanne's new chair on the final evening of the 2004 Lausanne Consultation.

Cedar "loaned" his Mission America communications director, Naomi Frizzell, to Lausanne for twenty hours a week. Naomi and I made up the entirety of the staff as we entered this new season. Though we only had a combined workforce of thirty hours a week and a budget of US$1,000 a month, it was quite apparent that many people were eager to be part of the revitalization of this great global movement.

Four Priorities for the Revitalization of Lausanne

Our new leadership team had four priorities for revitalizing Lausanne. Our first and highest priority was to elevate "theology" to its rightful place of prominence in Lausanne. We were concerned that by the end of the twentieth century, too much of the mission enterprise had been captivated by metrics, megaplans, money, and managerial paradigms. As a consequence, theology was often relegated to a secondary or subservient role.

Chris Wright agreed to serve as the chair of the Theology Working Group. He brought rich experience and impressive credentials as a missionary, Old Testament scholar, the former principal of All Nations Christian College, and the international director of Langham Partnership.

Our second priority was to enlist John Stott to serve as the honorary chair. Stott's engagement and strong endorsement sent signals of hope and confidence for Lausanne's future.

Third, we believed that the best and fastest way to give Lausanne visibility and vitality globally was to establish a new cadre of leaders from twelve regions of the world to serve as International Deputy Directors (IDDs). All twelve regions of the world had IDDs in place within six months of the conclusion of the 2004 Forum. These IDDs became the eyes and the ears for the Lausanne Movement, as well as being persuasive advocates for the vision and spirit of Lausanne.

Our fourth priority was to appoint leaders who could serve as chairs of the remaining three working groups: Strategy, Communications, and Intercession. Once Paul Eshleman, Steve Woodworth, and Sarah Plummer filled these positions, our new leadership team was in place. In just one year, we had a new executive chair, honorary chair, international director, twelve IDDs, four newly constituted working groups, and thirty-one issue group leaders and their newly gathered networks from around the world.

In June 2005, we gathered in Hong Kong with seventy-five members of our reconstituted Lausanne Movement Leadership. This included an Executive Committee made up of the twelve IDDs, and some 30 issue specialists who served as Lausanne Senior Associates. At that time, plans were made to bring together five hundred younger leaders, selected from the twelve regions of the world, for a Lausanne Younger Leaders Gathering in Port Dickson, Malaysia, in October 2006 (YLG '06). An exploratory team was also formed to consider the possibility of a third Lausanne Congress in 2010. In Hong Kong, we were also joined by Terry Douglass, an American engineer and business executive, who advised Lausanne and gave generously to the organization.

Preparing for a Third Congress

With the growing leadership strength, together with the successful completion of YLG '06 and significant progress in raising funds, the decision was made at our leadership team meetings in Kuala Lumpur in 2006 to convene the Third Lausanne Congress on World Evangelization in 2010. The year 2010 was chosen as it was the one hundredth anniversary of the 1910 World Missionary Conference. There was widespread recognition that the church around the world was facing new opportunities as well as daunting challenges that would impact the global mission of the church.

The year 2007 would prove to be a pivotal year in the work of revitalizing Lausanne. Early that year, the decision was made to hold the congress in Cape Town, South Africa. We formed a South Africa leadership team and a thirty-member Pan-Africa Advisory Committee. In June 2007, Lausanne convened a global gathering in Budapest – to discuss the dates, budget, and themes for the upcoming Congress – at which 350 Lausanne leaders, representing every part of the world and every major Lausanne gathering, were present.

During the next three years, the four thousand two hundred participants were selected, GlobaLink was built for six hundred sites around the world, and 18 million USD was raised for the revitalization of the Lausanne Movement and for the Third Lausanne Congress – Cape Town 2010. Over 120 gatherings and consultations were held in sixty countries around the world with mission leaders, denominational and church officials, college and seminary presidents, as well as leaders from other Christian bodies – including the World Evangelical Alliance, the World Council of Churches, Orthodox Patriarchs, the Vatican, African Indigenous Churches, and the China Christian Council.

The Cape Town Congress

Christianity Today called Cape Town 2010 the most globally representative gathering of Christian leaders in history. The 4,200 participants from 198 countries represented a microcosm of the global church. At the congress these 4,200 participants became 700 small communities as they sat together at tables for six during plenary sessions to pray, study, listen, discuss, and process the Bible expositions that began the day and the presentations that were made on the great themes of the Congress. Afternoons featured a wide array of breakout sessions on different topics. The evening plenary sessions, which were themed "God is on the Move," showcased God's work on each continent.

Impact of Cape Town 2010

In this section, I will highlight five ways in which the Cape Town Congress impacted the Lausanne Movement and the cause of world evangelization.

First, *The Cape Town Commitment*. *The Cape Town Commitment* consists of both theological affirmations and strategic priorities. The first section is entitled "For the Lord We Love" and the second part "For the World We Serve." Chris Wright, the chief architect of this congress document, was assisted by eighteen theologians representing every region of the world. *The Cape Town Commitment* was the first document of this kind to be written in the language of God's covenantal love.

Second, a revitalized Lausanne Movement in "the spirit of Lausanne." Given the growth of evangelicalism around the world, the huge multiplication of mission organizations, church movements, and leadership training models, and the individualistic and entrepreneurial nature of evangelicalism, Lausanne represents a gift to the global church by providing the space for meeting together to see what we look like and to hear what we are thinking about. It also provides national, regional, and global networks of friendship and trusting partnerships across regional, organizational, ecclesiastical, and theological boundaries.

Third, theologians and strategists working together. Theologians are people who think, analyze, write, and critique. Strategists are more inclined to plan, to initiate, to do, and to measure progress against stated goals. Both types of activities are necessary. In Lausanne, we believe that "all theological reflection must find expression in mission action, and that all mission action must be theologically grounded."[10]

Fourth, generous giving. The "spirit of Lausanne" manifested itself in an unanticipated spirit of collaboration and generosity through the impact of the newly formed Resource Mobilization Working Group. The result was an increase in giving for world evangelization, totalling to a sum of approximately 100 million US dollars a year – as documented by the National Christian Foundation and by Rob Martin, Lausanne's Global Catalyst for Generosity and architect of the "Lausanne Standards."[11]

Fifth, a new generation of leaders. More than one thousand of the participants at Cape Town were under forty years of age. Many of them are now in positions of leadership within the Lausanne Movement. In 2016, they convened a Younger Leaders Gathering in Jakarta for one thousand younger leaders who have further infused the Movement with vision, energy, and global connections.

Conclusion

Lausanne '74 was the seminal event. No global congress before or since has had its depth of impact or breadth of influence. It was a gift from God through the magnanimous spirit of people like Graham and Stott. Lausanne II and III built upon Lausanne's legacy and added to it. This is a legacy that the global church should cherish, steward, and carefully and generously pass on from one generation to the next.

Knowing our history shapes our future. Indeed, those who will best guide us into the future are those with the most comprehensive understanding of the past. Just as Graham, Stott, Ford, Osei-Mensah, and other leaders of the first generation learned from and drew inspiration from the Edinburgh 1910 conference, I trust that the next generation will be informed and inspired by

---

10. Peter Kuzmic, a longtime member of the Lausanne Theology Working Group shared this statement with me in my office at Gordon-Conwell shortly after I became the new chair for Lausanne. We were discussing a common tension that exists among theologians and strategists. Peter was seeking to underscore the fact they they must understand that distinctive role that each plays, and that they must work together.

11. This was shared by Rob Martin, Chair of the Lausanne Standards project, and by David Wills, the President of the National Christian Foundation, at the time of a 10th Anniversary of the Cape Town 2010 Congress. This came as a great surprise as this had not been a stated goal or anticipated outcome of Cape Town 2010. It was the result of a community of global donors and foundations that began to meet together in Oxford in 2006, and then in Budapest in 2007 where they would form the Lausanne Resource Mobilization Working Group.

what happened first at Lausanne '74 and subsequently by this movement that has continued to "light up the skies" in the fifty years since.

Bibliography

Stott, John. *Making Christ Known: Historic Documents from the Lausanne Movement, 1974–1989*. Grand Rapids: Eerdmans, 1997.

Time magazine, July 1974.

4

The Lausanne Covenant (1974), The Manila Manifesto (1989), The Cape Town Commitment (2010): The Foundation and Fruit of the Movement

Kiichi "Paul" Ariga and Kohei Takeda

> When the foundations are being destroyed, what can the righteous do? (Ps 11:3)
>
> no one can lay any foundation other than the one already laid, which is Jesus Christ (1 Cor 3:11)
>
> Therefore if you have any encouragement from being united with Christ, if any comfort from his love, if any common sharing in the Spirit, if any tenderness and compassion, then make my joy complete by being like-minded, having the same love, being one in spirit and of one mind (Phil 2:1–2)

What we believe shapes who we are and how we live. As believers, we know that this is true in our own lives since we have personally experienced continued transformation from the time we believed in Jesus as our Saviour. It is Jesus Christ and our faith in him that defines our whole being and life – our identity, attitudes, priorities, and actions towards God and others. On the other hand, we must note that throughout church history, God did not only shape believers' lives individually but also shaped the life of the church – that is, the global body of Christ – collectively. The Lausanne Movement is one of the historic ways in which God fundamentally shaped the life of the global church in modern history. Transformation was led by convening diverse Christian leaders, whose collective confession of faith deepened their identity – as those united as one in Christ – and shaped their trajectory of missional endeavours for more than half a century.

In July 1974, under Billy Graham's leadership, God convened 2,700 Christian leaders from nearly 150 countries to the International Congress on World Evangelization – as it was then called – in Lausanne, Switzerland. Along with the blessings of prayer, fellowship, and scholarship, God granted something special and historic to the global church – the formation of *The Lausanne Covenant*, with John Stott as its chief architect. *The Lausanne Covenant*, which is one of the significant fruits of the Congress, became the foundation that led Lausanne from a convention to a movement on a global scale that has continued to have an immense impact on the global church for over 50 years.

No sooner was Lausanne '74 convened and *The Lausanne Covenant* made than Lausanne emerged as a global evangelization movement. This bore two tangible fruits in the congresses that followed: *The Manila Manifesto* (Lausanne II, 1989) and *The Cape Town Commitment* (Lausanne III, 2010). Built upon the foundation of *The Lausanne Covenant*, these declarations of faith were the result of careful biblical and theological discussions on what the church is and what the church is called to do in order to obey the Great Commission and fulfil God's mission. History portrays *The Lausanne Covenant* as a united, humble, and yet articulate expression of faith with which God has blessed the global church. It is because of God's faithfulness in accordance with his divine story and purpose that the Lausanne Movement has been used to advance the kingdom thus far. By God's grace, each of the confessions created in a Lausanne congress has continued to shape and transform the life of the global church – by discerning who we are as the global church, revealing what we ought to do in fulfilment of God's mission, and deepening unity and collaboration for world evangelization.

In this chapter, we will reflect on the confessions of faith from each of the Lausanne congresses with which God blessed the global church, especially in regard to leadership development. Moreover, we will share how God led the Lausanne Movement to deepen leadership development over time based on the foundation of *The Lausanne Covenant*. This will give a clearer view of how the Lausanne Movement from 1974 to 2024 is a critical part of God's story and plan to bless the world even more. We hope that these perspectives would produce more faith, hope, and love among us even in this uncertain age. In sharing this chapter, our desire is to first glorify and give thanks to God by reflecting on how he led the Lausanne Movement to form and transform our faith and life. Second, with even greater hope in Christ, at Seoul 2024, through Lausanne 4 and beyond, we want to faithfully recommit ourselves to Christ for the future advancement of his kingdom.

The Lausanne Covenant (1974)

In modern church history, *The Lausanne Covenant* is widely known as one of the most significant and foundational documents that formed the missions of the global church. It has been a great rallying call to the evangelical church around the world. John Stott, architect of *The Lausanne Covenant*, wrote in his commentary that only history would prove whether or not *The Lausanne Covenant* is the most significant ecumenical confession on evangelism[1] – and after fifty years, we witness history's verdict that God truly did make this happen. As Doug Birdsall, chairman of Lausanne III states, *The Lausanne Covenant* has played a significant role in the modern church and its missions, just as the ancient confessions and creeds produced by church councils defined the identity of the church in relation to God, oneself, and others.[2]

The Lausanne Covenant defines what it means to be evangelical in terms of having Scripture as the final authority for what we believe and how we live. This is a covenant with God himself and, yet, also a covenant with one another as brothers and sisters in Christ, which challenges Christ-followers to collaborate in sharing the good news of Jesus with the whole world. Chris Wright, chief architect of *The Cape Town Commitment* explains that the uniqueness of *The Lausanne Covenant* lies in its emphasis on the wholeness of the gospel:

> There is a wholesome balance of biblical truth and mission imperatives. This is one reason why it is so appropriately called a covenant, since that is precisely true of the biblical covenants themselves. The *Covenant* makes many ringing declarations, strong affirmative statements of what the Bible teaches, and we joyfully raise our voices in agreement. Yet it never lets us rest content with signing a mere statement of faith. Again and again it

---

1. Stott, "Lausanne Covenant," https://lausanne.org/occasional-paper/lop-3.
2. Birdsall, "Lausanne Covenant," https://lausanne.org/content/lausanne-covenant-foreword-birdsall.

calls for commitments to be undertaken, for choices to be made, for promises to be kept, for sacrifice to be endured, for words to be spoken and actions to be taken.[3]

The well-known Lausanne slogan – "the whole church taking the whole gospel to the whole world" – is derived directly from *The Lausanne Covenant*, which Stott originally drafted. This means that *The Lausanne Covenant* defines evangelization in terms of "who," "what," and "where" or "how" to advance God's kingdom – a theological and practical application of sharing the good news, keeping with the authority of Scripture and expressed with a sense of urgency.

We see that *The Lausanne Covenant* aligns well with Billy Graham's vision of world evangelization, which views the Christian faith as both *being* united with God and *doing* God's missions. This is reflected in Graham's words: "In the struggle for righteousness, there is nothing more helpful than being passionately in tune with Christ through His Spirit and being passionately committed to doing His will."[4]

Confession of Failures in Leadership Development

Since this is a book on leadership development, we cannot ignore the section on "Education and Leadership" in *The Lausanne Covenant*. We find this in the eleventh chapter.

> We confess that we have sometimes pursued church growth at the expense of church depth, and divorced evangelism from Christian nurture. We also acknowledge that some of our missions have been too slow to equip and encourage national leaders to assume their rightful responsibilities.[5]

It is interesting that this chapter begins with a vulnerable confession of two shortcomings of the church in leadership development – Stott terms this "a frank double confession."[6] First, we confess that the church leadership becomes unhealthy when we pursue quantitative growth over qualitative growth or when we divorce evangelism from Christian formation that focuses on developing

---

3. Wright, "Lausanne Covenant: Foreword." https://lausanne.org/content/lausanne-covenant-foreword-wright.
4. Nelson, "Billy Graham in Quotes."
5. "Lausanne Covenant," 11. Education and Leadership.
6. Stott, "Lausanne Covenant," https://lausanne.org/occasional-paper/lop-3.

Christian character and lifestyle. Such actions result in the superficiality of our faith. Second, in the area of missionary work, we confess that we have been reluctant to equip national leaders to fulfil their rightful responsibilities. These two shortcomings could be the result of character flaws such as pride, hunger for power, and desire for control in the lives of leaders, which seem to be some of "the acts of the flesh" that the apostle Paul lists as being contrary to "the fruit of the Spirit" (Gal 5:19–23). In other words, these confessions acknowledge that there are some core issues that we underestimate and, therefore, fail to provide the necessary character formation in education and leadership development. *The Lausanne Covenant* calls for effective, contextualized, and well-balanced education – theologically and practically – for church leaders, which includes pastors and lay leaders of every nation.

It may surprise us to see such honest, vulnerable, and yet to-the-point self-assessment and confession in *The Lausanne Covenant*. However, we believe that this humble approach set the tone of the leadership culture of the Lausanne Movement, emphasizing humility and integrity. In his commentary, Stott explains that *The Lausanne Covenant* points to a twofold biblical solution.[7] First, we must pursue two biblical principals in leadership: (1) delegation to local leaders and (2) focus on Christlike character in leadership development. The former is evident in the apostle Paul's instruction to Titus to "appoint elders in every town" (Titus 1:5), thereby delegating authorities to local leaders. We must first realize that leadership structures should not be centralized in the global church, an idea that is supported by the biblical principle that Christian leaders should always be those who serve rather than seeking for others to serve them, which was ultimately exemplified by Jesus in his life. This means that the Christian style of leadership should always be countercultural to the world's secular style that aspires for and exerts power.

The second biblical solution to the modern leadership issue is theological education for both pastors and lay leaders in the church. Stott points out that most problems that churches are facing are theological. Thus, equipping church leaders with sound theology would help them to solve problems by applying theological principles. Furthermore, theological education is indispensable in teaching the word of God. At Lausanne I, there was extensive discussion on the need for such education, especially in the Majority World, followed by the suggestion to build networks and fellowship among theological institutions and have regional and national teacher exchange programmes.

---

7. Stott, "Lausanne Covenant," 11B(i.). https://lausanne.org/occasional-paper/lop-3.

The Manila Manifesto (1989)

Fifteen years after the International Congress on World Evangelization in 1974, the second congress on evangelization was convened in Manila, Philippines, with 4,000 global leaders from 173 countries. With its expansive global representation, the Congress provided what Edward Dayton, the programme director, called "a marvellous 'town meeting' of people from all over the world who could find new networks, new relationships, new challenges, and thus move toward the goal of the Lausanne Movement."[8]

The Manila Manifesto emerged from Lausanne II as an elaboration of *The Lausanne Covenant*. It begins with twenty-one theological affirmations that were distilled from *The Lausanne Covenant*, followed by the sections that declare the mission of the church in three categories: "the Whole Gospel," "the Whole Church," and "the Whole World."

Elaborate Repentance in Leadership Development

The Manila Manifesto has no section on "leadership" and does not even use this term. However, the section on the "Whole Church"[9] elaborates on roles, integration, and integrity in the ministry of witness in some partnerships – for example, pastors and lay leaders, men and women, and older and younger generations. First, pastors and teachers are to lead God's people to maturity and equip them for ministry, not by monopolizing the church but by encouraging others to use their unique gifts and multiplying Jesus's disciples who make disciples. For men and women, they are equal in dignity since God created them both in his image. Thus, we agree to serve with one another in partnership in world evangelization in accordance with what God intended. Finally, *The Manila Manifesto* recognizes the significance of children and young people, who enrich the church's worship and outreach. Thus, we need to train these groups in discipleship and evangelism so that they may reach their own generation for Christ.

Christlike integrity is indispensable in all this integration and unity of the church, whether between clergy and laity, men and women, or older and younger generations. In the ministry of evangelism and discipleship, we ourselves must first be obedient to Jesus Christ, our Lord, by denying ourselves and taking up our cross to follow him. This means that we must die

---

8. Dayton, "Manila Manifesto," Introduction. https://lausanne.org/content/introduction-2.
9. "Manila Manifesto." https://lausanne.org/statement/the-manila-manifesto, sections 6 and 7.

to self, ambition, dishonesty, and covetousness and live a life of simplicity, contentment, and generosity.[10] Section 6 says, "We repent of our share in discouraging the ministry of laity, especially women and young people. We determine in the future to encourage all Christ's followers to take their place, rightfully and naturally, as his witnesses." The subsequent section goes on to repent of our dishonesty: "We deplore the failures in Christian consistency which we see in both Christians and churches: material greed, professional pride and rivalry, competition in Christian service, jealousy of younger leaders, missionary paternalism, the lack of mutual accountability, the loss of Christian standards of sexuality, and racial, social, sexual discrimination."

This confession is sobering and surprisingly relevant even to the church today. In a spirit of humility and self-admonition, we must admit that Christian leadership development is still an unmet need. At the same time, however, we have greater hope in Christ since we believe in the gospel that promises continued transformation of our whole being into Christ's likeness through our faith. *The Manila Manifesto* is critical in that it acknowledges and elaborates on core issues in leadership and calls for integration and integrity in the church across professions, genders, and generations, whereas *The Lausanne Covenant* places greater emphasis on healthy relationships between global and local (indigenous) leadership. Though *The Manila Manifesto* may not have had the same historic impact as the foundational *Lausanne Covenant*, it represented a significant and necessary step forward in the church's journey to maturity.

The Cape Town Commitment (2010)

Under God's guidance, the Third Lausanne Congress on World Evangelization was convened in Cape Town, South Africa, in October 2010, and it bore the fruit of the greatly anticipated *The Cape Town Commitment*. With the attendance of four thousand Christian leaders, representing 198 countries, this Congress has been called the most diverse gathering of Christian leaders in the two-thousand-year history of the Christian movement.[11] One mark of uniqueness of Lausanne III was its diversity, not only in nationality but also generation and global representation, with 55 percent of participants being under the age of fifty and two-thirds of speakers and presenters being from Africa, Latin America, and Asia, where two-thirds of evangelicals lived. With

---

10. "Manila Manifesto," https://lausanne.org/statement/the-manila-manifesto, section 7.
11. Kennedy, "Diverse Gathering," https://www.christianitytoday.com/ct/2010/september/34.66.html.

the integration of generations and local leaders from across the globe, it could be said that the organizing of Lausanne III itself – led by the chairman, Doug Birdsall – was God's response to the confessions and the fulfilment of the needs set out in *The Lausanne Covenant* and *The Manila Manifesto*.

It was in such a setting that God blessed the global church with *The Cape Town Commitment*, which is immensely significant in terms of both its content and sphere of influence that defined the direction and focus of the mission work of the global church. And indeed, it also served as a roadmap for the Lausanne Movement over the next ten years. The heart of *The Cape Town Commitment* – which is demonstrated in the title itself – is its confession of faith and call to action. First, *The Cape Town Commitment* seeks to present a confession of Christian faith around the theme of love – love for God, love for one another, and love for the world – which is documented in Part I. The second half of *The Cape Town Commitment* is a call for action that clarifies the priorities of Christian mission that the global church should be addressing in the twenty-first century. This call to action was shared in the six themes that emerged after listening to the voices of each region and discerning major mission challenges facing the church. Chris Wright, the chair of the Cape Town 2010 Statement Working Group, comments,

> The Cape Town Commitment is not the memorial of a movement. It is the conviction of a Movement and the voice of multitude. It distils a vast quantity from the global Church. We profoundly hope and pray that we are hearing not just the voice of Cape Town 2010, but the voice of our Lord Jesus Christ who walked among us there.[12]

A Call for Action to Pursue Christ-Centred Leadership

"Leadership" is one of the key focuses of *The Cape Town Commitment*, which devotes comparatively more space for this specific topic than *The Lausanne Covenant* and *The Manila Manifesto*. The term "leadership development" was also first introduced in *The Cape Town Commitment*, though it clearly sets the concept apart from, and rejects, any secular connotation. The concept is most extensively articulated in *The Cape Town Commitment* in the section IID-3, "Christ-Centered Leaders" under the theme of "Discerning the will of Christ

---

12. Wright, "Cape Town Commitment," https://lausanne.org/statement/ctcommitment.

for world evangelization" in the Cape Town Call to Action. It is noteworthy that this call is motivated by love for God and for his people, as described in Part I.

The Cape Town Commitment uncovers two core problems regarding leadership: (1) appointing un-discipled leaders who aspire for power, status, and personal enrichment and (2) neglecting character formation in leadership development. Though this may sound blunt, it is painfully pertinent. Biblically speaking, only those whose lives have been transformed by mature discipleship should be appointed as Christian leaders. Un-Christlike or worldly leadership will only cause "reductionist evangelism, neglected discipling and shallow growth"[13] among the people being led. Furthermore, even Christian leadership programmes sometimes focus on equipping people with knowledge, skills, and techniques but miss out on developing godly character. Other times, leadership programmes fail to equip people with indispensable skills – that is, skills to teach God's word. These failures point to a lack of genuine discipleship in the church.

In light of this, *The Cape Town Commitment* calls for four concrete actions in leadership development: (1) Reinforce discipleship in the church so that only those who meet the standards of biblical maturity are appointed as leaders; (2) Commit ourselves to pray for our leaders; (3) Recognize our vulnerability and engage in an accountability group; and (4) Integrate spiritual and character formation in leadership training programmes in seminaries.

From Faith to Faith

Looking back on Lausanne's fifty-year history, God has indeed blessed each of the three confessions of faith – *The Lausanne Covenant*, *The Manila Manifesto*, and *The Cape Town Commitment*. In *The Lausanne Covenant*, the church discerned, acknowledged, and confessed failures in leadership. In *The Manila Manifesto*, the church elaborated on and sincerely repented of its failures in leadership and leadership development. Then, in *The Cape Town Commitment*, church leaders confessed their flaws – not the lack of leadership development but the loss of the value placed on godly character in leadership and leadership development. But with a greater faith and conviction in Christ, *The Cape Town Commitment* called the church to commit to practical actions to pursue Christlikeness. With God's grace and faithfulness, we bear witness to the fact that even though we are still far from perfect, God has blessed our faith to shape the life of the global church over time. As we desperately desire

---

13. "Cape Town Commitment," IID-3.

to advance God's kingdom until the coming of Jesus, all we want to do is cling to the gospel, the truth that transforms our lives and leads us to be part of God's mission.

> For in it the righteousness of God is revealed from faith for faith, as it is written, "The righteous shall live by faith." (Rom 1:17 ESV)

Bibliography

Birdsall, Doug. "The Lausanne Covenant: Foreword." *Lausanne Movement*. https://lausanne.org/content/lausanne-covenant-foreword-birdsall.

Dayton, Edward. "The Manila Manifesto: Introduction." *Lausanne Movement*. https://lausanne.org/content/introduction-2.

Kennedy, John W. "The Most Diverse Gathering Ever." *Christianity Today*, 29 September 2010. https://www.christianitytoday.com/ct/2010/september/34.66.html.

"The Manila Manifesto." *Lausanne Movement*. https://lausanne.org/statement/the-manila-manifesto.

Nelson, Thomas. "Billy Graham in Quotes."

Stott, John. "The Lausanne Covenant: An Exposition and Commentary." Lausanne Occasional Paper 3. *Lausanne Movement*. https://lausanne.org/occasional-paper/lop-3.

Wright, Christopher J. H. "The Cape Town Commitment." *Lausanne Movement*, 2010. https://lausanne.org/statement/ctcommitment.

———. "The Lausanne Covenant: Foreword." *Lausanne Movement*. https://lausanne.org/content/lausanne-covenant-foreword-wright.

5

Leadership Development in the Lausanne Movement

Nana Yaw Offei Awuku, Rudolf Kabutz, and Lars Dahle

The Word became flesh and made his dwelling among us. We have seen his glory, the glory of the one and only Son, who came from the Father, full of grace and truth (John 1:14)

He appointed twelve that they might be with him and that he might send them out to preach (Mark 3:14)

Again Jesus said, "Peace be with you! As the Father has sent me, I am sending you" (John 20:21)

Connecting missional leaders across generations is both historically and strategically at the heart of the Lausanne Movement. In 2017 the three authors collaborated to explore the history of developing younger leaders in the Lausanne Movement. Each of the authors have contributed into various multi-generational relationships while being closely involved in a variety of facets of the Lausanne Movement.[1] We here provide windows into unique stories that tell what key leaders have observed about the vision and modelling of leadership development through relationships within the Lausanne Movement

---

1. A major part of chapter originally appeared as an article entitled "Connecting Across Generations for Global Mission" in the October 2017 issue (https://lausanne.org/global-analysis/connecting-across-generations-global-mission) of the Lausanne Global Analysis and is published here with permission. To receive this free bimonthly publication from the Lausanne Movement, subscribe online at https://lausanne.org/global-analysis.

over the years. We listened to past and present leaders,[2] and our findings outline the key lessons for the global church.

Foundation: Learning from the Master

To provide insight into the deeply personal nature of leadership development, Nana Yaw shares his personal experiences of engaging with experienced leaders within the Lausanne Movement:

In 2017, a core group of Lausanne leaders met in Wittenberg, Germany, at the time the global church was marking the five hundredth anniversary of the Reformation. In one of the small group conversations about the strategic priority of disciple-making in global mission, a question was posed to Patrick Fung, who is serving as the programme team chair for Seoul 2024. The question asked what Patrick – in his busy role as the international director for OMF International – had learned about the most effective way to develop younger leaders. I was struck by the brevity of Patrick's response to such a profound question. He simply responded that it was by "being with" younger leaders, which pointed directly to Mark 3:14 that describes how Jesus called his disciples to "be with him." Then, on a slow tram ride down the beautiful mountains of Switzerland, I had a lovely conversation with Blair Carlson, who served for twenty-six years as Billy Graham's international congress director. What Blair shared with me is the closest window I ever had into the private life of Billy Graham, the world-renowned evangelist and founder of the Lausanne Movement. Blair shared fond private memories of his times with Billy after huge gospel crusades, when Billy would ask this young leader, "Blair, did I preach about the Cross?"

My friend Emmanuel Ndikumana, a regional director for the Lausanne Francophone region, shared with me that one of the most transformative moments in his journey as a younger leader with IFES in Burundi was when "Uncle" John Stott visited their country and, setting aside the arrangements made by the Anglican church in accordance with normal protocol, chose to stay with him at home. At almost ninety years old, Uncle Gottfried Osei-Mensah

---

2. In preparation for this article, the authors were privileged to obtain personal stories and reflections through direct personal electronic communication from many past and present Lausanne leaders. We also acknowledge, with gratitude, the assistance received from Paul Ericksen, director at BGC Archives and Museum, Wheaton College, who provided key material about leadership reflections of historic Lausanne leaders from "Records of the LCWE: Collection 46."

makes his regular home at the home of his younger leader friend Rev. Samuel Boateng every time he visits Ghana.

My own most cherished full day of leadership learning took place during the Cape Town 2010 Lausanne World Congress when I was Doug Birdsall's younger leader special guest for the day. At around 11:00 p.m., at the end of that busy day spent with Doug in his role as the executive chairman, he remarked cheerfully, and with memorable warmth, "Nana, this friendship is for a lifetime."

In the region of Africa, I cherish my relationship with Gideon Para-Mallam, who led the Lausanne EPSA Region, in nurturing me into the role of becoming regional director for EPSA after him. Through many conversations Gideon has shared his vast experience, has breathed his passion for justice and missions, and has spurred me on towards nurturing multi-generational leadership relationships.

I am sure you get a picture of the grand narrative that can be repeated around the world and across the generations – this very personal and incarnational approach, beautifully laced with stories of grace and truth, that has shaped the lives of individuals within Lausanne's history and its DNA of relational leadership development of almost fifty years!

The Vision: Developing Younger Leaders

The intergenerational emphasis was included from the very beginning of the Lausanne Movement, with many younger leaders present at Lausanne I in 1974. For many, their Lausanne story began with identification through a nomination, an invitation following a careful process of selection to a Lausanne gathering or committee, and then integration into a lifelong journey of transformative friendships with other peers and senior leaders over time and from across the world. There is an interesting story about two younger leaders who were involved in the 1974 Congress. Singaporean Wee Hian Chua, a former general secretary of IFES, served as the youngest member of the planning committee. With Billy Graham, John Stott, and other senior leaders on board, he was still given the opportunity to lead devotions at planning meetings – think about how the vision for intergenerational leadership was present right from the beginning! Chua then nominated Ramez Atallah from Egypt for an invitation to the Congress. But it was only recently that Ramez became aware that it was this friend and colleague on the IFES staff who had nominated him at that time, some forty-nine years before – and he wrote a note of gratitude to Chua, saying, "God used you to change my life through that recommendation." Ramez was twenty-eight when he attended the '74 Congress, becoming its youngest speaker; he was appointed the first "youth representative" on the Continuation Committee and later joined the permanent Lausanne Committee for World Evangelization (LCWE) led by Ajith Fernando and Brian Stiller. Founder Billy Graham, first chair Jack Dain, first executive secretary Gottfried Osei-Mensah, and leading theologian John Stott were all modelling intentional mentorship in their many influential relationships with younger leaders.

Atallah explains that the clear vision for younger leaders within the Lausanne Movement "developed after Leighton Ford's Sandy died and he wanted to invest in younger leaders in memory of his son." At an LCWE executive meeting early in 1983, Ford took Atallah, Fernando, and Stiller aside, sharing his emerging calling that he later formulated as "helping identify, develop, and network younger leaders of a new generation." During this historic conversation, the idea of a global conference for younger leaders came up. "I offered the observation," Stiller recalls, "that we faced a rising church generation which seemed to lack younger leaders."

Ford, as Lausanne chair and CEO (1976–1991), commissioned Stiller to undertake a global review process to prepare for decisions in the LCWE. A key feasibility study in this review process included the following essential observations: "Continuing world evangelization requires present leadership to encourage younger leaders to take their place. . . . For the Lausanne Movement to continue to influence world evangelization, it is essential that the younger leadership catch its spirit."

This growing vision of intergenerational partnership in global mission was shaped by the "spirit of Lausanne," representing a shared communal attitude and the practices of friendship, prayer, study, partnership, hope, and humility.

Singapore YLG 1987: "A Conference of Younger Leaders"[3]

Inspired by this growing vision and informed by the review process, decisions were made within the LCWE to arrange a global "Conference of Younger Leaders" in Singapore in 1987. The key appointments included Brian Stiller as chair, Steve Hoke as director, and Ramez Atallah as programme coordinator, as part of a wider global planning team of "dynamic, opinionated, entrepreneur-type younger leaders."

Singapore 1987 brought together nearly three hundred younger leaders from more than sixty nations to "provide networking, stimulate evangelism and raise awareness of resources and innovative ideas." Doug Birdsall – Lausanne Chair and CEO (2004–2012) – was a younger leader participant at YLG 1987 in Singapore, and he recalls that this gathering gave the participants a unique "window on the world." Lifelong gospel partnerships and personal friendships were formed across regions, cultures, and generations. The fact that John Stott was present only as a mentor and humble listener made a huge

---

3. See Singapore 87: A Conference of Younger Leaders – Lausanne Movement. https://lausanne.org/gathering/younger-leaders-gathering-1987.

impact. Many of the participants later became Christian leaders who were well known worldwide.

When retelling the Singapore 1987 story, Atallah reflects on why this Lausanne conference became such a turning point in the lives and ministries of so many influential Christian leaders. He points out that the process was as important as the event: "I firmly believe that one of the main reasons the conference was a remarkable success was because of what God did in each one of us in the planning group. . . . To me it was proof that a well-chosen group of 300 younger leaders can impact the global church."[4]

"Passing the torch" of leadership to the next generation[5] was a key concern at the first YLG in Singapore 1987, thus modelling the missional significance of intergenerational partnerships and friendships for the global church.

Malaysia YLG 2006: "Live and Lead Like Jesus"[6]

Following Lausanne II in Manila in 1989, the Lausanne Movement went through a challenging decade. It survived due to the faithful service of leaders such as John Reid, Tom Houston, Fergus Macdonald, and Paul Cedar.

---

4. Atallah, "Continuing the Vision," 78.

5. "Chris Wright observes that John Stott personally modelled 'the godly, wise, and humble handing over of leadership' to younger leaders, both at All Souls Church and in Langham Ministries." https://lausanne.org/content/lga/2017-11/connecting-across-generations-global-mission#endnote-ref-6.

6. See https://lausanne.org/gatherings/ylg/younger-leaders-gathering-2006-2.

A key factor in the revitalization of the Lausanne Movement was the second YLG in Malaysia in 2006, which brought together 550 younger leaders from over one hundred countries. The theme of this gathering was "Live and Lead Like Jesus," thus helping younger leaders "to lead more like Jesus, more to Jesus, and more for Jesus."[7]

Lausanne CEO Michael Oh (2012–present) was a younger leader at YLG '06 and led the planning team. He described the planning process for YLG 2006 as "the best, but not the easiest, team experience of my life."[8] Despite gaps in culture, calling, experience, gifting, and personality, a unique bonding emerged. Oh says,

> That experience taught me so much about the mission of the Lausanne Movement to *connect*. And it is not just a functional connection to do things together. As important as the *doing* of global mission is, it is the relational *being* together that really is a critical empowering dynamic to enable true, long-lasting *doing*.[9]

Through plenary sessions, small group discussions with mentors, workshops, and regional meetings, the programme focused on opportunities for – and barriers to – sharing the gospel. As Doug Birdsall pointed out at the time, the whole gathering was forward-looking, seeking "to be faithful to a rich heritage of the past just as it [was] committed to responsible obedience with the challenges and opportunities of the future."[10]

Christlike servant-leadership across generations was a central theme at Malaysia 2006, thus modelling the missional significance of character and partnership to the global church.

---

7. Leighton Ford coined this phrase; see https://www.leightonfordministries.org/leadership/.

8. Cited in Dahle et al. "Connecting across generations for global mission", 2017. https://lausanne.org/global-analysis/connecting-across-generations-global-mission.

9. Cited in Dahle et al.

10. See https://www.lausanneworldpulse.com/leadershipmemo/299/04-2006.

Jakarta YLG 2016: "United in the Great Story"[11]

After Lausanne III in Cape Town in 2010, the global need for a third YLG became apparent. A Younger Leaders Planning Team was appointed, with Sarah Breuel as chair and Ole-Magnus Olafsrud as senior coordinator.[12]

YLG 2016 took place in Jakarta in August 2016. More than one thousand young leaders and mentors from over 140 countries participated to connect, pray, learn, partner, and be equipped for holistic mission. The theme was "United in the Great Story" from Creation to New Creation via the cross, a story in which every continent and people group across history take part. There was a blend of younger and older plenary speakers and essential contributions from all Lausanne issue networks through workshops.

Breuel emphasizes the continuity with previous YLGs:

> Singapore 1987 deeply inspired us because of the stories we had heard of many of today's global leaders who were there and how critical this event had been in their lives. Malaysia 2006 was also important because we had read the feedback of how much the time in small groups sharing their life stories was the highlight for many; so we wanted to take a similar direction in this area.

---

11. See https://lausanne.org/gatherings/ylg/younger-leaders-gathering-2016.

12. See Breuel and Benson, "Six Leadership Lessons," https://lausanne.org/content/lga/2016-11/six-leadership-lessons-from-ylg2016.

"Connections were our highest value," Olafsrud points out. This became especially evident through the Connector App set up before the event and through the deep personal sharing of life stories during the event. He continues, "This brought us deep with one another and with the Lord – and United in the Great Story."

Learning from the biblical story and from one another's stories were key themes at Jakarta 2016, thus modelling for the global church a forward-looking intergenerational missional learning community.[13]

YLGen: A Global Intergenerational Commitment (2016–2026)[14]

A new global initiative was launched in 2016 to faithfully steward the connections and fruits from YLG 2016 for greater missional impact. This is a ten-year commitment to walk alongside younger leaders. The aim is to connect them more intentionally to Lausanne issue networks, regions, resources, and mentors, as well as to one another, through various interest groups.

YLGen is not just a commitment to younger leaders but also to building connections across generations. This is highlighted by Oh: "Through YLGen, relationships, and partnerships are being established across generations in our realms of regions and ideas."

---

13. See Awuku, "Engaging an Emerging Generation," https://lausanne.org/content/lga/2016-11/engaging-an-emerging-generation-of-global-mission-leaders.

14. See https://lausanne.org/ylgen.

Olafsrud makes a similar observation: "Both YLG 2016 and YLGen show – even stronger than at YLG 2006 – the hunger for and potential of mutually being equipped as leaders through relationships and partnerships across the generations."

This recent major initiative goes far beyond previous Lausanne younger leader initiatives in its scope and depth. It represents a unique long-term strategic investment in the YLG 2016 community and beyond to equip emerging generations of evangelical influencers to engage future missional contexts, tasks, and issues.

YLGen models intergenerational missional discipleship and partnership to the global church by focusing simultaneously on a character goal ("grow to live and lead like Jesus"), a missional goal ("so that the world may know Christ"), and a friendship goal ("inspire connections marked by the spirit of Lausanne").

Towards 2050: Lausanne Generations Together in Global Mission

The Lausanne vision for the ten-year YLGen commitment of investing in younger leaders has a strategic intent of connecting influencers and ideas across generations to accelerate global mission so that the world may know Christ. A good review enriches the fruit of reflection. It is evident from this chapter that the theme of connecting across generations is historically foundational to Lausanne's approach to leadership development. The vision of the Lausanne 4 process focuses on shaping the world of 2050 by accelerating the fulfilment of the Great Commission.

The Lausanne Generations Conversation (LGC23) was held from 30 May to 3 June 2023 at Biola University as part of a series of global gatherings in preparation for Seoul 2024.[15] The participants, carefully selected from some forty countries, were between the ages eighteen and eighty-one. A key concern was to ensure that a balanced generational representation was convened and to engage in carefully designed conversations to explore core relational dynamics and best practices in connecting across generations. The five core values that framed the conversation were biblical foundation, missional calling, friendship, mutuality, and collaboration. The outcomes of LGC23 have been phenomenal and hold great promise for the sustainability of the Lausanne 4 process towards 2024 through healthy intergenerational leadership and collaboration. Russ Martin, Lausanne's chief communication officer, who participated in LGC23, shares this appreciation and insightful observation:

---

15. https://lausanne.org/gathering/lausanne-generations-conversation.

I really enjoyed the focus at LGC23 on what mutuality and collaboration across five generations looks like as we participate in God's mission. **It will greatly accelerate the global mission to make progress on this important topic.** It was really helpful to hear from younger leaders in Gen Z about the challenges they face in making a meaningful contribution to God's mission. Having the older generations seek to unleash these key generations of leaders is a mission-critical task for accelerating great commission work.

Moving forward into the future, leadership development in the Lausanne Movement will hopefully bear the even richer fruit of strategic and sustainable models of intergenerational friendships, mutuality, and collaborations in maximizing acceleration in the work of the Great Commission towards 2050.[16]

The journey towards YLG 2026 has already begun, with a clear generational roadmap looking over the horizons to YLG 2036 and YLG 2046. The Lausanne Movement sees the task of healthy leadership development as critical to fulfilling the Great Commission of making disciples of all nations to the ends of the earth (globally), within each sector of society (across all issues) and to the end of the age (generationally).

Five Key Lessons for the Global Church

It has often been said that the fruit of the Lausanne Movement grows best on other people's trees and that its most effective role is to serve as a catalyst.

We sincerely hope that the following five key lessons – from the distinctive story of the Lausanne younger leader initiatives – may inspire the global church in its leadership development for global mission:

1. Shared personal commitments to holistic mission across generations lead to global Christian friendships and gospel partnerships.

2. Shared evangelical convictions across generations, as expressed in *The Lausanne Covenant* and *The Cape Town Commitment*, lead to shared global missional reflections and strategic ministry collaborations.

3. Mutual trust may be developed through intentional relational processes, with more experienced leaders mentoring younger leaders to take on missional tasks according to their personal callings and

---

16. https://lausanne.org/generations.

gifts and with younger leaders inspiring experienced leaders to embrace thinking and acting from new paradigms.

4. Innovative space is created for younger leaders to develop personal character and skills with biblical integrity for transformative ministry in complex and rapidly changing future contexts.

5. These intergenerational relationships are characterized by the "spirit of Lausanne," with a shared focus on prayer, study, partnership, hope, and humility.

A deep and prayerful implementation of these five lessons will equip the global body of Christ across generations of younger and experienced leaders "to bear witness to Jesus Christ and all his teachings – in every nation, in every sphere of society, and in the realm of ideas."[17]

Bibliography

Atallah, Ramez. "Continuing the Vision from Lausanne 1974." In *The Lausanne Movement: A Range of Perspectives*, edited by L. Dahle, M. S. Dahle, and K. Jørgensen, 74–85. Oxford: Regnum, 2014.

Awuku, Nana Yaw Offei. "Engaging an Emerging Generation of Global Mission Leaders: Embracing the Challenge of Partnerships," *Lausanne Global Analysis* 5, no. 6 (November 2016). https://lausanne.org/global-analysis/connecting-across-generations-global-mission#endnote-ref-12.

Breuel, Sarah, and Dave Benson. "Six Leadership Lessons from YLG2016." *Lausanne Global Analysis* 5, no. 6 (November 2016). https://lausanne.org/content/lga/2016-11/six-leadership-lessons-from-ylg2016.

"Cape Town Commitment: Foreword." *Lausanne Movement*, 2010. https://lausanne.org/content/ctc/ctcommitment#foreword.

Dahle, Lars. "Mission in 3D: A Key Lausanne III Theme." In *The Lausanne Movement: A Range of Perspectives*, edited by L. Dahle, M. S. Dahle, and K. Jørgensen, 265–79. Oxford: Regnum, 2014.

Dahle, Lars, Nana Yaw Offei Awuku, and Rudolf Kabutz. "Connecting across generations for global mission, Lausanne Movement" (2017). https://lausanne.org/global-analysis/connecting-across-generations-global-mission (Accessed: 15 July 2024).

---

17. "Cape Town Commitment: Foreword." https://lausanne.org/content/ctc/ctcommitment#foreword, and Dahle, "Mission in 3D," 265–79.

Section II

The Gospel for Every Person

6

Leadership Development for Unreached People and Places

Joshua Bogunjoko

Introduction

The angel instructed Philip the Evangelist, "Go south to the road – the desert road – that goes down from Jerusalem to Gaza." So, Philip went, and there the Holy Spirit instructed him to "stay near" the chariot of an Ethiopian eunuch. Philip did so, and he overheard the man reading from Isaiah. Philip asked the man if he understood what he was reading. "How can I," the man replied, "unless someone explains it to me?" Then he invited Philip to sit with him in his chariot and explain the passage. "Philip began with that very passage of Scripture and told him the good news about Jesus." Later, as they passed a body of water, the eunuch requested baptism. After this, the Spirit took Philip away, and the eunuch "went on his way rejoicing" (Acts 8:26–39).

Surely this is one of the most straightforward examples of reaching the unreached. The Ethiopian's heart and mind were clearly prepared by the Spirit before the moment of Philip's arrival. He immediately welcomed Philip, invited him to come up alongside him, and then listened to the good news that Philip shared. The Ethiopian was an ideal "unreached person" – spiritually hungry, open to learning, and prepared by the Holy Spirit. And Philip was the ideal missionary – in tune with God's instructions, obedient, and equipped to expound on Scripture at a moment's notice. If only every unreached person was like the Ethiopian and every missionary team member just like Philip, then our vision to see the whole world worshipping the Lord would be quickly accomplished! However, more often than not, God sends us to people who are more like the Ninevites, and God sends people – you and I – who are more like Jonah.

God called his prophet Jonah to go and prophesy to Nineveh, a wicked Assyrian city known for its oppression and extreme cruelty to conquered people such as Israel and Judah. Understandably, Jonah had no desire to witness to his enemies. Instead, he invested his time and money in boarding a ship that was sailing in a different direction. We all know the story of the violent storm, how Jonah was thrown overboard, and how he survived inside a large fish, where he had plenty of time to reflect and to pray.

After the Lord commanded the fish to vomit Jonah onto dry land, the reluctant prophet obeyed God's command. He walked the streets of Nineveh and warned its people that the Lord would bring calamity upon them. To Jonah's utter surprise, these wicked people – everyone, including the king – yielded to his warnings. They proclaimed a fast and humbled themselves before God. God, in turn, had compassion and turned away the disaster he had planned for them.

I believe that the biggest challenge in reaching the unreached lies less with the unreached and more with the reached, particularly with church leaders whose hearts are not truly connected with God's compassionate heart, as revealed in his dealings with the Ninevites. People are unreached because God's people are "unsent." We must not mistake "unreached" with "unreach-able"; these words are not synonymous. The unreached only become unreachable when the unsent are unsendable. Let us look more closely at some reasons for this.

Leaders on a Ship to Tarshish

Many leaders today have figuratively boarded ships to Tarshish, investing time and money in sailing to many places except towards the unreached. This can be because they are deliberately rebelling against the voice of the Lord, but it can also be because they are uninformed or misinformed. The first obstacle is lack of awareness or inaccurate knowledge, which is a stewardship issue.

We are not always wise stewards of the information and resources we have at hand. Many capable and missions-minded leaders and churches have no idea that so many people in the world still lack the most basic access to the gospel in a language or form that they can understand. A surprising 77.3 percent of missionaries today are serving among the world's reached, and another 19.4 percent among the unevangelized. Only 3.3 percent are living among the 3.28 billion people who have never heard the name of Jesus. Jesus commanded, "Go into *all the world* and preach the gospel to *all* creation" (Mark 16:15 emphasis added) and Acts 1:8 emphasizes a witness to the remotest part of the earth. The Lausanne Movement calls for "the whole Church to take the whole gospel *to the whole world*" (emphasis added). If we truly believe that the gospel is meant for the whole world, then why are missionaries going in the opposite direction from where the largest concentration of those with no access to the gospel are living?[1]

Leader development for unreached people and places must be informed by the right data, which in turn will inform the right priorities. Questions can reveal our awareness levels and stewardship priorities: *How many of your resources are actually going towards making the gospel accessible to those who have no access?* Questions can trigger a learning orientation: *Is it right to continue sending more workers to contexts where the gospel is present, and even strong, and to ignore contexts where the gospel is not heard at all?* Unless an organization's purpose, mission, and vision deliberately focus on those who live with no access to the gospel, it is almost inevitable that resources and priorities will drift towards the low-hanging fruit of existing and "easy" places. Remember, no one among the unreached will advocate for themselves to be a priority.

In these disruptive times in our world, leaders who champion priority changes are made, not born; they are developed, rather than being spontaneously produced – hence the urgent need for leader development for unreached people and unreached places. Such intentionality will lead many leaders who are presently steering their ships to Tarshish to gather the courage of conviction, implement a higher standard of stewardship, and use their leadership skills, under the direction of the Holy Spirit, to humbly turn the ships of their churches and organizations towards the urgent needs of "Nineveh."

Another reason the unsent might be unsendable is a lack of character formation. When the Lord resolved not to send calamity upon Nineveh because the people had repented, Jonah – himself a recent recipient of the Lord's compassion and miraculous salvation – was furious at the Lord's compassion towards Nineveh. Jonah was so angry that he literally wanted to die. In the climax to this story, Jonah left the city and sat nearby to watch what might

---

1. See: "Mission Stats." *The Traveling Team*. https://www.thetravelingteam.org/stats. "How Hard Can it Be To Find Someone Who Knows Jesus?" *mark4.co*, 19 September 2019. https://mark4.co/blog/how-hard-can-it-be/. Crowson, Natalie. "Perfect Strangers: Christians Living among Buddhists, Hindus and Muslims." *Lausanne World Pulse Archives*, 2007. https://bit.ly/3mcQCg6.

happen to it. There, the Lord provided a plant to shade Jonah, followed the next day by a worm to eat the plant, then a scorching wind and blazing sun to beat down on Jonah so that, once again, he wished for death. Initially "very pleased" with the shady plant, Jonah was now angry because the plant died. God asked, "Do you have good reason to be angry?" (Jonah 4:9 NASB 1995).

Jonah's story concludes with a question that reverberates through time and eternity: "Should I not have compassion on Nineveh, the great city in which there are more than 120,000 persons who do not know *the difference* between their right and left hand?" (Jonah 4:11 NASB 1995, emphasis original). Jonah had compassion for himself, yet he could not connect with God's heart of compassion for people just like himself. While feeling entitled to the personal comforts that God had provided for him, he was outraged at the salvation God provided for 120,000 people.

If we are to develop leaders who do not sail their ships to Tarshish and do not sit in shelters outside the city, then what should we do?

Leaders with Paul's Vision

The apostle Paul relates his vision of the risen Christ, speaking to him:

> For this purpose I have appeared to you, to appoint you as a servant and a witness not only to the things in which you have seen Me, but also to the things in which I will appear to you, rescuing you from the Jewish people and from the Gentiles, to whom I am sending you, to open their eyes so that they may turn from darkness to light, and from the power of Satan to God, that they may receive forgiveness of sins and an inheritance among those who have been sanctified by faith in Me. (Acts 26:16–18 NASB)

Christ's description of transformation to Paul sounds much like the descriptions of the transformed Ethiopian eunuch and the people of Nineveh. This is also a good starting point to address the gap that now exists in developing leaders for unreached peoples and places in the world. The heart of Christ's message to Paul is the transformation of all those to whom he will be sent – from blindness to clear vision, from darkness to light, from the dominion of Satan to God, from sin and guilt to forgiveness, and from alienation from God to an inheritance among those who are sanctified by faith in Christ. Christian leaders are empowered by divine resources, and their primary focus must be people and God's purpose for them.

Leaders Who See Themselves and Others as Image-Bearers

A leadership development philosophy must begin with creation itself in order to lay a solid foundation for its conclusions and practices. Genesis 1:26–27a (ESV) tells us, "Then God said, 'Let us make man in our image, after our likeness. And let them have dominion over the fish of the sea and over the birds of the heavens and over the livestock and over all the earth and over every creeping thing that creeps on the earth.' So God created man in his own image."

However, by Genesis 3, that perfection was exchanged for sin and corruption. Adam and Eve disobeyed God and became subservient to Satan in enmity to God. Despite their fallen state and their need for redemption and reconciliation (Rom 3:23), human beings retained their position as image-bearers of God. This is evident in God's words to Noah: "For in the image of God has God made mankind" (Gen 9:6). Nevertheless, "every inclination of the thoughts of the human heart was only evil all the time" (Gen 6:5).

Human leadership now includes not only stewardship of the earth but also a mandate to draw people back to God through Christ, "the Lamb of God, who takes away the sin of the world!" (John 1:29). Christian leadership must take its cues from Christ's own purpose in coming: "I have come that they may have life, and have it to the full" (John 10:10). It must also consider the conclusion of all things: the worship of the Lamb by people "from every tribe and language and people and nation" (Rev 5:9).

The core of Christian leadership, like Christ's leadership, should be the transformation of the leader and the led, including their families, communities, and societies. This applies even more so for unreached peoples. *The core being of the leader* is central to the entire development process. The leader must first experience the transformative work of the Holy Spirit before he or she can lead transformation where Christ is not yet known. Authentic and lasting change for the led only comes from within, and so change must first be realized in the leader.

Like Paul, leaders must carry the burden of the lostness of the unreached, almost wishing themselves accursed for the sake of the lost. Such leaders do not just lead *from* the heart; they lead *to* the heart. Missions to and among the unreached and in unreached places is born from the heart, from the deepest part of our emotions, and is complemented in its outworking by the strategic and the cognitive side – data, methods, hard skills. It is also communal, not just personal.

Addressing a leader's entire being includes their life experiences, the world view from which they come, the shaping influences of others, and their experiences of Christ in their lives. Leader development is a life-on-life process of formation rather than a classroom impartation of knowledge. Leaders who are formed in this way become like Philip – willing to be used of God in any way he chooses. Jack Hayford writes,

> Although I have no suspicion or criticism to make of any zealous leader's effort to seek help from leadership methods or systems, true leadership ultimately is found at Jesus' feet and is shaped and kept only in the heart. Fruitful leadership is not getting others to fulfill my goals (or even my God-given vision for our collective enterprise and good), but helping others realize God's creative intent for their lives – personally, domestically, vocationally and eternally. My character is not shaped by the sum of my information, but by the process of a transformation that is as unceasingly needed in me. . . . to generate a dynamic, wholehearted, clear-eyed people, people who possess the character of Christ! My character as a leader seeking to reflect the highest of values will distil truth from God's Word to be woven into the fabric of my life. My ultimate objective is to grow, slowly but surely, into the image of Christ-only as I "walk in the Spirit."[2]

This has to be the ultimate goal, purpose, and focus of leader and leadership development for unreached peoples and places.

Leaders as Shepherds, Servants, and Stewards

When engaging in leadership processes such as strategic planning, problem solving, and change management in times of disruption, these principles must be borne in mind: the leadership focus is on people and their purpose to glorify God; the leadership heart is that of a shepherd; the leadership attitude is that of a servant; and the active expression of the servant attitude and shepherd's heart is stewardship.

Shepherds

Psalm 78 says, "From the care of the ewes with nursing lambs He brought him to shepherd Jacob His people, and Israel His inheritance. So he shepherded them according to the integrity of his heart, and guided them with his skillful hands" (Ps 78:71–72 NASB). Shepherds focus on God's people. They nurture,

---

2. Hayford, "Character of a Leader," 71.

care, and protect God's people as under shepherds of God. Their vision is to see people honour God, grow in grace, and fulfil God's purpose for their lives and their communities. They do accomplish tasks, but such tasks are a means of growth in grace and a means of blessing others as they put their gifts and skills to use. Developing leaders for unreached places means investing in the grace of developing a shepherd's heart for the people of God. This requires leaders with hearts of integrity and skilful hands.

Servants

Paul says, "In your relationships with one another, have the same mindset as Christ Jesus: Who, being in very nature God, did not consider equality with God something to be used to his own advantage; rather, he made himself nothing by taking the very nature of a servant, being made in human likeness" (Phil 2:5–7). Leadership development for unreached places must produce leaders who have the mindset of servants and who demonstrate this attitude through their humble relationships, actions, and character traits. Through discipleship and mentoring, they pour their lives into the lives of others. They use leadership processes with the attitude of servants.

Stewards

There is no true servanthood without stewardship, and real stewardship comes only from a servant heart. A true shepherd is a servant. Just as a good servant must be a good steward, so also true stewardship expresses itself in servanthood. In disruptive times, those who would lead for unreached people and places must be equipped to express themselves through stewardship as a core attribute or characteristic of their actions. The statistics cited earlier point to the lopsidedness of the stewardship of mission resources today in favour of places where the gospel is already present. A heart of shepherding, an attitude of servanthood, and the attribute of stewardship will serve to renew organizations and refocus their priorities.

Leaders for unreached people and places will view their lives as a continuous state of being and becoming, during which time they steward their gifts, talents, resources, and the trust of others as the Lord's provision for his redemptive purposes. Such leaders are always growing and developing, while also growing and developing others into true stewards of gifts and grace. Jonah was in a leader development process even as he was God's messenger to the unreached. God was disciplining and discipling him through his ordeals in the belly of the fish and by removing his shade. Although we do not know the rest of Jonah's story, we can be sure that God was shaping him to skilfully steward all that he had experienced into his calling as a prophet. Developing leaders for unreached places must embrace a developmental perspective on the leadership journey.

Leader development for unreached people and places involves diverse people, churches, and organizations working together collaboratively to spread the good news of Christ. On the paradigm of control, Araujo, Lederleitner and Mischke write,

> We in the West have been so successful in taming the material world to serve our needs and aspirations that we have assumed a paradigm in which control of resources and processes is also the default mode for ministry. Consider . . . we often express our obedience to God in terms of methods and management – assuming a high level of control, taking charge of tasks, and measuring outcomes. We set dates, create timetables, and identify numeric results by which to evaluate how well we serve the Lord and his church.[3]

They continue, leaders who function from a paradigm of control and a base of material power hinder mutuality. Relationship is primary, accomplishment secondary. In God's service, the standard is faithfulness more often than measurable results. The ability to embrace vulnerability and live with ambiguity creates opportunities for trust building. Sensitivity to context and commitment to learn about people, their history, world view, and way of life creates opportunities for relationship, mutual understanding and partnership.[4]

Change is fundamental to transformational leadership and leaders with hearts that are open and committed to change are desperately needed if unreached peoples and places are ever to be reached with the gospel. The ability to change and adapt in times of disruption is the most important survival – and even flourishing – strategy needed by organizations today. Leaders for unreached people and places must be learners who "walk the walk and talk the talk."

Leadership for the unreached, which embraces the necessary deep change, applies to all levels of leadership in the church and in Christian organizations.

---

3. Araujo, Lederleitner, and Mischke, "To Catch the Wind: A New Metaphor for Cross-Cultural Partnerships, 68.

4. Araujo, Lederleitner, and Mischke, 70.

Developing such leaders will involve heart, head, and hands, and will embrace the biblical metaphors of leaders as shepherds, servants, and stewards. This will involve refocusing leadership – not just using the business models of measurable goals and an individualistic view of leadership development but seeing leadership development as collective wisdom towards a deep spiritual, emotional, and intellectual journey of change for the sake of the gospel. It is a humble learning attitude that recognizes the giftedness of all peoples and the critical contribution that is inherent in the diverse peoples and cultures in Christ's global church. Considering that the most unreached places in the world today are in societies based not on individualism but collectivism, the embrace of such a broad-based understanding of leadership is critical for the development of leaders for unreached peoples and places in disruptive times.

Conclusion

At first pass, the story of Philip and the Ethiopian eunuch seems enviably effortless, almost too easy to be instructive for us today. But I believe that there is more than meets the eye behind this "success story." Philip spent time in the Scriptures and in relationship with Jesus and was part of the community of those who followed Christ. This slow and steady journey of following Jesus contributed to the formation of his spiritual state, a state in which an angel could specifically direct him and he would obey without resistance. Time with Jesus and other disciples would also have imbued in him a profound and thorough knowledge of Scripture. In a world where false teachings, cults, and heresies thrive, a love for and a deep grounding in the word is a basic ingredient of any leader development process. Philip was able to pick up a thread of Scripture selected by the Ethiopian and, beginning with that, share the good news. Philip was also chosen as a deacon based on his being filled with the Holy Spirit and with wisdom (Acts 6:3). Philip was a servant of God and also a servant of the Ethiopian. He travelled to where the Ethiopian was, climbed up into his chariot, and, in a demonstration of mutuality, both asked and answered questions.

Is leader development for the unreached categorically distinct from leader development for other situations? No. Biblical leaders are called to be stewards, shepherds, and servants. There is no alternate leader profile for those who oversee the formation of vision, strategies, and activities for and among the unreached. Rather, the reality of the unreached makes the need for leader development exceedingly acute and exposes the dire consequences of not having well-formed leaders.

The focus of leadership development for unreached peoples and places is the transformation of individuals, families, communities, peoples, and nations from blindness to seeing, from darkness to light, and from the dominion of Satan to the dominion of God, that they may receive the forgiveness of sin and an inheritance among those who are sanctified by faith in Christ Jesus. Many peoples and places are still in need of this work of salvation. Therefore, there is an urgent need for godly leaders, both men and women, who can engage leadership processes from diverse cultural perspectives, cultural understandings, and cultural imagery. Let the investing in the development of such leaders begin. Amen.

Bibliography

Araujo, Alex, Mary Leaderleitner, and Werner Mischke. "To Catch the Wind: A New Metaphor for Cross-Cultural Partnerships." In *The Beauty of Partnership Study Guide*, edited by Werner Mischke, 67–72. Scottsdale: Mission One, 2009.

Crowson, Natalie. "Perfect Strangers: Christians Living among Buddhists, Hindus and Muslims." *Lausanne World Pulse Archives*, 2007. https://bit.ly/3mcQCg6.

Hayford, Jack. "The Character of a Leader." In George Barner (1997) *Leaders on Leadership: Wisdom, Advice and Encouragement on the Art of Leading God's People* edited by George Barner. Grand Rapids: Baker, 1998.

"How Hard Can it Be To Find Someone Who Knows Jesus?" *mark4.co*, 19 September 2019. https://mark4.co/blog/how-hard-can-it-be/.

"Mission Stats." *The Traveling Team*. https://www.thetravelingteam.org/stats.

7

Learning from New Believers

Abigail Abok and Sarah Breuel

Introduction

In an ever-evolving world, the truth of the Bible is never-changing. Making the gospel available to every person is still as much an imperative today as the day Jesus said the words of the Great Commission over two thousand years ago. The Great Commission as recorded in Matthew 28:19–20 is a command that Jesus Christ gave to his disciples after his resurrection and before his ascension into heaven. By extension, all Jesus's followers, including those of us who are alive today, have been given the same command. Every church is expected to work towards getting the good news to the ends of the earth. This is so important that pastor and author Oswald J. Smith once said, "Any church that is not seriously involved in helping fulfil the Great Commission has forfeited its biblical right to exist."[1] The parable of the lost sheep illustrates the premium God places on the salvation of one soul. As children of God, finding the lost sheep is as much a duty as it is a privilege; it is something that should be in our consciousness always. God wants all humanity to be saved. That is why Jesus had to die on the cross – so that, through him, we might obtain salvation and have eternal life (John 3:16). Therefore, spreading the gospel of Christ is an integral part of the Christian faith. However, it is not enough to spread the good news; we are to make disciples by teaching and preaching. When new believers are made disciples, they take on the responsibility of the Great Commission and help lead others to Christ. Sadly, the common practice in many churches today is to recruit new believers and baptize them to become church members. Once this

---

1. Smith cited in Greene, "Why is the Great Commission Important?," https://www.keystoneproject.org/blog/why-is-the-great-commission-important.

is done, the church moves on to win more new believers and repeat this cycle. The discipleship aspect is missing in this practice, and this is something that the church should prioritize. After all, it is through discipleship that we can engage with new believers, listen to them, learn from them, and groom them to become leaders. Lack of proper discipleship makes it easy for some new believers to slip through the cracks and go back to their old ways. The Bible, through the parable of the sower, shows us that the seed of God's word may not always germinate in every person – that is, the ground or soil it falls on – and that we have to do our part. This is why we need to engage in evangelism with foresight and with a vision that transcends the numerical growth of the church. Making disciples who will make disciples – as we have seen Jesus do – is the standard for missions and evangelism. This means listening, learning, and fostering the leadership capabilities of new believers with the ultimate goal of achieving the Great Commission.

Who Is a New Believer?

When a person accepts Jesus into their hearts, they become new creatures. This is possible because God has had humanity on his heart since the dawn of creation. Even after human beings strayed from God by disobeying his command in the garden of Eden, God did not give up on them.

Jesus's death on the cross was the means God chose to restore humanity's relationship with God. Through Jesus, what was lost – our relationship with God – is restored. Without Jesus, human beings are inherently lost to God. Thus, when someone accepts Jesus as Lord and Saviour of their life, that person is found. A new believer is, therefore, someone who has just recently found their way back to God's ever waiting and open arms. No matter the age of the person, a new believer is akin to a baby in the Christian faith. This does not mean that new believers are less important – only that they are younger and less experienced. New believers have so much to learn as they journey to maturity in Christ. Regardless of their inexperience in the faith, however, new believers can be involved in the church even as they grow in the faith.

The Church's Role in a New Believer's Life

Growth requires nourishment. When a child is born into a family, the members of the family are responsible for grooming that child and teaching that child to become a functional member of that family. Within a few years, that baby become familiar with the ways of the family and is able to teach these ways to others. It is the same with the family of God. When a person accepts Christ, it is the responsibility of the church to teach the person what it means to be a member of the family of God. Members of the church have the important role of loving, supporting, and helping one another. When new believers do not receive these things, their growth is stunted.[2] It is the responsibility of mature members of the church to help new believers grow in their relationship with Jesus. The church leadership and other members of the church – who have already grown in maturity – then serve as elder siblings to the new believer and are responsible for teaching and nurturing the faith of the new believer. This is where discipleship comes in. The church has to do more than preaching and teaching the gospel; they must also model how new believers should obey all the teachings of Christ, thereby leading the believer towards maturity. Such discipleship "goes beyond expounding a few basic truths to nascent believers and leaving them to their own devices in figuring out the entirety of Christian life alone."[3]

What the Church Can Learn from New Believers

New believers, who are often considered babies in Christ, are sometimes relegated to the background or sidelined in churches. Often, even where the church has a discipleship plan for new believers, the new believers are expected to listen to and obey instructions. Communication is often one-way, flowing from the disciple to the one being discipled. Many churches do not realize how much new believers can contribute to missions if church leaders would just listen to them and involve them in their missions plans. New believers have many things to teach older Christians and can contribute to church growth.

One of the things we can learn from new believers is how to develop a fresh fascination with Jesus. The enthusiasm of their first love and their excitement over the new light they have seen can encourage and help long-standing believers to rekindle their love for God. Many who have walked with Jesus for a long time may, over the years, have lost that flame of excitement they had when they first believed in Christ – and new believers can infect them with a new and fresh burst of energy that reminds them why they believed in the first place.

---

2. Wiltshire, "8 Areas of Discipleship for New Believers," https://research.lifeway.com/2023/05/10/8-areas-of-discipleship-for-new-believers/.

3. Harless, *Transformational Discipleship*, 14.

New believers also make some of the best evangelists because of the boldness with which they share their faith with both authenticity and simplicity. Their zeal for evangelism and faith is contagious. They are quick to tell their friends about their new-found faith in Christ, often with an enthusiasm that more mature believers lack. When the Samaritan woman met Jesus at the well and was convinced Jesus was the Messiah, she ran back to the town to share the good news. She did not think about being ridiculed or whether she was competent; the joy of her salvation overflowed, and many believed in Jesus because of her.

New believers also remind us not to come to God with preconceived ideas. Like children, they approach God with genuine curiosity. When they open the Bible and ask questions about God, they do so with childlike honesty and simplicity. They are not afraid of being laughed at or ridiculed. When we have been Christians for a long time, we may get to a point where we start thinking that some things are too silly or too basic to seek God's guidance. We become self-conscious and begin to believe that some questions are off the table. But God is willing to meet us in our authenticity and is not angry when we express our curiosity. What we need is real honesty with God, and this is something that some Christians find difficult because they feel that they have to be put together before they can ask God questions. This childlike quality of new believers is refreshing, and we can learn from this to be more real with God, not thinking that we must be perfect before we can approach God or work for God. When we look at the ministry of Jesus, many of the people who were attracted to him were those considered sinners at that time – for example, the tax collectors. But Jesus maintained contact with such people, giving us a clear message. As Jesus himself said, he came for the sick, not for the healthy.

As believers, losing touch with what God is doing through new believers makes us less mission-oriented and shifts our focus away from the Great Commission. Learning from new believers can help us to remain more rooted in God. We can do this by opening the channels of communication so that these flow both ways and by listening to new believers, who, in many instances, have important contributions to offer to the church.

Fostering the Leadership Capabilities of New Believers

As the global church strives to be obedient to the Great Commission by getting the word of God to the ends of the earth, it may be of immense benefit for church and mission leaders to listen and learn from new believers even as they are groomed to maturity through discipleship. The Great Commission goes beyond the followers of Christ preaching for conversion alone; it goes beyond teaching new believers some fundamental truths about life in Christ and leaving them to their own devices to figure out the entirety of Christian life on their own. Discipleship places a demand on the church to engage in preaching, teaching, and building accountable relationships with new believers. However, discipleship is not meant to be a checkbox that church leaders tick off after a few classes with new believers. Rather, it is a process through which new believers are transformed into disciple-makers. This is what we see in the apostle Paul's admonishment to Timothy: "And the things you have heard me say in the presence of many witnesses entrust to reliable people who will also be qualified to teach others" (2 Tim 2:2). Discipleship includes the process of mentoring to equip new believers to impact further generations of new believers and disciples.

Though nascent in Christ, new believers need to be given a sense of belonging while their faith is nurtured to maturity in Christ. This can be done by listening to them and getting them involved in missions, which can potentially yield immense rewards for global missions. The testimonies of those who have just recently come to Jesus has the fresh quality that is needed to encourage seekers – who are unsure about taking the plunge and accepting Jesus Christ – or even unbelievers who have no interest at all in Christianity. In this context, the testimonies of new believers become a tool for directing seekers or softening the hearts of non-believers. When someone who was just recently a sinner speaks of the joys of becoming a Christian, their testimony becomes ten times more powerful. New believers, by telling their stories, become preachers. The testimonies of new believers can also inspire and encourages missionaries, church leaders, or Christians who have begun to feel weary after years of evangelism without great results. In such cases, the testimonies of new believers become oil in the wheels of continuous evangelism, galvanizing the church to continue to press on. Part of discipleship is assigning responsibility to the disciple. It is, however, wise to let them mature through discipleship before entrusting any leadership responsibilities to them. As in the parable of the sower, some new believers may not end up becoming rooted in the faith. This is why we must disciple to ensure maturity before assigning responsibility. Yet involving new believers in short-term missions helps to boost the effectiveness of such undertakings. But this cannot happen unless church leaders and missions leaders become more Christlike in disposition.

While church leaders must think strategically, they must also recognize that there is no one single strategy that works for every new believer. As Dietrich Bonhoeffer notes, "We must be ready to allow ourselves to be interrupted by

God. God will be constantly crossing our paths and cancelling our plans by sending us people with claims and petitions."[4] The ultimate goal of reaching everyone with the gospel of salvation will depend a lot on how the church and church leaders view their roles. According to Bill Hull, "Obedience to the Great Commission hinges on the three qualifiers: an intentional plan that defines and trains disciples, a commitment to reproduction by training in evangelism with accountability, and a commitment to multiplication by special training in order to produce disciple-making leaders."[5] This was the kind of leadership that Jesus exhibited. If Jesus had not reproduced within his disciples the disciple-making characteristic that he possessed, the gospel would have long been forgotten. There is an urgent need for current global missions leaders to do the same kind of replication in those they disciple.

An extensive research study by Christian Schwarz and the Institute for Natural Church Development,[6] showed that leadership has been shown to either facilitate or inhibit growth in peoples. Leaders are like gardeners who, though powerless to create growth from seeds or plants, can create conditions that might make such growth more likely. From the research, Schwarz found that thriving churches have eight qualities or characteristics that are absent in declining churches.[7] The first significant characteristic he highlights is empowering leadership. Empowering leadership is the kind of leadership that is focused on equipping and releasing Christians for ministry. The absence of such leadership compromises the health and vitality of any local church and severely restricts its capacity to thrive and grow. Another finding from the research was that the particular leadership factor with the strongest direct correlation to the overall quality and growth of a church is a leader's readiness to accept help from others. The kind of leadership that helps churches and missions thrive is collaborative and responsive as opposed to a more heroic style of leadership. The importance of leadership is further buttressed by the research conducted by Professor David Voas and Laura Watt among English Anglican churches.[8] One of their findings was that while the role and contribution of clergy as visionary and inspirational leaders is clearly significant, of equal significance is good

---

4. Bonhoeffer, *Life Together*, cited by Tenney, "Interruption Is God's Invitation," https://www.desiringgod.org/articles/interruption-is-gods-invitation.

5. Hull, *Disciple-Making Pastor*, 71.

6. Cited in Parkinson, *Understanding Christian Leadership*, 9.

7. Cited in Parkinson, *Understanding Christian Leadership*, 9.

8. Voas and Watt, *The Church Growth Research Programme Report*. https://www.churchofengland.org/sites/default/files/2019-08/report_strands_1_2_rev2-from-cgr-website.pdf.

quality lay leadership, which correlates directly with church growth. Thus, a church where volunteers are involved in leadership and where roles are rotated regularly is likely to be a growing church – especially where younger members and new members are included in lay leadership and service.[9] Leadership should enable followers to lead. This means leadership should be dispersed within the organization in a way that goes beyond leadership positions or titles. That is collaborative leadership where followers' strengths are maximized for growth and more impact. Doing this will have a positive impact on an organization's fruitfulness.

As modelled by Jesus in his ministry, leadership is intended to serve the needs of others. Any leadership that does not influence or facilitate ministry by others will lead, inevitably, to a diminished church. Thus, "the mark of effective ministry is that others are helped; the mark of effective leadership is that others are enlisted and enabled to share in the work of ministry."[10] Similarly, Simon Walker observes that the only proper goal of leadership is enabling people to take responsibility. Leadership is concerned with the task of helping people to move towards fully mature and responsible personhood.[11]

Throughout Jesus's ministry, he demonstrated his concern for the development of the capabilities of others, with the aim of equipping workers for God's kingdom. He spent time enabling his disciples to take responsibility. This, above all, should serve as a pattern for productive Christian leadership. With love and humility, church leaders should invite new believers into their lives to learn from them. Like Barnabas, leaders should patiently encourage new believers. When mission and church leaders listen to new believers and engage them in leadership, there is a multiplication of people who can be used as a means to reach and inspire even more people around the world with the gospel of salvation. Here are some of the ways in which this can be done:

- empowering people in the congregation for personal witness
- identifying those among new believers who have gifts that can be used for the gospel
- producing a vision of what is possible for new believers
- inviting new Christians to participate in Lausanne meetings

---

9. Voas and Watt, *The Church Growth Research Programme Report*, 3.

10. Parkinson, *Understanding Christian Leadership*, 20.

11. Walker, *Undefended Leader*, quoted in Parkinson, *Understanding Christian Leadership*, 21.

Church and mission leaders sometimes have reservations about allowing new believers to get involved in leadership, and such reservations are often valid since a leader cannot be sure what a new believer is able to do without first assigning responsibility. The leader might have concerns over the stage of maturity of the new believer and whether he/she seeks to take advantage of the church for personal gains. This is why leaders need to pray for a discerning spirit that will enable them to recognize when new believers are simply seeking to take advantage of the weaknesses of the church. The goal must be to let new believers lead but without overwhelming them, without letting them take on tasks that they are not yet mature enough to undertake, and without exposing the church to danger.

Conclusion

Learning from new believers and letting new believers lead may make many uncomfortable, but we need to remember that we have not been called to feel comfortable and do only those things that make sense to us. When called to leadership, we need to ask ourselves, as C. T. Studd did, "How could I spend the best years of my life in living for the honours of this world, when thousands of souls are perishing every day?"[12]

As Christians, bringing others to the saving grace of Christ is our duty. Missions is not optional for anyone who calls themselves a child of God. Taking missions seriously is a sign that we have the spirit of God in us for, as Henry Martyn rightly states, "The spirit of Christ is the spirit of missions. The nearer we get to him, the more intensely missionary we become."[13] We need to remember that with each passing day, the souls of men and women continue to perish and that it is our duty as believers to lead them to salvation.

Bibliography

Barna, George. *Growing True Disciples: New Strategies for Producing Genuine Followers of Christ*. Colorado Springs: WaterBrook, 2001.

Bonhoeffer, Dietrich. *Life Together*. London: SCM, 1954.

---

12. Message Ministries & Missions, "Missions Quotes." https://messagemissions.com/missionary-quotes/.

13. Message Ministries & Missions, "Missions Quotes." https://messagemissions.com/missionary-quotes/.

Campbellsville University. "GUIDE: A Pastor's Guide to Mentoring New Believers." *CU Online*, 20 September 2020. https://online.campbellsville.edu/ministry/guide-to-mentoring-new-believers/.

Davis, Andy. "6 Practical Steps for Discipling New Believers and How They Matter to the Great Commission." *IMB*, 31 October 2016. https://www.imb.org/2016/10/31/6-practical-steps-for-discipling-new-believers/.

Earley, Dave, and Rod Dempsey. *Disciple Making Is . . . How to Live the Great Commission with Passion and Confidence*. Nashville: B&H, 2013.

Greene, James, "Why is the Great Commission Important?," *The Keystone Project*, 2023. https://www.keystoneproject.org/blog/why-is-the-great-commission-important.

Harless, Jon Thaddeus. *Transformational Discipleship: A Model for Sermon-Based Small Groups for Life Transformation*. Lynchburg: Lambert Academic Publishing, 2012.

Harrington, Bobby. "Four Disciple Making Essentials." *Discipleship.org* (blog). https://discipleship.org/blog/four-disciple-making-essentials/.

Hull, Bill. *The Disciple-Making Pastor: Leading Others on the Journey of Faith*. Rev. and exp. ed. Grand Rapids: Baker Books, 2007.

Laloux, F. *Reinventing Organization*. Brussels: Nelson Parker, 2014.

Parkinson, Ian. *Understanding Christian Leadership*. London: SCM, 2020.

Schwarz, C. A. *Natural Church Development Handbook*. Moggerhanger: British Church Growth Association, 1996.

Tenney, Joseph. "Interruption Is God's Invitation." *Desiring God*, 28 October 2015. https://www.desiringgod.org/articles/interruption-is-gods-invitation.

Voas, D., and L. Watt. (2014). "The Church Growth Research Programme Report on strands 1 and 2. Numerical change in church attendance: National, local and individual factors. London: Church of England Archbishops' Council." https://www.churchofengland.org/sites/default/files/2019-08/report_strands_1_2_rev2-from-cgr-website.pdf.

Waggoner, Brad J. *The Shape of Faith to Come: Spiritual Formation and the Future of Discipleship*. Nashville: B&H, 2008.

Walker, Simon P. *The Undefended Leader*. Austin: Piquant, 2010.

Wiltshire, Kyle. "8 Areas of Discipleship for New Believers." *Lifeway Research*, 10 May 2023. https://research.lifeway.com/2023/05/10/8-areas-of-discipleship-for-new-believers/.

8

Developing Outward-Looking Leaders

Kavitha and Jeyakaran Emmanuel

Introduction

Jennifer has struggled all her life with her skin colour. From childhood, she faced verbal abuse and discrimination from various family and church members. Her skin colour was seen by her Christian community as an impediment to being successful in life. Statements like "Who will marry you? You are so dark!" kept Jennifer from realizing her potential. She is a regular churchgoer, who is passionate about mission and serves as a producer working with a Christian television channel. But all along, she carried the pain of believing that she could never be enough – all because of how her world and her church related to her because of her skin colour. What does the gospel mean to a person like Jennifer? How can the church rise up to be a culture-transformer?

Biblical discipleship should produce outward-looking leaders with a vision and passion to transform all aspects of life. Dietrich Bonhoeffer describes Jesus as "the man for others" and says that "the Church is only the Church when it exists for others."[1] Unfortunately, we often see around us leaders and churches that are inward-looking, with a consumeristic posture, existing for themselves and even allowing the toxic postures of the world to seep into the life of the church. There is a great need to intentionally develop Christlike leaders who are outward-looking. Some of our observations about outward-looking leaders are described in the rest of this chapter.

---

1. Bonhoeffer, *Letters and Papers from Prison*, 40.

Outward-Looking Leaders Address the "Divides"

In Powerhouse, the church we planted in Chennai over two decades ago, we realized, quite early on in our journey, that if we were to raise outward-looking leaders, we would have to intentionally bridge at least three great divides: the sacred-secular divide, the clergy-laity divide, and the gender (male-female) divide. We emphasized the priesthood of all believers and the call of every believer to be salt and light wherever God has placed them. This resulted in catalyzing several "lay" leaders – from artists and film makers to doctors and social workers – to make a difference outside the four walls of the church, living with a vision to see kingdom impact in their spheres of influence. Another area that we felt God was calling us to champion was the issue of the full inclusion of women in ministry to bridge the gender divide. Women, despite making up a large majority of the Indian church, are, sadly, often the frozen assets of the church. We were greatly concerned to see that over half the church was being immobilized. Hence, over the years, we have also prioritized developing outward-looking women leaders by equipping and releasing women to function in all roles in the church alongside men, with the conviction that function and leadership in the church is based on gifting and calling, not gender.

Outward-Looking Leaders Are "Double Listeners"

Developing outward-looking leaders begins with teaching people to look outward until this becomes a way of life. It is not enough for the church to talk the talk, we must also walk the walk. Developing outward-looking leaders begins with nurturing a posture that asks critical questions about how the gospel can permeate into the world and influence the healing of people, places, and spaces. John Stott called this "double listening"[2] – a spiritual discipline of "listening to the word" and "listening to the world" in an attempt to make the God of the word relevant to God's world. The faculty of "double listening" enables us to see the world with God's kind of eyes. We read God's word to know God, and we read the world around us to figure out how to make his word relevant to the world.

As a church, we began to ask hard questions about the issue of colourism that is highlighted in Jennifer's story. Eventually, in 2009, our response was "Dark Is Beautiful," a nationwide campaign launched by Women of Worth – a non-profit that I (Kavitha) founded – to address the toxic belief that a person's worth is measured by the colour of their skin. The campaign went viral on

---

2. Stott, "Double Listening," 347.

social media. News media from over eighteen nations called us to talk about the campaign. While writing this article, I called Jennifer – who was one of our poster girls for the campaign – to ask her what the campaign meant to her. Here is what she said: "The campaign helped me change my thinking. I learned to embrace my skin colour and celebrate it. The affirmative voices helped me see the toxic belief system that I thought was the way of life until then." Today, the campaign continues to have a ripple effect in restoring to people everywhere – even those outside the church – their God-given worth and value.

Outward-Looking Leaders Are Devoted to the Great Commission

I (Jeyakaran) interviewed a few pastors in my city of Chennai to identify several key principles and practices they were employing to develop outward-looking leaders in their churches. A common thread was their deep devotion to the Great Commission.

Chadwick Mohan is the lead pastor of the English congregation – numbering over four thousand – of the New Life Assemblies of God Church. He shared that he had been developing outward-looking leaders based on his core convictions: the Great Commission is for all believers, the priesthood is for all believers, and training is for all believers, not just for a few. He believes that the DNA of the local church is missions and that "missionless" churches and "churchless" missions are not biblical because we see in the Scriptures that the Great Commission unfolded through the planting and multiplication of authentic, relational, and transformational communities of disciples.[3]

City Rock Church, founded by Ranjith Isaac, is one of the radical churches in the city, reaching young people. Ranjith shared how he has led by example with an outward-looking posture as a leader. He has created a culture within the church that is positively biased to "outsiders" – those yet to know Christ from other faiths or no-faith backgrounds. His church's slogan is "Be with Him. Go for Him," based on Mark 3:14: "He appointed twelve that they might be with him and that he might send them out." According to Ranjith, the passion and vision to be missional is both caught and taught. It is caught as potential leaders are encouraged to function alongside outward-looking leaders in a team so that the DNA of the Great Commission rubs off on them. The biblical mandate is also taught intentionally and consistently at various levels, ranging from sermons to one-on-one mentoring conversations. Every church member is encouraged to make a list of five friends and pray regularly for these people

---

3. Personal interview, December 2023.

to encounter Christ. The church budget is biased positively towards investing in building friendships with non-Christians and in various evangelistic efforts – from pre-evangelistic bridge-building events to mission-exposure trips.[4]

Max Premson, the founding pastor of the God's Army Church, was called by God to church planting while he was working as a senior management professional in the corporate world. He initially began with an attractional "come and see" model of church but soon felt compelled by biblical convictions to transition to an incarnational "go and be" model of church that is more community oriented. Premson has planted twenty-five churches in the city, reaching mainly young people in the slum communities of the region where he pioneered his work. He is influencing these slums, which are notorious for violence, alcoholism and drug addiction. His model for developing outward-looking leaders is what he calls the "Jesus model of 3–12–70," where every leader is encouraged to invest intentionally in three primary leaders, twelve secondary leaders, and, eventually, in shepherding a larger community of disciples (the seventy). His church is constantly engaged in community outreach – from literacy classes to football coaching – that has kept the outward-looking temperature of the church community at very high levels.[5]

Outward-Looking Leaders Are Disruptors

Being outward-focused leaders is a call to be disruptive! As Mac Pier, the founder of Movement.org, says, it takes gospel disruption to transform cities.[6] The word "disruption" means stopping a pattern that is normative. It is interrupting something that is in its default mode. A disruptive posture is critical for outward-looking leaders. The call to disrupt is a call to transform what is toxic and unjust. It is a call to be part of the co-creation process with God in restoring his world. Building outward-focused leaders takes mentoring leaders who will listen to the voices of those calling out for help. It takes the willingness to have bold and difficult conversations to disrupt. The cries of pain of this generation are constantly reaching God's ears. God expects us to coach and develop leaders who are willing to be disruptive, who are not afraid to "uproot" and to "tear down" just as much as they "build" and "plant" (Jer 1:10).

One of the disruptions that the church is required to respond to at such a time as this is gender-based discrimination and violence. The UN predicts

---

4. Personal interview, December 2023.
5. Personal interview, December 2023.
6. Pier, *A Disruptive Gospel*.

that it will take another three hundred years to see women live without fear of violence or discrimination.[7] Women and girls represent not just half the world's population but also, therefore, half its potential. Women and girls constitute not just half the world's population, they also make up more than 50 percent of the global church today. Gina Zurlo, the co-director of the Center for the Study of Global Christianity at Gordon-Conwell Theological Seminary, says that the future of the church is women (and African).[8] A recent survey by TRACI (Theological Research and Communications Institute) in India revealed how women became more silent about their abuse after they become Christians because of the teaching they constantly hear in their churches that "women need to be silent in the churches." A call to disrupt by speaking out about injustice and discrimination against women is undeniable.

One of the most recent initiatives that we facilitate is called the Disruptive Women's Network, an expression of Movement.org in cities to mobilize kingdom men and women to disrupt the status quo of women and girls, both within the church and in the cities. It is a movement supporting the mission of taking the *"whole gospel to the whole city by the whole church."* This is about disrupting gender-based violence in churches and acting in a concerted way to create churches as safe spaces in cities for women and girls across South Asia. The missional strategy here is to develop women as leaders and influencers in the city. City movements and networks are being encouraged to intentionally include women as co-leaders across the region. Close to twenty cities are warming up to this movement and intentionally bringing together women who are being developed as "outward-looking" city leaders. The goal is to see one hundred women enabled each year as pastoral leaders, church planters, marketplace influencers, culture transformers, non-profit leaders, and leaders who are part of city movements.

Outward-Looking Leaders Are Drivers of Change in the Marketplace

Over two decades ago, Billy Graham prophetically said, "I believe that one of the next great moves of God is going to be through believers in the workplace." This seems to be happening in Chennai! Chennai has a long history of Christianity, ever since the coming of the apostle Thomas, who is believed

---

7. United Nations. "Why It Matters: Gender Equality." Sustainable Development Goals, 2020. https://www.un.org/sustainabledevelopment/wp-content/uploads/2016/08/5_Why-It-Matters-2020.pdf.

8. Zurlo, "Why the Future."

to have been martyred on St. Thomas Mount in Chennai. Today, Chennai is blessed to have around six thousand churches. One unique phenomenon in Chennai is the presence of hundreds of workplace fellowships in almost every workplace domain. Christians gather for regular prayer and fellowship at their workplace or in a location near their workplace. One key reason these workplace fellowships are thriving is because of outward-looking leaders who lead them with a vision to see the gospel impact their workplaces. I (Jeyakaran) spoke to the leader of one such fellowship that meets in one of India's largest information technology companies (names withheld for security). Much like the early church, this corporate fellowship meets every working day (Monday to Friday) for thirty minutes during their office lunch break. They have a clear purpose for each day: Mondays and Tuesdays are Bible study days for discipleship, Wednesdays and Thursdays are evangelistic focus days, and Fridays are for prayer. The leader said that many non-Christians from orthodox other-faith backgrounds attend their fellowship and that this gathering is their only point of contact with Christian fellowship and witness. So, in many ways, such fellowships function as marketplace churches. Several who come to Christ in their workplace fellowship remain secret Christians for fear of persecution and ostracization from family and community. The leadership development strategy of such workplace fellowships includes getting everyone to do the S.H.A.P.E. gifts assessment test and forming various gift-based teams, including an evangelism team that regularly organizes prayer walks around their corporate offices and various outreach programmes such as regularly distributing thousands of evangelistic tracts to workplace professionals. Their recent Christmas evangelistic event – themed "Christ GPT" – attracted over three hundred non-Christians from various IT companies. All these strategies continually reinforce a contagious outward-looking ethos in their workplace movement.

Another workplace forum – the Chennai Corporate Fellowship (CCF) – seeks to network all the corporate fellowships on a common platform. The vision statement on their website captures their outward-looking posture:

> CCF is having the vision of raising an army of "Corporate Evangelists" who can witness for God with their "Work Excellence" and "Spiritual Excellence" in workplaces. CCF is anchored by workplace believers from various workplace fellowships across industries like IT, BPO, Manufacturing, Automobile, Transportation, Energy and Natural Resources, Construction, Media, Banking and Finance Insurance, Logistics, Healthcare

and the like – who are burdened to reach their co-workers, who cannot be reached by any organization functioning outside the workplace.[9]

Danny, one of the senior leaders of CCF, shared how they have developed outward-looking leaders who are encouraged to demonstrate work excellence, ethics, and integrity in the workplace, which earns them the credibility and respect of their non-Christian colleagues with whom they desire to share Christ.

Outward-Looking Leaders Are Developers of Transformational Strategies

In the last decade, we have seen the emergence of several city transformation networks in over twenty major cities in India, including the mega cities of Delhi, Mumbai, Chennai, and Kolkata. These are interdenominational, intergenerational movements of prayer, unity, and collaboration, where city-facing outward-looking leaders from the "3-legged stool" of the church, marketplace, and non-profit sectors are uniting to work together for the transformation of their cities.

At the Chennai Transformation Network (CTN), where we serve on the leadership team, we have been envisioning and equipping hundreds of pastors and church leaders to be outward-looking using the 4-S framework tool of *Streets, Spheres, Segments, and Stages*:

- Streets: outward-looking leaders developing strategies for the transformation of geographic areas (for example, streets, neighbourhoods, and zip codes)
- Spheres of Influence: outward-looking leaders envisioning kingdom influence in all spheres and sectors of society (for example, the arts, entertainment, media, business, education, health services, and government)
- Segments of people: outward-looking leaders being mobilized to reach all kinds of people groups living in the city (for example, language groups, socioeconomic segments, and migrants)
- Stages of life: outward-looking leaders focusing on impacting people across all stages of life, spanning all generations (for example, Gen Alpha, Gen Z, Millennials, and Gen X)

---

9. "About Us." *Centre for Catalyzing Change*. https://www.ccf.org.in/aboutus/.

This 4-S tool is one of the many tools that has helped church leaders to envision and develop an intentional, holistic, outward-looking posture and to raise outward-looking leaders in their churches.

Outward-Looking Leaders Embrace Diversity

Diversity and inclusion are buzz words anywhere you look – especially in the world of social media – and are seen as a foundational value that drives human rights. The world defines "diversity and inclusion" without boundaries and without a plumb line with which such inclusion must align. Over the years, along with a group of like-minded women, I (Kavitha) worked on training modules for workplaces with a biblical narrative of "diversity and inclusion." Although the modules do not mention Scripture verses or the name of Christ, embedded within are messages carrying godly perspectives that can influence the professional world. We are regularly invited for speaking engagements and workshops on topics such as "Gender Mainstreaming," "Diversity and Inclusion to Combat Colourism," and "Transforming Workplace Culture."

In today's context, diversity and inclusion require biblical thinking and a biblical response. Embracing a diversity of cultures and people groups is our God-given mandate. The Great Commission demands that we embrace diversity so that *all* the world may know Christ. From Genesis to Revelation, God's heart for all people and all the world is clear.

One of the most critical aspects of the biblical narrative is what Christ demonstrated in the way he included both the rich and the poor, the literate and the illiterate, the Samaritan and the Jew, and women and men. He subverted culture in radical ways to show us where God stands when it comes to inclusion. Jesus hated sin but loved the sinner. He hung out with drunkards and tax collectors, but he also transformed their way of life. As outward-looking leaders, we are called to emulate Christ's way of inclusion and spur others to do the same.

In conclusion, it is critical that we facilitate processes that catalyze the formation of leaders who are outward-looking like Christ. Catalyzing a generation of outward-looking leaders begins with developing a diverse group of leaders – both male and female – from various backgrounds. It requires embracing voices from various cultures and ethnicities to reach the world for Christ.

Bibliography

Bonhoeffer, Dietrich. *Letters and Papers from Prison*. Edited by Eberhard Bethge. Macmillan, 1971.

https://lausanne.org/about/blog/christians-work-missing-link-fulfilling-great-commission

Corporate Fellowship Foundation. "About Us." CCF. https://www.ccf.org.in/aboutus/ (accessed 2 July 2024).

Dark Is Beautiful Campaign. https://www.darkisbeautiful.in/.

"Gender Equality." United Nations. 2020. https://www.un.org/sustainabledevelopment/gender-equality/.

"The Gender Gap in Religion around the World." *Pew Research Center*, 22 March 2016. https://www.pewresearch.org/religion/2016/03/22/the-gender-gap-in-religion-around-the-world/.

Pier, M. *A Disruptive Gospel*. Grand Rapids: Baker Books, 2016.

Stott, John R. W. "Double Listening: A Theological Reflection." In *Making Christ Known: Historic Mission Documents from the Lausanne Movement*, edited by John R. W. Stott, 343–53. Grand Rapids: Eerdmans, 1996.

Zurlo, Gina. "Why the Future of the World's Largest Religion is Female – and African." *The Conversation*, 23 March 2022. https://theconversation.com/why-the-future-of-the-worlds-largest-religion-is-female-and-african-178358.

9

Digital Technology to Accelerate Capacity for Leaders Worldwide

Andrew Feng, Jonah Jala, and Nick Wu

Introduction

Digital technology is reshaping our human social experiences and increasing accessibility to people in previously hard-to-reach places. Because of the internet, the increase in mobile phone users, and emerging technologies, there are new ways for Christians to engage in sharing the gospel with unreached peoples. "Digital missions" – which is the use of tools, resources, and strategies for the spread of the gospel – is an effective and natural way for the larger Christian body to be involved in mission. Believers can be involved in digital evangelism, whether it is by using a mobile app to help with gospel conversations or by building a digital resource to help with disciple-making movements on the ground.

The term "digital transformation" has been used in the marketplace to describe the adoption of new technology to make processes more efficient and effective. This may also be true for many missions organizations. For leaders looking to innovate in missions and fulfil the task of the Great Commission, new strategies need to be experimented with and implemented. Digital spaces, tools, and resources offer new opportunities for innovation and capacity building. For leaders aiming to adopt digital transformation, a shift to a growth mindset is necessary. Such a mindset helps leaders to reimagine failure as steps to growth and encourages leaders to innovate and experiment in their ministry to reach new people. In terms of capacity building, leaders adopting new digital technologies can become more efficient in their processes and increase the scale of their involvement of digitally skilled workers.

However, many believers with these digital skills are often unaware of the needs of missionaries. Fewer than 1 percent of Christians work in full-time ministry, and these people are often operating beyond capacity. Digital technologies and spaces offer opportunities for the 99 percent of Christians who are not working in missions to also join in fulfilling the Great Commission.

Digital spaces can invite more Christians to co-labour with ministry workers and on-the-ground missionaries. For example, digital resources can help with training, networking, and mentoring across geographical boundaries. Leaders can be raised and equipped with knowledge of innovative ideas, and they can share effective practices using new technology and connecting online.

Digital spaces are also opening up access to new peoples, especially through digital evangelism and discipleship. Any believer with access to the internet or social media has a platform to connect and share the gospel with others. Many believers of the next generation can connect with others on social media platforms and, thereby, cross-cultural boundaries. Young believers want to make an impact in a way that lets them utilize their digital and marketplace skills, and digital missions offers a new avenue for their involvement. Not only does this support older generations of missionaries, it is also effective for reaching younger generations with the good news. This will thus increase the capacity of current leaders and enable the next generation to be developed into leaders in the missions world.

However, while digital technology offers many potential solutions in the context of missions, some important caveats must be noted. Digital technology cannot replace incarnational ministry, and it cannot spiritually transform lives. Additionally, many digital strategies also require an offline component for continued discipleship and growth in Christ. New technologies must be closely monitored because ethical or long-term issues may arise. On the other hand, as Christians, we should not avoid technology but, instead, approach new opportunities with curiosity, wisdom, and discernment. In this way, we can model what using technology for good looks like.

In this chapter, we will explore examples of digital missions including media strategies, disciple-making movements, social media outreach, messaging apps, mobile tools, micro-experiences to engage the next generation, and remote work.

Digital Mission Trips: Online and Offline

As of January 2023, there were 5.16 billion people in the digital space.[1] If we want to share Jesus with people, then we must go digital.

A 2014 initiative called Digital Outreach used direct messaging on social media. Later, others also began to use language learning apps and webinars. These activities can be incorporated into evangelism and discipleship efforts. Digital mission trips can last a week or even a month. Strategic conversations, online events, and offline interactions sometimes ensue as a result of initial online contact.[2]

For online mission trips, teams craft experiences and activities that resonate with the target audience. One team in Singapore reached out to students in Thailand during COVID-19. They collaborated with local missionaries to get to know the audience and held a series of cultural and language exchange webinars. Each day, the conversations centred around faith, hope, and love. This enabled the team to speak about biblical topics. As a result, students initiated spiritual conversations. The team found opportunities to share more about the gospel, and local missionaries connected to those who were interested in further conversations.[3]

There are different variations of similar activities. Mobilizing followers of Jesus can go beyond a face-to-face interaction. As we make disciples, we should seek to use communication platforms wisely.

Engaging Next Gen from Hackathon to Cohorts

For leaders who are looking to expand beyond traditional missions, innovation and capacity building are major needs. The intersection of faith and technology presents a meaningful opportunity for young adults to collaborate in the missions world. The next generation is made up of digital natives who can offer unique insights to engage unreached peoples. At the same time, engaging in digital missions can deepen their passion to live out their call to fulfil the Great Commission. While young adult Christians may be willing to go overseas for short-term missions, these opportunities can be costly and, to be effective, require a higher level of cross-cultural training. Digital missions

---

1. DataReportal, "Digital 2023," https://datareportal.com/reports/digital-2023-global-overview-report.

2. Lukens, "Students Do Digital Outreach," https://indigitous.org/article/students-do-digital-outreach-in-a-new-kind-of-mission-trip/.

3. Tai, "Exploring the New Frontier," https://thirst.sg/exploring-the-new-frontier-how-we-started-going-on-digital-mission-trips/.

micro-experiences offer a new pathway for all Christians to connect, engage, and support the needs of the missions world; and since people can be involved remotely, this increases accessibility, enabling Christians to serve the missions world from wherever they are.

Indigitous (indigenous+digital) is a global movement that is taking the gospel to new people, places, and spaces. The largest digital missions micro-experience is #HACK, a global Christian hackathon gathering believers to brainstorm, innovate, build, and collaborate in tackling some of the biggest challenges in the missions world. Since Urbana's #HACK4Missions event in 2015, Indigitous have continued to host the hackathon annually. Thousands of technologists, creatives, and entrepreneurs have participated in these events, and multiple missions organizations have also been involved. Leaders from the missions organizations bring global challenges for hackathon participants to "hack" and prototype solutions.

A notable project that was launched out of #HACK was a Bible story app made by Upstream, a tech ministry of Pioneers. This simple app aims to share Bible stories with unreached peoples. The first few apps were created for persecuted groups of field workers among a marginalized people group. Although limited gospel resources were available, these stories were in the heart language of the community. Indigitous and Upstream collaborated with the local missionaries and a remote digital missions cohort made up of young developers, coders, and UI and UX designers. While the cohort grew in their app development skills, they also experienced real-time feedback during on-the-ground testing with the missionaries and local leaders. As their tech skills were being refined, their passion for the unreached also grew.

This cohort demonstrated how the next generation can be involved in digital missions. Faced with a crucial need to provide a digital tool and resource for evangelism and discipleship, these young adults saw their impact magnified beyond their imagination. Rather than going overseas themselves, they used their digital skills to contribute and support the needs of the missionaries remotely. Through their time, work, and dedication, these young adults increased the capacity of both Upstream's ministry and the missionaries on the field.

Upstream has since adopted the Indigitous cohort model to establish their own internship programme to invite both remote and in-person team members and volunteers to join digital missions micro-experiences. Upstream's team is continuing to grow and expand. They are now working on new Bible story apps in different languages to assist different missionaries in reaching the unreached.

Remote Work with Switchboard

One common challenge that many ministry leaders face is meeting operational needs that enable their incarnational ministry work to flourish. This includes back-end support, building new strategies, marketing, storytelling, and building resources. Many of these challenges can be solved with remote work provided by the larger body of Christians, especially those who have expert skills in these areas.

Switchboard has taken this solution and built a platform to match believers' skills with ministry needs. Christians with expertise and skills, who are dubbed Kingdom Consultants (KCs), lend a helping hand to serve alongside Great Commission Organizations (GCOs). With the accessibility of remote work, KCs can reach GCOs that have various needs and problems by consulting with them or even taking on work like freelancers.

Through a platform like Switchboard, believers can find a role wherever they are and be part of God's global story; thereby, more people are mobilized to join missions work. As a result, missions organizations can continue to strive towards sustainability and scale ministry efforts.

Boiling Waters: Memes and Discipleship

Many movements are starting in the world of social media as a result of memes and direct messages. Boiling Waters (BW) in the Philippines is one such movement. Since sharing their first meme on social media in 2016, they have grown their audience to two million followers.

Their first post delved into one of the most captivating and widely discussed topics – romance. This post received an unexpected surge of engagement overnight, surprising even its creators. Many people resonated with similar relationship challenges, which led BW to grow their presence online.

The process involved meticulous groundwork, posting content three times a day, and diligently monitoring reactions to align with platform algorithms. The influx of messages from people seeking help on issues – ranging from minor dilemmas to complex issues like unplanned pregnancies – prompted the team to maintain anonymity. It also led the team to become active in supporting and ministering through direct messages. Some followers were also referred to professional counsellors. Due to the muscle work required to make sure that every person's story was heard, the BW founders decided to invite more people to support their social media page.

As Boiling Waters continued to grow, the team diversified its touchpoints. They created a website, an Instagram account, and a podcast series. Their twice-weekly "Ask Me Anything" (AMA) Facebook Live videos engaged hundreds of followers and fostered a sense of community. Their commitment to their followers also led to the creation of a dating app that countered the prevailing hook-up culture.

The rising engagement also created a need for more spiritual and community leaders. Engaged followers of BW transformed from mere consumers to creators. BW inspired content to be crowdsourced, including the creation of the "Cactus Community" Facebook group. Spaces like this serve as a source of content and provide a safe space for followers to share and connect. As engagement continued to grow, additional moderators were enlisted to maintain a healthy community. Moderators not only managed content but also provided nurture and care for the community. In these unique spaces, the value of developing smarter relationships can be seen. As people engage with a caring community, opportunities for discipleship open up.

The Gospels say that the harvest is plentiful but the labourers are few. As we pray for the Lord of the harvest to send labourers into the harvest field, may we also ask the Lord for wisdom on how we can enable those in online spaces.

Using Messaging Apps to Spread the Message Together in Africa

Technology enables faster and smarter communication. Every platform has a different purpose and is influenced by culture. To reach all people with the gospel, we need to go where people are spending their time.

According to IMB, this is the fourth era of missions.[4] This era is not driven by a compass to the coastlands, a move to the interior, or an understanding of the complexity of peoples. Instead, this era introduces a new dynamic – unleashed by the connectivity technology provides – that allows every disciple to play a part in the Great Commission. Anyone who has a smartphone can share the gospel. However, newer technology does not always guarantee increased effectiveness. The key is meeting people in the right place.

Smartphones may be widespread, but Wi-Fi access is a challenge for many. One ministry leader in Togo developed creative ways to overcome this challenge. He and his team carried out an SMS campaign to reach out to people who do not have smartphones. They were able to share the gospel with many people.[5] One person of another religion was interested and asked questions

---

4. Davis, "Missions History," https://www.imb.org/2017/09/07/have-we-entered-a-new-era-of-modern-missions/.

5. Indigitous, "Togo," https://www.youtube.com/watch?v=hZHg2kEe4PY.

about Jesus. The more this man understood about Jesus, the more convinced he was of the truth. Eventually, he gave his life to Christ. For this man, the good news arrived at just the right time, in just the right place.

A man called Kyle, from Africa, used WhatsApp to minister to others. He shared testimonies and Scripture verses to engage people in spiritual conversations. He also shared Scriptures with friends until more and more people wanted to receive these messages. One person who received a Bible verse from Kyle was convicted by the Lord to live a righteous life. He began a relationship with Jesus, and Kyle began discipling him. As the Bible reminds us, "So is my word that goes out from my mouth: It will not return to me empty, but will accomplish what I desire and achieve the purpose for which I sent it" (Isa 55:11). Kyle wanted to share his walk with God in the simplest way he could. God used his obedience to speak to many about repentance, encouragement, and hope.

The Telegram community is not a stranger to conversations about God either. Such movements are happening in central Africa. A group of young people are simultaneously sharing about Jesus via Telegram by posting and sharing stories, videos, and podcasts with their friends and contacts. Some of them even use the same worship song as a ringtone. When people nearby hear the song and ask questions, this becomes an opportunity to talk about Jesus.

A co-founder of Indigitous once said, "There isn't going to be just one approach, tool, site, app, video, or link that connects 5 billion hearts to Jesus."[6] This mindset can encourage people to embrace the context where God has placed them and reach others with the gospel of Christ.

Finding Seekers Online through Media to Movements (M2M)

Every day, there are 3.5 billion Google searches worldwide, adding up to 1.2 trillion searches per year. Millions of those searches are about Jesus. People are searching for truth. When people turn to the web instead of seeking out face-to-face interactions, what do they find?

God has raised up people to make his word known in the digital space. Media to Movements (M2M) is a coaching team committed to helping to develop a contextual digital strategy. They lead movements of disciples making disciples among the unreached people groups. End-to-end media strategy

---

6. Cochrum, "Why Indigitous? By Ken Cochrum," https://youtube/JXRpAYdGu4E?si=8 6HOS6MTGdQZ3VUS.

begins with the end in mind. The goal is to multiply movements of disciple-makers to identify and connect with people who are spiritually open.

Various media components and people play a part in a seeker's journey of discovering Jesus online. Media content and advertisements may grab their attention first. Then, as they continue their search, digital conversations take place. As a result of these conversations, discipleship happens as seekers are connected with disciple-makers. Face-to-face follow-up fosters the discovery of Jesus, leading to obedience to his call. Ultimately, this process leads to a movement built one person at a time.

In both online and offline communities, it is important to build up leaders to come alongside individuals at every step in their journey. With groups like M2M, there are more opportunities for Christians to get involved in sharing the gospel when people search online for truth.

Digital EV with GodTools App

Many relationships today are established and developed exclusively in an online context. People have integrated screens and smart devices into their personal routines and social lives. Despite some ethical considerations, new technology is an opportunity for deeper gospel connections.

Evangelism can be supported by digital tools and apps. GodTools, an app with over one million downloads, is helping Christians to start conversations with contextualized evangelistic resources in multiple languages. The app includes translated tools for sharing your God story, the "Four Spiritual Laws," and conversation starters.

One user of GodTools was a Vietnamese woman who became friends online with a young man in Germany. Their conversation led to talking about God and an invitation to hear the gospel. The woman used GodTools via screen-share to effectively share the gospel from across the world. Such a tool for evangelism helps to connect Christians with new people and aids them in taking ownership of their part in the Great Commission.

Conclusion

As we navigate these digital opportunities, it is imperative to move forward with wisdom and discernment. These digital strategies must complement the incarnational aspect of missions, and we must ensure that these strategies enhance rather than replace the personal and relational nature of evangelism and discipleship. The digital realm, while vast and full of potential, calls for intentional and thoughtful engagement as we innovate and extend the reach of the gospel in this digital era. Digital transformation and a growth mindset are critical for the development of leaders. As leaders embrace innovation and build capacity with the involvement of the 99 percent of Christians who do not work full time in missions, we can accelerate the impact of the gospel on the unreached.

The rise of social media and other digital platforms has accelerated movements of faith and transformed online spaces into vibrant communities for spiritual guidance and leadership development. These platforms have proved instrumental in creating meaningful conversations and nurturing a counternarrative to prevailing cultural trends.

Moreover, in regions with limited internet access, the innovative use of basic digital tools like SMS and messaging apps has bridged significant gaps in gospel outreach. These simple yet effective methods have led to transformative encounters, demonstrating the power of digital engagement in missions work.

Leveraging the strategic use of digital tools and platforms has opened new pathways for Christians – especially those not engaged in full-time ministry – to actively participate in evangelism and discipleship efforts. These tools foster innovation and collaboration at the intersection of faith, technology, and missions. Digital avenues are crucial for reaching unreached peoples, facilitating spiritual growth, and building capacity for ministry leaders worldwide.

The increasing involvement of tech-savvy Christians in mission-oriented projects showcases the significant impact that digital skills can have in supporting missions leaders and advancing the Great Commission. Collaborative efforts highlight the crucial role of technology in nurturing the next generation of mission-minded individuals.

Bibliography

Cochrum, Ken. "Why Indigitous? By Ken Cochrum." YouTube, 21 April 2014. https://youtube/JXRpAYdGu4E?si=86HOS6MTGdQZ3VUS.

Davis, D. Ray. "Missions History: On the Cusp of a New Era of Modern Missions." *IMB*, 7 September 2017. https://www.imb.org/2017/09/07/have-we-entered-a-new-era-of-modern-missions/.

"Digital 2023: Global Overview Report." *DataReportal*, 26 January 2023. https://datareportal.com/reports/digital-2023-global-overview-report.

Global Switchboard. https://www.globalswitchboard.io/.

GodTools. "GodTools App." https://godtoolsapp.com/en/.

Indigitous. "Togo | indigenous + digital." YouTube video, 6:27, posted by INDIGITOUS, 13 November 2023. https://www.youtube.com/watch?v=hZHg2kEe4PY.

Lukens, Jeremy. "Students Do Digital Outreach in a New Kind of Mission Trip." *Indigitous*, 21 September 2020. https://indigitous.org/article/students-do-digital-outreach-in-a-new-kind-of-mission-trip/.

Tai, Janice. "Exploring the New Frontier: How We Started Going on Digital Mission Trips." *Thirst*, 20 September 2021. https://thirst.sg/exploring-the-new-frontier-how-we-started-going-on-digital-mission-trips/.

Section III

Disciple-Making Churches for Every People and Place

10

Collaboration for Disciple-Making and Church Planting

Ken Katayama and Idris Mammadov

One of the greatest honours in my (Ken's) life has been to serve on the board of directors of Missio Nexus, which is the North American Missions Association. As this association serves by catalyzing relationships, ideas, and collaboration within the Great Commission community, one core value is foundational for the constituency:

> The Great Commission is too big for anyone to accomplish alone and too important not to try to do together.[1]

What an inspiring concept for collaboration! Therefore, the task at hand is urgent and we need each other. However, an inspiring concept does not make a task easy; in fact, collaborative partnership is hard. Good and effective cross-cultural collaborative partnership is even harder.

In this chapter, Idris Mammadov – my teammate – and I are excited to share with you three key lessons that we have learned during the last fifteen years of working together at Crossover Global to make disciples and plant churches among the unreached.

While Crossover Global is not the focus of this chapter, it is important to introduce the organization in order to explain the context in which these lessons were learned. Crossover Global, a church-planting organization established in 1987, seeks to multiply church planters to plant multiplying churches among

---

[1]. Missio Nexus. https://missionexus.org/the-great-commission-big-important.

the unreached. At present, Crossover Global's team has planted over 3,700 churches among 246 unreached people groups in 34 countries.

The founders of Crossover Global set out a clear direction for the mission – not the "West to the rest, but from the reached to the unreached." This mentality has been our guide over the past three decades. Naturally, if you consistently do and lead others to the same thing, eventually you will see results. Consequently, our ministry focus on "reached people reaching the unreached peoples" turned Crossover Global into a highly diverse and cross-cultural team. Today, we have a team of 185 people from 33 nationalities serving a total of 53,880 church members.

Idris and I are honoured to give executive leadership to this amazing team. We set out below the three key lessons that we, as a global team, have learned about disciple-making, church planting, and collaboration.

Lesson 1: Disciple-Making – Think Maturity over Activity

Jesus commissioned his disciples to make disciples (Matt 28:19–20). While the commission is clear, the method is not. We believe that this was intentional since each person will be reached and will learn to become a follower of Jesus within their own culture and language. This unchangeable reality poses a big problem for collaboration: When making disciples, do we actually know what we are trying to do together?

One of the foundational lessons we learned as we collaborated was the importance of clarifying concepts. This was a must for disciple-making. How do we know when a new disciple is "made?" We know that this process begins with repentance and the lordship of Christ, but when does it end? Is it a programme? A Bible study? Or a lifetime journey?

When collaborating in cross-cultural contexts, the Bible became the final authority in decision-making. In fact, one of our values as a team is that the authority of the Scriptures is our "supracultural" guidance.

> We call this bridge the supracultural gospel because it can transcend the limited cultural and theological understandings of the gospel in both the West and East.
>
> The word gospel means "good news." The prefix supra indicates going above or beyond. So the supracultural gospel is above all cultures. It is not limited to one worl view or one set of religious constructs.[2]

---

2. Codman-Wilson and Zhou, *Supracultural Gospel*, 4.

The clarity for our work together came in focus when the measurement became spiritual maturity instead of activities.

When I (Idris) met Ken for the first time, I – along with two other key leaders – had recently started a small network of churches in my country, Azerbaijan. At that time, this network consisted of thirty-five church members, who came from a Shia Muslim background and were meeting in house churches. We had a vision to reach our nation with the good news of Jesus. We wanted to start ten thousand churches in our country. We did not know how to do so, and we were focusing on activities instead of maturity! During that first meeting, Ken shared Crossover Global's strategy of multiplication.

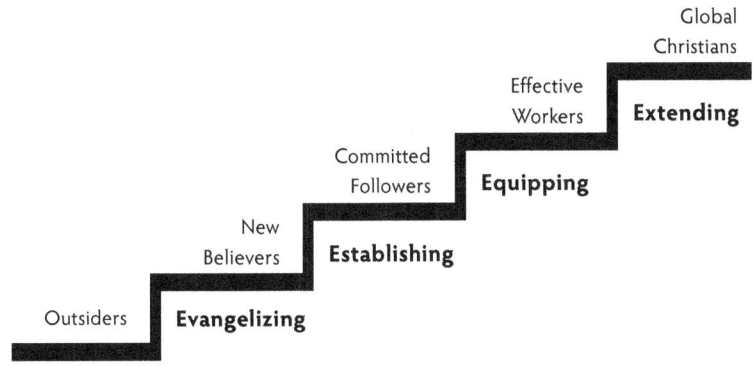

Stairsteps of Spiritual Maturity[3]

Scripture provides clear direction for Christ's followers to help others move up the stairsteps of spiritual maturity. After an outsider (Col 4:5) is *evangelized* and comes to repentance in Christ, we must focus on *establishing* the new believer as a committed follower of Christ.

> Therefore, as you received Christ Jesus the Lord, so walk in him, rooted and built up in him and established in the faith, just as you were taught, abounding in thanksgiving. (Col 2:6–7 ESV)

This step, *establishing*, focuses primarily on helping new believers to grow in their walk with Christ. The next step, *equipping*, trains committed followers for ministry to others. This step move these disciples to become effective leaders.

---

3. Adapted from Jones, *The Ministry Multiplication Cycle*, 37.

> And he gave the apostles, the prophets, the evangelists, the shepherds and teachers, to equip the saints for the work of ministry, for building up the body of Christ. (Eph 4:11–12 ESV)

The final step, *extending*, mobilizes effective leaders to become "global Christians" – people who take personal responsibility for the Great Commission by understanding that they serve as goers or senders to reach the hundreds of millions of people who do not have access to the gospel.

Our founder, Dr. Bill Jones, cites Mark 3:14:

> And he appointed twelve (whom he also named apostles) so that they might be with him and he might send them out to preach.

Dr. Jones believed that this verse touches on the last two steps – equipping and extending – by highlighting three critical actions necessary to make the name of Christ known among the nations.

> The first critical action, "He also appointed 12," emphasizes the importance of wise selection. Luke 6:12–13 notes that before Jesus selected His team, He spent the entire previous night in prayer.
>
> Further, when He chose His team, Jesus did not choose strangers. He had met five of them through John the Baptist about a year earlier (Jn 1:35–51). He even went on a ministry trip with four of them (Mk 1:13–14) before selecting them. Note, too, that from His many disciples (2:15), He only selected twelve. Having a small number allowed for personalized training. Similarly, as the Church equips future missional leaders, we must follow Christ's example by covering the selection in prayer, choosing only those whom we know well, and limiting the training to a small number in order to maximize the impact.
>
> The second necessary action, "to be with Him," focuses on Jesus' preferred method of a preparation. They experienced on-the-job training. They watched the Lord as He ministered in public and listened as He debriefed them in private (4:10). Later, as His team developed, Jesus sent them out to practice ministry two by two (6:7,12). Likewise, we must realize that no better training method exists than involving future ministers in ministry with us: no contact, no impact.
>
> The final action, "to send them out to preach," stresses Jesus' ultimate goal, the mobilization of effective workers who could reach the nations with the message of the Gospel. Throughout

His ministry, Christ demonstrated God's love not only for the Jews, but also for the Samaritans (Jn 4) as well as the Gentiles (Mk 7:24–30). Later, as this vision of God's heart for all peoples grew into a sense of urgency, the Twelve traveled to the ends of the earth proclaiming God's love and forgiveness.[4]

Maturing believers in their walk with Christ became more important than the activities we engaged in as local house churches. We realized that the newly created network of churches in Azerbaijan were trying to plant churches but only had a church full of new believers.

By learning and applying these simple but profound biblical steps for disciple-making, our small network of churches grew from just three to 113 house churches (to date) in Azerbaijan. Since discipleship does not end with establishing a person in their faith and equipping them for ministry, we began intentionally mobilizing reached Azerbaijanis to reach the unreached. The local network of churches planted a total of sixty-eight churches in several countries – Iran, Turkmenistan, the Republic of Georgia, and the Northern Caucasus in Russia.

We believe that disciple-making is a maturing process for every new believer, and we call this process the "Phases of Discipleship."[5]

Phases of Discipleship

Establishing Phase (Colossians 2:7)	Equipping Phase (Ephesians 4:11–13)	Extending Phase (Acts 13:1–3)
Came after Him Mark 1:16–20	Co-laboured with Him Mark 3:13–19	Commissioned by Him Mark 16:16
Shaped their Values	Shared their Ventures	Sharpened their Vision
Master-oriented	Ministry-oriented	Mission-oriented
Emphasis on Maturity	Emphasis on Multiplication	Emphasis on Missions
Established in their Walk	Equipped for their Witness	Extended to the World
Focused on the Great Commandment	Focused on the Great Commitment	Focused on the Great Commission

---

4. Jones writing in: Stetzer and Nation, *Mission of God*, 1238.
5. Adapted from Jones, *Ministry Multiplication Cycle*, 28.

Lesson 2: Church Planting – Think Multiplication over Growth

We believe that church planting is the result of evangelism and disciple-making. Missiologist J. D. Payne defines church planting as "evangelism that results in new churches" and goes on to say, "There are many ways to plant churches; however, the model in the Scriptures is one that begins with evangelism and ends with those new churches following the Lord in obedience."[6]

Pioneer church planting among the unreached is difficult. It takes church planters to plant churches. Paul and Barnabas, who planted new churches, give us great practices to imitate. They not only evangelized new cities but returned to each city to encourage the believers, appoint elders, and entrust that new church to the care of these leaders.

> When they had preached the gospel to that city and had made many disciples, they returned to Lystra and to Iconium and to Antioch, strengthening the souls of the disciples, encouraging them to continue in the faith, and saying that through many tribulations we must enter the kingdom of God. And when they had appointed elders for them in every church, with prayer and fasting they committed them to the Lord in whom they had believed. (Acts 14:21–23 ESV)

Later, Paul returned to Lystra, where the local church that he had planted now served as a sender of Timothy as a church planter to join Paul in the task of proclaiming Christ to the nations.

> Paul came also to Derbe and to Lystra. A disciple was there, named Timothy, the son of a Jewish woman who was a believer, but his father was a Greek. He was well spoken of by the brothers at Lystra and Iconium. Paul wanted Timothy to accompany him, and he took him and circumcised him because of the Jews who were in those places, for they all knew that his father was a Greek. As they went on their way through the cities, they delivered to them for observance the decisions that had been reached by the apostles and elders who were in Jerusalem. So the churches were strengthened in the faith, and they increased in numbers daily. (Acts 16:1–5 ESV)

Crossover Global has created a vital component within our organizational culture of multiplication. We talk about multiplication at every level. When it

---

6. Payne, *Discovering Church Planting*, loc. 87, Kindle.

comes to church planting, multiplication is a must! Our team seeks to plant Christ-centred, biblically founded, and culturally relevant churches that have multiplication in their DNA.

New Churches Planting New Churches

After all these years, the focus on multiplication is starting to pay off. On average, 68 percent of all churches planted by our team are at least second-generation churches. In others words, churches we planted have planted daughter churches. In some parts of the world, we have begun to see a third, fourth, or even fifth generation of churches being planted.

Now we face a new problem. One of those so called "good problems." New churches are being planted. Churches are multiplying. Churches are growing. When is our job finished?

We knew that the pioneering nature of our work would require us to start new churches. The vast majority of these new believers come from animist, Muslim, Hindu, or Buddhist religious backgrounds and had never experienced "church" until gospel access was provided to them. The majority of them are first-generation believers among their own people group. Consequently, there are no local networks of churches to welcome these newly established churches into their care.

As a church-planting organization, we did not want to remain too long, thereby creating unhealthy dependency, or leave too soon, thereby risking the creation of syncretistic churches. In collaboration with our local teammates, we found the answer to our problem. After much conversation, translation, time, and prayer, we finally understood what we were seeking to communicate to each other.

This is what local church leaders were asking of us:

- We desire to be coached, not controlled.
- We desire to give relational authority, not organizational authority.
- We desire to be guided, not driven.

Wow! What a powerful finding about how we could continue to serve them as local and newly established churches. We also had the opportunity to share our hearts and vision with them in the following ways:

- We desire to affirm authority, not seize authority.
- We desire to empower, not enslave.
- We desire to serve you, not take advantage of you.

After discussion, the local leadership told us that the best way to fulfil these expectations was for us to help them to organize themselves into what we call "networks of churches."

What a beautiful surprise! We asked them to explain what they meant by a "network of churches" and, together, we created the following definition:

> A network of churches is a group of local churches that are committed to support encourage and keep one another accountable. They are located in the same geographical location, belonging to the same ethnic group with the same language, culture and customs. They also share the same biblical principles of ministry and service.
>
> These networks are based on friendly relations, support fraternal fellowship, mutual assistance, and share the same principles of ministry based on biblical truths. Church planting and ministry methods are adopted according to the culture, customs, and language of the people they serve.
>
> The purpose of the network of churches is to help the local churches fulfill its mission and thus the Great Commission of the Lord Jesus Christ, realizing that we have the responsibility to be obedient by going and making disciples while remembering that it is He who is building His church.
>
> The work of a network of churches is focused on ensuring that local churches are strengthened on Biblical foundations and meet the four characteristics of a fully mature church:

1. Self-governed

Local churches are managed by local ministers. They consistently gather the local believers for worship, Bible study, prayer, and providing accountability (membership).

2. Self-supported

Local churches meets the need of members by caring for them as well is able to support itself by covering the expenses necessary for the activities of the church.

3. Self-propagating

Local churches grow by practicing local evangelism and multiplying to serve as senders of members who are called to plant new churches.

4. Self-expressing

Local churches learn to express their faith according to their own cultural backgrounds thus creating their own style on Biblical practices such as communion, worship, study of Scripture, day of the week for gathering, etc.[7]

Lesson 3: Collaboration Requires Coordination

How have we worked together to use these biblical concepts and practices? The answer came when a dear friend challenged our thinking a few years ago, boldly stating that collaboration is overrated and coordination is underrated!

At first, we did not realize how profound and deep these words were. We reflected on his words for a couple of months and then asked the leadership team at Crossover Global for their views. Our friend gave us clear terminology for our collaboration model, which we termed "the Art of Coordination."

Let me explain. Being Brazilian-born, I (Ken) have seen how Europeans in Southern Brazil exercise control over the ministry. I am afraid that my personal experience in Brazil with Europeans missionaries is not an exception. In missions, it seems that collaboration became a reaction against control. As missions strategies moved from a top-down model to a flat model of collaboration, much kingdom progress was made – for example, think tanks, networking conferences, and global consultations. But, unfortunately, moving from one extreme to another also caused kingdom loss. For instance, a lot of good ideas have been proposed and discussed at network meetings, but little has been done in the way of implementation. The mentality when no one gets the credit normally equals nothing gets done.

At Crossover Global, we have learned that the proper tension between control and collaboration is a better model when partnering with the Majority World. We call this the "Art of Coordination" because there is a swinging back and forth, with control and collaboration interacting and complementing each other.

A good example of how this works is our human body, specifically the body of an athlete. For an athlete, hand-eye coordination is not only a fundamental skill but crucial for a successful performance. Take cricket, for example. It is important for the batter to have excellent hand-eye coordination to take the

---

7. Mammadov, Crossover Global Internal Documents, Church Planting Network definition, 2021.

best shot they can with the ball travelling at up to 160 kilometres per hour towards them. Or take a professional golfer, who can hit a ball with spin, altitude, and distance in order to get as close as possible to the hole. When we come across people who excel in such sports we do not think of them as having great hand-eye "collaboration," or hand-eye "control" – we describe it as hand-eye "co-ordination."

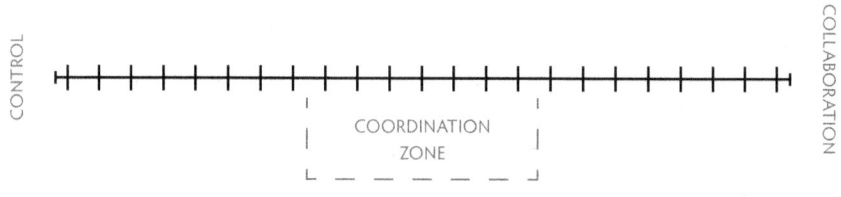

Art of Coordination[8]

We have learned that in order for great collaboration to take place, we need great coordination. Just as an eye does not become a hand or a hand become an eye in order to work together, we learned that by remaining true to who we were and allowing our partner to be who they were, together, through a coordinative effort, there was greater kingdom advancement. Power lies in the ability to coordinate each other's strengths and weakness.

We began this chapter with a quote:

> The Great Commission is too big for anyone to accomplish alone and too important not to try to do together.[9]

We truly believe this statement, and we have tried to live it out by remaining focused on maturity rather than activity and multiplication rather than growth and by applying the art of coordination. We hope that this chapter has encouraged you and given you some ideas to discuss with your own ministry team.

Bibliography

Codman-Wilson, Mary Lou, and Alex Zhou. *Supracultural Gospel: Bridging East and West*. Pasadena: William Carey Publishing, 2012.

---

8. Katayama, Crossover Global Internal Documents, Crossover Global Model of Operations, 2021.

9. MissioNexus. https://missionexus.org/the-great-commission-big-important.

"The Great Commission: Big and Important!" *Missio Nexus*, 20 September 2014. https://missionexus.org/the-great-commission-big-important.

Jones, Bill. *The Ministry Multiplication Cycle*. Eugene: Wipf & Stock, 2020.

Payne, J. D. *Discovering Church Planting: An Introduction to the Whats, Whys, and Hows of Global Church Planting*. Downers Grove: InterVarsity Publishing, 2012. Kindle.

Stetzer, Ed, and Philip Nation, eds. *The Mission of God Study Bible*. Nashville: Holman, 2012.

11

Moving beyond Silos: Energizing Partnerships in Leader Development

Peter Tarantal, with help from Evi Rodemann and Michael Kaspar

Introduction

The well-known saying "It takes a village to raise a child" originated in Africa. I grew up in South Africa, and this was certainly true for me. In the Cape Town township where I grew up, the philosophy was that every child is everyone's child. Our parents would take comfort from the fact that we would be safe if we were playing with other children in the community and overseen by any one of the adults. If any child misbehaved while out in the community and one of the aunties or uncles saw this, they would discipline them – and complaining to your parents about this would result in further discipline. Not that I ever misbehaved growing up!

My world view, belief system, values, and thinking were greatly shaped by this community. In addition, there is the strong African philosophy of "ubuntu" – "*umuntu ngumuntu ngabantu*" or "I am a person through other human beings" – basically means that I am what I am because of who we all are. One of the key aspects of the ubuntu philosophy is a deep interconnectedness and interdependence.

It Takes a Village

When it comes to leadership development, it is pivotal to recognize the contribution of a host of entities in this development process. In my own case, here are a couple of examples of people who have helped to shape me:

I became a follower of Jesus at the age of twenty. The church that I attended did not have a formal discipleship programme, but the older men took us younger men under their wings. They took us to some of the different ministries they were involved in and gave us opportunities to share. During this time, I gave my first testimony and preached my first sermon at an open-air meeting. It was only later that I learned the term "mentorship," but that is what these older men were doing. This is where I learned to take people with me and give them as much exposure to different leadership experiences as possible.

There are so many others who contributed to my development as a leader, but I will just mention George Verwer, the founder and former international director of OM (Operation Mobilisation). George's passion for world evangelization, his deep love for people, and his immense heart of generosity were all characteristics that I wanted to emulate. I recall a number of occasions when some of us in OM leadership gave up on a person who had repeatedly violated trust, but George would go the extra mile to engage with that person. George also modelled vulnerability for me when it was taboo for Christian leaders to talk openly about their failings and weaknesses.

From these experiences, I learned the value of community and that I am who I am through others.

Silo Mentality Defined

The Western Cape is known as the wheat capital of South Africa. I often drive past large grain silos that, in my experience, stand alone. Paul Van Zandt, writes, "Silo Mentality is defined as a mindset of exclusivity that exists when people in different teams refuse to share information with other departments or team members. This restrictive attitude seals off communication creating an isolated work environment and often sees employees hoarding knowledge for their own benefit."[1]

---

1. Van Zandt, "Silo Mentality," https://ideascale.com/blog/silo-mentality-definition/.

The Negative Impact of Silo Thinking

"Alone we will go fast, together we will go further" is another popular saying in Africa. In the short term, individualistic thinking may seem effective and efficient. But will such thinking yield the desired outcomes in the greater scheme of things? Some leaders do not share important information. Their reasons for such behaviour may vary, but one possible reason is fear. Fear that someone else will get the credit. Fear that the other person will not do something as well as they themselves would do it. Fear of "letting go of my baby" and losing control or ownership. Fear of losing power. Or, perhaps, fear that bringing others on board will slow me down as a leader. As Van Zandt says above, a silo mentality is restrictive and will hold us back from accomplishing so much more than we could otherwise achive.

My siloed thinking could also be a result of my own insecurity as a leader. In his short book entitled "Becoming a Secure Leader," Rev. Dr. Geoffrey Njuguna of Kenya – leader of the East Africa region of MANI (Movement for African National Initiatives) – says this:

> A secure leader will always recognize and promote those under him, without fearing for his job. He acknowledges that those under him need to be encouraged to exert their energies for the common good of the organization. He is never intimidated by the exceptional performance of those working under him, because he sees the big picture; the overall performance of the organization. He identifies and affirms the gifting evident in the emerging leader.[2]

What Geoffrey says so well is that the insecure leader may miss out on the joys of seeing a new generation of leaders emerge. Indeed, it takes maturity to encourage new leaders to step forward and to empower them to do so.

Soumitri Das – founder and CEO of Propcore, a property development company – writes, "Organisational silos are a dangerous business barrier. They create an environment where teams do not work well together, duplication occurs, there is no synergy, and knowledge is not exchanged effectively." He continues, "Yes, siloed work environments are bad for two primary reasons: first, because they destroy information transfer; second, because they create an environment where people can't share ideas."[3]

---

2. Njuguna, *Secure Leader*, 75.

3. Das, "Dangers of Organizational Silos," https://www.linkedin.com/pulse/dangers-organisational-silos-importance-collaboration-soumitri-das/.

We live in an interconnected and complex world, and we simply cannot afford siloed thinking. As Das says, a silo mentality often results in unnecessary duplication. When I consider the Christian organization and church world in which I operate, I lament unnecessary duplication, especially in the face of scarce resources. When Christian leaders who work in the same space see others, even subconsciously, as competitors rather than kingdom comrades, much potential fruit is torpedoed. Such behaviour also short-changes what Jesus taught through his prayer for our unity *so that* the world may believe that the Father sent him to be the Saviour of the world (John 17:21). In fact, as Patrick Fung writes,

> The model of *perichoresis* in the Trinity is to cascade down from God to the believers as Jesus prayed for the disciples "May they also be in us so that the world may believe that you have sent me" (John 17:21). Unity thus cascades down from God to the believers, one form of unity a derivative of another.[4]

What a powerful witness it was to the whole of South Africa when Christian leaders prayed together with believing politicians in our parliament building for our unity and the unity of the country as a whole. We openly declared that we are children of God and that – despite barriers such as race, gender, and class – we are one. That event solicited attention from the national news media and, in a small way, Jesus's prayer "that they may all be one . . . so that the world may believe" (John 17:21 ESV) became a reality that day. My own life has been enriched by a wide variety of people, and I have often learned most from those who think very differently to me. I believe that if we partner well in leadership development, the recipients of those efforts will benefit immensely as they will be exposed to leadership development from a variety of places and perspectives. As Lausanne's *The Cape Town Commitment* says, "A divided church has no message for a divided world."[5]

Another danger of silo thinking is our – sometimes hidden – desire to develop leaders in our own image. It is arrogant to believe that if only every leader could be like me, they would be successful. For all leaders the humility to develop leaders who have different ways of expressing their gifts and skills in leadership to us is vital. This is another reason we need to be committed to partner with others in developing leaders.

---

4. Fung, "Cooperation in a Polycentric World," 2.
5. *Cape Town Commitment*, IIF-1.

Importance of Collaborative Thinking in Leadership Development

I find it critical to keep in mind why I am in leadership and why I believe that developing leaders is a noble desire.

First, and speaking personally, leadership is not something I ever strived for. Growing up and at school, I was never the leader type. Truthfully, that served me just fine as I just wanted to be "one of the boys." At school, being in leadership meant responsibility and, sometimes, having to discipline fellow students. I wanted to be popular with the guys . . . and maybe the girls! At the age of twenty, I had a radical conversion experience. Within months of joining the church's young adults group, I was asked to join the leadership team. Somehow, God had plans for me regarding leadership. After joining OM South Africa in 1987, I was soon made the men's team leader and subsequently joined the leadership team of OM South Africa. I held various leadership roles in the organization and, in 1995, became the national director of OM in South Africa. I was one of the first Black leaders of a national Christian organization in South Africa. Since then, I have had the privilege of serving the Lord in various leadership roles globally.

Therefore, I strongly believe that Christian leadership is a calling and that God anoints us for leadership – although it is our responsibility to develop ourselves as leaders and also to develop others for leadership.

The second reason for which I believe that I am in leadership is to serve God's purposes by serving others. It is not about having a title for, as Jesus said, "Not so with you. Instead, whoever wants to become great among you must be your servant" (Mark 10:43). As Hwa Yung says,

> Our striving should never be after leadership itself. Rather, we should be striving to be faithful to our callings or vocations through which we are to love and serve others. Striving for leadership in itself will invariably lead to our being seduced by ambition and power; seeing ourselves as leaders rather than as servants will inevitably result in hubris and an unwarranted sense of self-importance.[6]

It is both helpful and necessary to constantly remind myself that the greater kingdom value is to serve others. In fact, Jesus himself said, "He who is greatest among you shall be your servant. And whoever exalts himself will be humbled, and he who humbles himself will be exalted" (Matt 23:11–12 NKJV). Therefore, if I operate from the kingdom value that it is all about

---

6. Yung, *Leadership or Servanthood?*, 132.

God's kingdom, it is easier for me to join hands with others when it comes to working collaboratively in leadership development.

Through the lens of kingdom collaboration, I see others not as competitors but as fellow pilgrims on this leadership journey. As John Maxwell says, "The sad truth is that when a leader sees another organization as competition, he focuses his attention on building his own case or championing his cause and forgets to learn from what the other group is doing."[7]

Ken Blanchard and Phil Hodges put it well: "The journey of life is to move from a self-serving heart. You finally become an adult when you realize that life is about what you give, rather than what you get."[8] There is so much joy in working with others.

Kingdom Collaboration in Leadership Development

Michael Kaspar of VisionSynergy shared this helpful definition with me: "A mission network is a group of individuals or organizations with a common interest, who connect, communicate, and collaborate together for mutual benefit toward a shared vision or purpose . . . and ultimately, to accomplish together what none could do alone."

One example of kingdom collaboration in leadership development is the National Christian Leadership Development Forum of South Africa, which was established in the early 2000s. I had the joy of chairing this group, which comprised leaders – from many different organizations – who had a heart to see leaders being developed. Our main goal was to foster and promote leadership development in South Africa. Our main focus areas included the following:

- helping people to develop as leaders
- developing a culture of mentorship
- skills development
- developing leadership resources

We hosted training events on topics such as mentoring and leadership competence, as well as reflections on the character of a leader. One of the things I appreciated most about this time was the shared learning. On one occasion, Johannes Malherbe – currently a senior academic at the South African Theological Seminary (SATS) – conducted a case study on two prevalent leadership models in Africa. We studied the life of Shaka Zulu –

---

7. Maxwell, *Indispensable Qualities*, 78.
8. Blanchard and Hodges, *Servant Leader*, 22.

former king of the Zulu tribe – and Mohlomi – former king of the Basuto tribe. Shaka ruled with an iron fist and believed that he should only give up power if someone cut off the hand which held his sceptre. He ruled authoritatively, from a power paradigm. Mohlomi, on the other hand, believed in the power of the collective and would listen to the counsel of others.[9] We reflected that, sadly, many African leaders – both in the political sphere and in Christian circles – operated from a Shaka paradigm when it comes to leadership.

Nelson Mandela – the founding father of South Africa's democracy and one of the global leadership icons of the last century – definitely did not engage in silo thinking. Mandela was Xhosa, and he said that "my notions of leadership were profoundly influenced by observing the regent and his court."[10] National issues such as drought, the culling of cattle, or new laws decreed by the Apartheid government were discussed during these tribal meetings. Everyone had an opportunity to speak and even to disagree with the Chief. The meeting would continue until some kind of consensus was reached. Majority rule was a strange concept. A minority was not to be crushed by the majority. Mandela says that he, Mandela "always followed that example of giving people an opportunity to speak before venturing my own opinion."[11] He always remembered the Chief's axiom: "A leader is like a shepherd. He stays behind the flock, letting the most nimble go on ahead, whereupon the others follow, not realizing that all along they were being directed from behind."[12] On several occasions, when praise was heaped on Mandela, he deflected it by giving the credit to his teammates. He truly believed in the collective.

I experienced another example of kingdom collaboration in August 2006 when I walked into the Kenya College of Communications Technology Convention Centre, Nairobi, Kenya, to attend the MANI (Movement for African National Initiatives) Consultation. I was immediately struck by the excitement and energy of the 520 leaders from across Africa. We had come together to take up the baton of providing leadership for the church's mission endeavours in Africa. I sensed that here was a group of leaders who were answering the call for the church to take responsibility for the challenges on our continent; and since then, I have been encouraged to see more and more leaders involved in this work. Especially heartening was the formation of the MANI Emerging Leaders group, which is designed to promote collaboration

---

9. du Preez, "African Socrates."
10. Mandela, *Long Walk*, 20.
11. Botha and Baron, *Majority World Perspectives*, 10.
12. Mandela, *Long Walk*, 22.

in developing the next generation of African Christian leaders. I feel more optimistic about the future of the church in Africa because of this initiative.

One of the things that I especially appreciate about being part of the MANI initiative is the opportunity to collaborate with leaders who have a great kingdom vision. I believe that one of the Christian African leaders who had a major prophetic voice in the last century was Tokunboh Adeyemo, former long-time general secretary of the Association of Evangelicals in Africa. Adeyemo writes, "Working together was the genius of the traditional African community before Africa was introduced to the destructive philosophy of divide and rule. We express it in many of our proverbs and pithy comments such as: 'One hand cannot put the roof on the mud shed.'"[13]

Evi Rodemann shares yet another example of collaboration from Germany:

> More than 100 youth ministries and organisations got together to offer a Christian youth festival for Germany's teenagers and young people in May 2022. Instead of each of them doing smaller events, they organized and offered a nationwide 4-day event and with a united effort welcomed fourteen thousand teenagers with their youth group leaders. Teenagers gave their lives to Jesus and youth groups across the nation have been impacted on a scale none of them could have achieved on their own.

Principles for Effective Collaboration

Effective collaboration requires intentionality. Working together does not always come naturally. John Maxwell says of collaboration that "each person brings something to the table that adds value to the relationship and synergy to the team. The sum of truly collaborative teamwork is always greater than its parts."[14]

Further we need to be convinced that we do not always need to be right, but need to hear what other people say. In his book entitled "The Need to Be Right," Dr. Arnold Mol writes, "The need to be right is one of the most powerful forces in human nature. It determines the way we think, the way we act and especially the way we relate to others."[15] When Arnold, who is a dear friend, sent me a copy of his book, he inscribed my copy with these words: "May you always

---

13. Adeyemo, *Africa's Enigma*, 100.
14. Maxwell, *Essential Qualities*, 13–14.
15. Mol, *Need to Be Right*, 11.

be right on the things that matter and allow others to be right on the things that don't." These are profound words. In the chapter entitled "Must We Be So Dogmatic?" in his book "More Drops," George Verwer writes, "How hard it is for us strong-minded, committed, Bible-believing Christians to ever change. But we need to be willing to change if we have been wrong." He continues, "On the very basics of the Christian faith we must remain unmoveable, but on many issues in which there are a variety of interpretations, I believe it is better to not be so dogmatic."[16]

Finally if we are to collaborate well, we will need to keep the bigger picture in mind and focus on what we are looking to achieve. It will be vital to remember that we cannot do this alone, but we need other people. Most importantly we need to remember that all our collaboration together is about God getting the glory, and therefore we must learn to get out of our silos and work together in authentic partnerships.

Conclusion

We will be so much more effective and God-honouring in developing leaders if we move beyond and outside our silos and collaborate well with others. Remember, "together we will go far!"

Bibliography

Adeyemo, Tokunboh. *Africa's Enigma and Leadership Solutions*. Nairobi: WordAlive, 2009.

Blanchard, Ken, and Phil Hodges. *The Servant Leader*. Nashville: Thomas Nelson, 2003.

Botha, Nico A., and Eugene Baron, eds. *Majority World Perspectives on Christian Mission*. George, South Africa: Kreativ SA, 2020.

The Cape Town Commitment. https://lausanne.org/statement/ctcommitment.

Das, Soumitri. "The Dangers of Organizational Silos and the Importance of Cross-Functional Collaboration." *LinkedIn*, 21 September 2022. https://www.linkedin.com/pulse/dangers-organisational-silos-importance-collaboration-soumitri-das/.

du Preez, Max. "The African Socrates." In *Of Warriors, Lovers and Prophets: Unusual Stories from South Africa's Past*. Cape Town: Penguin Random House South Africa, 2009. https://books.google.co.za/books?id=fAtbDwAAQBAJ&pg=PT49&source=gbs_toc_r&cad=3.

Fung, Patrick. "Cooperation in a Polycentric World." Paper presented at the Majority World Christian Leaders Conversation, Malaysia, 2017.

---

16. Verwer, *More Drops*, 57.

Mandela, Nelson. *Long Walk to Freedom*. New York: Little, Brown & Co, 1994.

Maxwell, John C. *The 17 Essential Qualities of a Team Player*. Nashville: Thomas Nelson, 2002.

———. *The 21 Indispensable Qualities of a Leader*. Nashville: Thomas Nelson, 1999.

Mol, Arnold. *The Need to Be Right*. China: Christian Art, 2018.

Njuguna, Geoffrey K. *Becoming a Secure Leader*. Nairobi: self-published, 2015.

Van Zandt, Paul. "What Is Silo Mentality? Definition, Consequences, and Remedies." *Ideascale*, 21 July 2021. https://ideascale.com/blog/silo-mentality-definition/.

Verwer, George. *More Drops*. Farnham: CWR, 2015.

Yung, Hwa. *Leadership or Servanthood?* Carlisle: Langham, 2021.

12

Platforming Fresh Expressions of Ekklesia

Mark Williamson

In the 1990s, fresh expressions of church began to spring up across the UK. These new forms of church were pioneered by leaders who wanted to reach people who would never consider joining a traditional church. Many of these expressions have a niche focus so that they can reach a particular community. In the UK, we now have a plethora of Café Churches, Messy Churches, and Forest Churches, as well as new church communities serving surfers, car enthusiasts, justice warriors, storytellers, and many, many more. Fresh Expressions "are new forms of church that emerge within contemporary culture and engage primarily with those who don't 'go to church.'"[1]

But the key is not to create a niche worship experience. One of the major mistakes Fresh Expressions (FX) pioneers often make is to design an alternative worship experience and hope that this will attract an unchurched community. The traditional church-planting approach is often to begin with a worship service, then seek to disciple those who attend, and, ultimately, point those people outwards towards mission. Although this approach works in many contexts, and this attractional church model can be a very successful method of church planting, there are always some people who will never be reached through this method.

FX turns this process around by having church pioneers begin with mission – finding ways to love and serve members of a specific community. As relationships are built, the pioneer seeks to disciple these people. Eventually,

---

1. Lings, "Fresh Expressions of Church," https://churcharmy.org/blog/2018/02/23/fresh-expressions-of-church/.

a new form of worship will come into being that is culturally relevant and appropriate for the community. This FX model has been adopted by many mainstream UK churches (core partners include the Anglican, Methodist, Baptist, Salvation Army, URC, and Church of Scotland denominations), resulting in thousands of new missional communities and fresh expressions of church across the nation.

> Nothing else, as a whole in the Church of England has this level of missional impact and the adding of further ecclesial communities, thereby feeling ecclesial re-imagination.[2]
>
> The fresh expressions movement within the Methodist Church has been extremely successful in welcoming previously unaffiliated people into Christian faith exploration and participation. Nearly two-thirds of the participants in ... Methodist fresh expressions are new to Christianity! I know of few other missional orientations that bear such amazing fruit.[3]

FX is also increasingly being looked at by newer house church and charismatic denominations. And there are now national FX teams supporting this form of missional pioneering – not only in the UK but also in Germany, Sweden, Switzerland, South Africa, Austria, Australia, Norway, the Netherlands, and the United States.

In this chapter, I will share some FX practices and wisdom that I have picked up over the last twenty years that have been most helpful for me in the fresh expressions and missional communities that I have led; and I will also share the current practices of our Sanctuary FX community in central London. The point is not to try and implement all this in your context – some of these practices will be relevant, others may not. Take what could be useful, adapt it as necessary, and see if any of these practices can help you or your colleagues in the development of missional communities.

Authentic Faith

In 2013, a research piece was commissioned by a group of UK FX leaders to look into successful practices for reaching young adults across the nation. Beth Keith from the Church Army did a thorough job of studying Fresh Expressions and talking with FX leaders to learn best practices. The findings have proven

---

2. Lings, *Day of Small Things*, 10.
3. *Methodism's Hidden Harvest*, 2.

remarkably helpful for many church pioneers and, although over ten years old, remain just as relevant today.

The full *Authentic Faith* report made a number of recommendations for the UK church and gave examples of differing types of fresh expressions. But what I found most helpful was the identification of five common values across all these different types of church communities. The fruitful churches were fruitful because they embraced these five concepts.

There were a number of common values and realities seen across all or most churches involved in the study. These realities shaped their practice, their faith, and how these communities organized themselves. While the outworking of these realties was different, their presence across all or most of the expressions of church investigated suggests a commonality across ministries with this age group. These five common values are described below:[4]

- **Community:** Community was a key value within these churches. Food, socials, and hospitality were all key components of church life rather than additional activities. The term "family" was used frequently, particularly in reference to church as family – either to those from broken family backgrounds or as a family away from home for those who had recently moved away from their parents' home to attend university or for a job.
- **Authenticity:** Honesty, integrity, and "realness" were emphasized over "rightness." Church was described as journeying together and working out faith together in the messy realities of life rather than as the teaching of truths. Leadership was characterized by honesty and connecting with others in their struggles rather than being detached or idealistic about faith. Discipleship was described as working out how to do life well rather than how to believe the right things.
- **Doubt (or questioning):** Across most of the churches, value was placed on an openness to express doubt, to question, and to deconstruct. This was often understood as a valuable formational phase in the church's life, enabling members to develop and own its vision and ethos. Churches reaching people with no previous church experience or closed de-churched young adults allowed more freedom in this area, with some leaders describing discipleship as moving through doubt towards faith.

---

4. Keith, *Authentic Faith*, 12–13.

- **Spirituality:** Across the range of churches, most leaders interviewed emphasized the emotive or "felt" nature of a spiritual encounter with God. Creative and experiential worship during church services was rated as a high value for young adults with previous church experience. For churches reaching those who were closed, de-churched, or non-churched, the term worship was not used; instead, there was reference to "spaces" where people could experience God. These spaces often looked very different from the sung worship happening within a traditional church service environment.
- **Change:** All the leaders interviewed discussed how change was an ongoing reality of their church. They described a continuous transition of people in and out of the community, which was caused by people moving geographically for work, studies, or resettlement. Transition was also caused by people moving to a new life stage. These ongoing transitions affected both members and leaders and had a significant impact on the development of the church. Larger churches emphasized the need for robust and supportive structures to balance the negative effects of transition. Smaller churches emphasized the strength of relationships and the important role the wider church can play, especially during leadership transitions.

While there is evidence of commonality across the churches examined, these realities of community, authenticity, doubt, spirituality, and change were worked out in very different practices. Though these realities shaped their faith and practice, there were noticeable differences between the types of churches, their contexts, and the kinds of young adults reached.[5]

So, while churches looked different and were doing very different things to reach very different types of people, these five common values were always present.

If you are involved in pioneering a church work, have you recognized the importance of these five values? Is your church a place where people encounter real community and can have authentic conversations – which go deeper than the surface level – with other believers about God? Is church a place where people can share their doubts and frustrations with the faith but also a place where they have an opportunity to explore genuine spirituality and encounter the presence of God? And do you recognize and embrace the reality of constant

---

5. Keith, *Authentic Faith*, 12–13.

change? The more urban your environment, the faster will be the pace of change and the turnover in your membership.

Other Research Reports

There are several other research pieces and books that have studied fresh expressions over the last twenty years. I found three of these especially helpful as a pioneer: *The Day of Small Things* by George Lings, *Not as Difficult as You Think* by the Church of England, and *Holy Grit* by James Poch.

The wisdom offered by *The Day of Small Things* suggests that two key elements should always be present in a fresh expression:

> Always work within the framework that fresh expressions of Church [fxC] are made of two elements. Water is hydrogen and oxygen, and fxC are mission and church. Neither element replaces the other; both work with the other; developing both elements is essential.[6]

Basically, mission and discipleship are key – we want to reach new people and then help them become mature and radical followers of Jesus. And going through this process will help us to pioneer new forms of worship services that are relevant to these communities. Lings shares several other key insights to help pioneers:

False assumptions to avoid:[7]

- **Buying an fxC off the shelf really works.** While this can be done, it is usually a mistake. Do not slavishly copy what others have done because this ignores context and discernment.
- **Settling on an act of worship is the best starting point.** Experience says that it is better to follow a longer process – listening and loving, serving people and building relationships, and then, naturally engaging in spiritual conversations. Only after that does public worship evolve.

---

6. Lings, *Day of Small Things*, 213.
7. Lings, *Day of Small Things*, 213–14.

Lessons on mission and church:[8]

- **Be clear about reaching outsiders.** Ensure that the leader and the team are focused on connecting with those beyond the church. Disaffected Christians joining causes problems.
- **Choose the venue and day for meetings according to what suits the context and the people,** not by the habits or the preference of existing Christians.
- **Start with the end in mind.** The goal is a community that is mature in Christ. As soon as it is appropriate, encourage the young church to take responsibility for its finances and local leadership. Look out for gifts and potential ministries in the team and in newcomers.
- **Start with discipleship, and not just attendance, in mind.** While being apprentices of Jesus can happen in many ways, it should be intentional and relational.
- **It is not wrong** – and in fact, quite normal – **to be a young, small church that is still maturing.**
- **Do not go it alone** – having a critical friend or consultant is very helpful.
- **Finding ways to develop discipleship can take time** and may involve experimenting with a number of different approaches. The test is the fruit of lives that are more like Jesus.
- **Resist complicating the life of the fxC.** Keep it simple, especially if you are leading in your spare time. Share the tasks with others – make it a working boat, not a passenger ship.[9]

So, once again, there is a strong reminder not to start with worship but with mission and to remain clear that your primary objective is to reach unchurched people. Second, prioritize discipleship. And after focusing on discipleship, develop your own worship style rather than simply copying what other people elsewhere may be doing. That progression of mission leading to discipleship leading to worship is crucial when trying to reach the unchurched.

The 2008 Anglican report *Not as Difficult as You May Think* contains more helpful wisdom.

Reflecting on stories we heard during our interviews, the following common themes stand out:

---

8. Lings, *Day of Small Things*, 213–14.
9. Lings, 213–14.

- For many, the start was having Christian friends who had invited them to some event.
- Others had been particularly impressed by the example of Christians involved in community projects and social action.
- Some had followed the case study churches "from a distance" on social media before deciding that they wanted to become more involved.
- Many also commented that they found the powerful sense of "community," "family," or "belonging" attractive.
- Having a safe space to ask – and honestly discuss – difficult questions was very important: "I've had these thoughts and questions for years but never had the confidence to say them out loud before."
- For some, this involved meeting regularly for coffee with a Christian – typically a church worker or chaplain – to study the Bible or discuss faith.[10]

The findings of this report confirm the importance of community, authenticity, and doubt – which were also emphasized in *Authentic Faith*. The report also brings out four fresh concepts to consider: the importance of using social media consistently, the value of members inviting friends to events or programmes, the powerful link between spirituality and social justice projects, and the importance of a place for intentional, one-to-one conversations about faith to help people mature as disciples.

At a workshop to discuss this report, a conversation with Jason Poch – author of *Holy Grit* – led to the identification of three other discipleship best practices that were key in our own lives and that we also wanted to provide for others as they grew in faith:

- **One-to-one conversations:** giving people an opportunity to talk about faith, Scripture, and God, and to grow through reflecting and being challenged by such conversations.
- **Holy role models:** the importance of people being able to see and interact with mature Christians who have a zeal for the things of God – prayer, Scripture, personal holiness, and the presence of the Holy Spirit.
- **Giving people responsibility:** people grow in faith and in capability through getting involved and also by being given slightly more

---

10. *Not as Difficult*, 9.

responsibility than they feel ready to take on – which pushes them towards prayer and reliance on God.

Current Practices at Sanctuary Westminster

In the light of all that has been said above, let me share how we are trying to implement some of these practices at our own Sanctuary community in central London. We are a fresh expression trying to reach people in their 20s and 30s – primarily young professionals – in London.

First, we describe ourselves as a community of young adults who are exploring spirituality, justice, and leadership. The terms "Christian" and "church" are binary and can be off-putting to many. If we introduce ourselves as a church, then many people respond by saying that they do not go to church and the conversation quickly stops. But saying that we are exploring spirituality, justice, and leadership opens up more of a conversation – people want to learn more and are often keen to explore these areas themselves.

We are clear that we are *very* Jesus-focused in each of these areas. We believe that Jesus is genuinely the expert in each of these concepts, and so someone taking any of these concepts seriously will have to consider how to respond to Jesus at some point in their journey.

- If spirituality is all about having a healthy relationship with God, then Jesus is clearly the expert; no one comes to the Father except through him (John 14:6).
- If justice is all about how to strive, in a healthy way, for a better and fairer world, then Jesus is the expert, with his teaching on loving our enemies (Matt 5:43–48) as a means of overcoming evil without being overcome by evil (Rom 12:17–21).
- If leadership is all about developing mature relationships with other people so that we can work together more effectively, then Jesus is the expert here, too, for he calls us to serve rather than to lord it over others (Mark 10:42–45).

So, community, spirituality, justice, and leadership give us a language to start having conversations about Jesus in a way that makes sense to those who are unchurched and also creates interest in what we are doing. And most important, it is authentic – since we genuinely do want to help people to grow in these areas of their lives.

The justice focus led us to create a series of Justice Groups. These groups meet roughly monthly, either to do a service project or to work on campaigning for justice. At present, we have a Financial Justice Group starting a campaign to shut down money laundering through tax havens and a Homeless Justice Group that volunteers with a local soup kitchen, collects for a food bank, and supports a winter night shelter accommodation project – since each of these projects are run by other local churches, we simply send volunteers to join them without having to take on project responsibility ourselves. Previous Justice Groups have focused on racial justice and climate change. These groups enable us to emphasize and lead with mission – rather than worship – as we talk about who we are so that we can build relationships alongside people as we serve and, together, try to turn the world upside down.

We try to maintain a credible online presence, with a modern website and regular content on our Twitter, Facebook, YouTube, and Instagram channels. We use these media to share with others the work of our Justice Groups and to invite them to join us.

As part of our discipleship focus, we offer monthly coaching conversations so that people can talk about their life of following Jesus with another member. Through One Rock International, we use the Pathway modules of coaching-based curriculum that can be used freely by churches and ministries to help their discipleship. Current modules available include *How To Pray* and *Jesus on Leadership*, and more modules are being developed.

Central to our discipleship focus is a "Rhythm of Life" – consisting of practices that help us to grow in spirituality, justice, and leadership – that we encourage all Sanctuary members to follow. There are a total of twelve practices, split into four groups of three:

- Each *day*, members are encouraged to (1) pray, (2) read the Bible, and (3) reflect on what they are grateful for and so, worship God.
- Each *week*, members are encouraged to (4) do an act of kindness for a stranger, (5) attend our Thursday evening meeting, and (6) invite someone new to a Sanctuary event or mission group.
- Each *month*, members are encouraged to (7) have a coaching conversation, (8) join a Justice Group activity, and (9) attend a Sanctuary social activity.
- And each *year*, we provide for members (10) a weekend retreat, (11) a one-day mission activity, and (12) a weekend of meditation and worship reflections.

This "Rhythm of Life" has now become the core element towards which, ultimately, we point all members or visitors. It is a slight refinement of our mission-discipleship-worship strategy. If people join a Justice Group (mission), then we invite them to get more involved, invite them to a relationship with Jesus, and point them towards the "Rhythm" as a means of developing that relationship. If they are already Christians and initially join Sanctuary through our Thursday evening meeting (worship), then we point them towards the "Rhythm" to help disciple them towards Christian maturity and then get involved in a Justice Group. So now, discipleship through the "Rhythm" becomes the core goal.

Whether people join through mission or through worship, we encourage them to join the twelve discipleship practices that will help them to follow Jesus and help to bind us all together as a community.

That was a whirlwind introduction to the concept of fresh expressions and to the practices in place in our Sanctuary community. Are any of these relevant and helpful to you and your church community as you seek to reach out to the unchurched with the gospel of Jesus?

Bibliography

Church Army Research Unit. *Not as Difficult as You Think*. Sheffield: Church Army, 2018.
Cray, Graham. *Mission-Shaped Church*. London: Church House, 2004.
Horsley, Graham, ed. *Methodism's Hidden Harvest*. London: Methodist Church, 2017.
Keith, Beth. *Authentic Faith*. Sheffield: Fresh Expressions, 2013.
Lings, George. *The Day of Small Things*. Sheffield: Church Army, 2016.
Poch, James. *Holy Grit*. Preston: Zaccmedia, 2017.
Wier, Andy. *Sustaining Young Churches: A Qualitative Pilot Study of Fresh Expressions of Church in the Church of England*. Sheffield: Church Army, 2016.

Sample of UK Fresh Expressions of Church:

An up-to-date list is available at https://freshexpressions.org.uk/examples-of-fresh-expressions/

Helpful information is also available at https://freshexpressions.org.uk/story-archive/

A sample list of communities and their websites are given below:

- StoryHouse in Liverpool: https://storyhouse.community/
- Kahaila in East London: https://kahaila.com/
- Sanctuary in central London: https://sanctuary-westminster.org/
- Sorted in Bradford: http://sortedcommunity.org.uk/
- Revs online: https://www.facebook.com/groups/revslimiter

- Explore in Leicester: https://www.leicester.anglican.org/news/explore-fresh-expression-of-church-brings-people-together-in-houghton.php
- Sacred Space Kingston: https://sacredspacekingston.com/
- Moot in central London: https://www.mootcommunity.org/
- Kairos Movement, Yorkshire: https://www.kairosmovement.org.uk/

Further websites:

- www.freshexpressions.org.uk
- www.onerockinternational.com
- www.sanctuary-westminster.org

13

Elevating Women in Ministry and Leadership

Funmi J. Para-Mallam

Introduction: The "Woman Question" in Ministry and Leadership

The question of women in ministry and leadership is fraught with controversy both in religious and secular spaces – but more so in the former. People tend to be quite polarized in their convictions as to whether women should be allowed to be pastors, to teach, or to hold other leading roles in church and society. In view of such contestations, I approach this topic from the standpoint of lived human experience held in creative tension with my Christian faith in the context of a strongly patriarchal Nigerian society. Yet it is a society in transition, shaped by conflicting influences of African traditional customary beliefs, Christian and Islamic theologies, as well as the secularizing effects of modernization.[1]

The convergence of these influences produces a dynamic social reality that is marked by ambiguity, anomaly, and paradox. For example, my home church, Evangelical Church Winning Africa (ECWA), does not consider it theologically appropriate to ordain women as pastors. Neither does it appoint women to serve as elders or deaconesses. Within the church setting, the roles of women in ministry are limited to teaching Sunday school, singing in the choir, playing in the band, serving as ushers, or serving on committees, which

---

1. Nweze and Takaya, "Relative Deprivation of the Nigerian Female Personality as Gender Violence: A Nigerian Overview," 1; Para-Mallam, "No Woman Wrapper in a Husband's House: The Cultural Production of Hegemonic Masculinity in Nigeria," 107.

they may chair. Some women who felt called to leadership roles have left for other denominations.

Yet, women teach at the Jos ECWA Theological Seminary and serve on its governing board, as I have also done. In another church in the same city, a dear friend of mine is one of three female senior pastors. Some Christian denominations permit women to serve in any ministry calling and to hold highly placed positions, including the office of bishop. All these groups use the Bible as a reference point to justify their theological standpoint. My personal reality reflects the same ambiguity and paradox: ecclesiastical restrictions conflict with my senior management and leadership training role in Nigeria's apex policy think tank and with my roles in teaching a theological course in gender and ministry, preaching, and mentoring Christian youth.

In view of such diversity of opinions and practices, I find the praxis model within a contextual theological approach particularly useful in understanding and interpreting scriptural intent and meaning based on lived experience. The story of a twelve-year-old girl I once taught in an ECWA Sunday school is a good place to begin. One day, around 2008, I was assisting another teacher, who posed a question to the class: "Why did Jesus have to become a man?" This little girl raised her hand and said, "Because if he had come as a woman, his message would have been lost; nobody would have listened to or respected what he had to say." The teacher brushed her response aside and said, "Oh no, that's not what I meant." As he pointed to another child, I requested that we pause to consider the deeper implications of what the girl had said.

Her observation highlights an important reality: being female means that you are less likely to be seen, heard, and respected and, therefore, less likely to play a leading role in church or society. The little girl was right. Christian ministry is often viewed through the lens of the call to full-time Christian service, which is largely a male enterprise. Even in missions, the discourse in our church is often about, "missionaries and their wives." This is not to suggest that the situation in ECWA is applicable in the larger Nigerian church. Ministries like Calvary Productions (CAPRO), the Nigeria Fellowship of Evangelical Students (NIFES), the Nigerian Evangelical Missionary Association (NEMA), and a host of church and parachurch ministries recruit and commission female ministers and missionaries in their own right. This has encouraged many young women to catch the vision for kingdom service across a broad range of callings in both paid and voluntary positions, sometimes in the midst of societal controversy and disapproval. These varied experiences are not limited to Nigeria; they occur in the church worldwide and underscore the need for a contextually relevant scriptural foundation for elevating women in ministry and leadership.

Theological and Conceptual Foundations

The praxis model of contextual theology is concerned with doing theology reflectively in a way that anticipates and facilitates social change. Indeed, God's divine presence is revealed in the "dynamic" process of historical development and change.[2] The context in which theology is done is understood to be problematic and requiring transformation. In this instance, it is the problem of social, cultural, and theological barriers to women entering and flourishing in ministry and leadership. The praxis model is associated with liberation theologies and similar emerging theologies that problematize the status quo and seek to promote change. Such theologies include feminist theology, Black theology, eco-sustainability theology, and disability theology, among others.

The praxis model has provided a powerful platform for Christian theology to bring about change in social, cultural, economic, and political systems. It is a viable means for an "alternative vision" of what society could become.[3] At the very heart of the praxis model lies Karl Marx's axiom: "The philosophers have only *interpreted* the world in various ways; the point is to *change* it."[4] The biblical foundation of the praxis model rests on the prophetic tradition of linking ideas or thoughts and words to practical action. Furthermore, it draws inspiration from New Testament passages such as James 1:22 and James 4:17 that enjoin hearing and believing the word that is backed by obedient action to ensure Christian impact. In this model, both *orthodoxy* and *orthopraxy* are equally vital.

Within the praxis model, a feminist theological lens is a helpful tool for interpreting Scripture from the lived experiences of women in the Bible, in history, and in contemporary society. To a large extent, women's experiences have been obscured and silenced by a dominant "malestream" narrative. Women's genealogies, personal walk with God, and individual struggles are not as visible as those of men. Using a feminist theological analysis that subscribes to the supreme authority and authenticity of the biblical revelation – albeit enculturated within a Middle Eastern and Judaic setting – I highlight the liberating message that the Bible has for women. That is, the underlying

---

2. Bevans, *Models of Contextual Theology*, 70.
3. Bevans, 77.
4. Bevans, 72, citing Marx, "Eleven Theses on Feuerbach," 15 (Emphasis original).

assumption that all believers – regardless of race, ethnicity, gender, or any other identity marker – are called to ministry and to play an influential part in building God's kingdom. First, however, it is important to clarify what is meant by "ministry" and "leadership."

What Is Ministry?

The word "minister" comes from a Latin word for servant, indicating that ministry entails service. God's prophetic promise in Joel 2:28 (fulfilled in Acts 2:1–21) to pour out the Holy Spirit on all people, both men and women, indicates that Christian ministry (or service) is mediated by the Spirit who indwells and empowers the believer to build God's kingdom and accomplish his divine purposes. There is a growing realization that Christian ministry encompasses all facets of worship and daily life and is not limited to the conventionally recognized fivefold ministry of apostle, prophet, evangelist, pastor, and teacher (Eph 4:11). The Bible is replete with stories of women and girls in diverse ministries such as helps (for example, Dorcas in Acts 9:36), gospel work financiers (for example, Mary Magdalene, Joanna, and Susanna in Luke 8:1–3), and hospitality (for example, the Shunamite woman in 2 Kgs 4:8–10).

Women like Leah, Rachel, and Ruth played powerful and active home and nation-building roles (Ruth 4:11). The import of women's ministry in the home and its critical link to nation-building tend to be overlooked, understated, and undercompensated – there are no national awards for being an exemplary homemaker. A Christian medical doctor once visited our home. When I asked him about his wife's occupation, he replied, "Nothing serious. She's not working right now. She just stays at home." The planning, energy, resourcefulness, and time that go into homemaking are so often perceived and treated as "nothing serious." Yet it is a critical ministry without which neither the world nor the church could survive. Although some Christian denominations do emphasize the importance of homemaking ministry, they often insist that this is a woman's sole and exclusive preserve. In such a context, women may be guilt-tripped into refraining from working outside the home or engaging in what are traditionally male roles. I had a friend in North America who graduated *magna cum laude* – at the top of her class – from a prestigious Christian college alongside her husband. Their denomination upheld the full-time homemaker ideal. Her husband went on to get a well-paid job while she raised their three children and slid into severe depression. In my conversations with her, it became clear that she was torn between a strong desire to be a career woman and the church-bred conviction that she should remain at home.

The important point to note is that all Christian ministry is about serving humanity in diverse ways and contexts and that this requires the guidance and inspiration of God's Spirit. Even Stephen and the six other men chosen to serve tables by distributing food in Jerusalem were required to be full of the Holy Spirit and wisdom (Acts 6:1–7). So, all ministry is meaningful, valuable, and potentially impactful. To elevate women in ministry and leadership calls for rethinking what we perceive as valuable ministry and who we perceive as valuable ministers – not in word alone but in demonstrable ways that give value, visibility, and voice to women and their varied callings. This will enable the church to increase women's capacity to influence their world and lead change for God's kingdom in ways God calls them to do.

What Is Leadership and How Should People Lead?

Leadership is essentially about influence.[5] It is also a process and a relationship that facilitates human organization by exercising various forms of influence towards the achievement of common goals.[6] The little captive girl in Naaman's household influenced him to seek medical help in Israel while his servants – junior officers – influenced him to follow the prophet Elisha's instructions to obtain healing (2 Kgs 5:1–14). These people demonstrated a level of leadership. Feminist praxis frowns on the conventional understanding of leadership as implying occupying a position or wielding authority over others in a domineering manner. Instead, leadership is an opportunity to be empowered from within and, in turn, to empower others.[7] This perspective coincides with the biblical injunction to ministers: "Don't lord it over the people assigned to your care, but lead them by your own good example" (1 Pet 5:3 NLT). In other words, ministers are called to be servant-leaders, as Jesus so aptly explained:

> But Jesus called them together and said, "You know that the rulers in this world lord it over their people, and officials *flaunt their authority over* those under them. But among you it will be

---

5. Maxwell, *The 21 Irrefutable Laws of Leadership*, 11.

6. Eklund, Barry, and Grunberg, "Gender and Leadership," 134 referring to Northouse, *Leadership: Theory and Practice*, 2007.

7. Rowlands, "Word of the Times, but What does it Mean? Empowerment in the Discourse and Practice of Development," 15–18.

different. Whoever wants to be a leader among you must be your servant." (Matt 20:25–26 NLT, emphasis added)

Servant-leaders exercise authority and may occupy positions of power, but they are expected to use that authority in God-responsive stewardship of creation, not in prideful, domineering, or selfish ways. According to Eklund, Barry, and Grunberg, there is an incongruity between the stereotypical agentic leader role that depicts male status, autonomy, authority, and power, and the gender role typically assigned to females, which is culturally constructed as passive and submissive under authority.[8] N. T. Wright believes that this gender-coded patriarchal understanding of leadership, power and authority its related is the basis for a faulty interpretation of isolated verses such as 1 Corinthians 14:34–35 and 1 Timothy 2:11–15.[9] Such passages have instigated widespread opposition to women occupying leadership positions and prompted the delegitimization of female leaders and the devaluation of their leadership styles. Katia Adams argues that, ultimately, such opposition contradicts the original divine mandate to all humans. She writes:

> The reality is that, in many church circles today, we have become so confused on gender roles and what the Bible is trying to tell us about women in leadership that we have encouraged our women to abdicate their purposes as revealed in Genesis 1:28. We have instructed generations of Eves to abdicate their God-given mandate to rule, in favour of an alternate church-given mandate to follow and serve Adam as he rules. And the results of this are catastrophic.[10]

Women's ability to exert influence in any capacity is often curtailed by defective exegesis of Scripture. This undermines their ability to overcome the double bind of not being perceived as possessing legitimate authority on the one hand and the demand to maintain self-effacing feminine qualities on the other. Such stereotypes run contrary to actual human experience in which factors other than gender shape personality and circumstances. These stereotypes also generate frustration and hurt in those who feel that their callings, gifts, and talents are not validated.

---

8. Eklund, Barry, and Grunberg, "Gender and Leadership," 133–34.

9. Wright, "Women's Service in the Church: The Biblical Basis," https://ntwrightpage.com/2016/07/12/womens-service-in-the-church-the-biblical-basis/.

10. Adams, *Equal: What the Bible Says about Women, Men and Authority*, 29.

> What is important is to recognise is how intensely angry and disenfranchised our young adult children and their Christian friends are about gender stereotypes. They get angry that a woman may be stopped from reaching her full potential due to gender; but they also see that men are locked into a toxic masculinity where they are perceived as weak if they dare to serve with compassion or gentleness, or give "power" away. We honestly believe that we will lose the next generation if we keep arguing over the roles and leadership of men and women.[11]

Proponents of servant-leadership argue that gender-integrative leadership education provides a gender-inclusive space to bring women's unique and urgently needed giftings, talents, and styles into leadership and ministry.[12]

Why Should Women Be Elevated in Ministry and Leadership?
God Uses Women: Women in the Bible

It is clear from Scripture that God, at various times, and for important reasons, placed great confidence in women.

The true and living Word, the Lord Jesus Christ, was the promised seed of the woman (John 1:1, 14; Gen 3:15). He was sired by the Holy Spirit and then entrusted to be nurtured in the womb of a woman, and nourished at her breast (Luke 1:26–35).

The Lord Jesus accepted various forms of help and sustenance from women: Mary anointed his feet with expensive perfume and wiped them with her hair (John 12:3); the Samaritan woman gave him water to quench his thirst (John 4:4–7); other women financed his ministry (Luke 8:1–3); and Martha offered him hospitality in her home (John 12:1–2).

The Lord Jesus permitted Mary to sit and learn at his feet with other male disciples and refused to let this privilege be taken away from her (Luke 10:38–42). He committed the sharing of the gospel message to the Samaritan woman and to the women who were the last to leave the Saviour at his crucifixion and the first to see him risen at the tomb (John 4:28–30, 39; Matt 28:1–10). He enabled women to serve in many different ways. For example, Lydia hosted a church in her home (Acts 16:40), Euodia and Syntyche served as co-workers alongside the apostle Paul (Phil 4:2–3), Priscilla, an itinerant gospel worker,

---

11. D & D, "Men and Women in Partnership for the Kingdom of God."
12. Reynolds, "Servant-Leadership as Gender-Integrative Leadership: Paving a Path for More Gender-Integrative Organizations through Leadership Education," 155.

taught and preached along with her husband and the apostle Paul (Acts 18:18–19, 24–26; Rom 16:3), and Phoebe served as a deacon (Rom 16:1–2). There is no doubt that God anointed and empowered women by the Holy Spirit to serve in the church in diverse ministries and spheres of influence.

Although the Holy Spirit's work may be mediated by a person's gender, God's choice of whom to use and for what purpose is not restricted by biological or sociocultural identity. Biblical accounts reveal how women served in atypical, even countercultural, roles, including prophetic (Huldah, Deborah, the four daughters of Philip), priestly (Hannah, Phoebe), political (Deborah), apostolic (Junia), evangelistic (Samaritan woman), and teaching (Priscilla) ministries. These women's callings were not due to the absence of qualified men but, rather, by divine ordination and commission.

God Uses Women: Women in History and in Contemporary Times

There is no space here to relate the landmark stories of the French prophet-warrior Joan of Arc (born c. 1412), African American abolitionist and author Sojourner Truth (born c. 1797), prolific American hymn writer Fanny Crosby (born 1820), British social activist Josephine Butler (born 1828), German medical doctor and theologian Katharine Bushnell (born 1855), and Dutch peace advocate Corrie Ten Boom (born 1892). A story that has greatly inspired me is that of Jackie Pullinger – a 22 year-old British woman who, against all advice, became a missionary to Hong Kong in 1966 in the dangerous Walled City of Kowloon, which was notorious for poverty, drugs, prostitution, and crime. She preached, taught, cared for drug addicts and prostitutes, and also initiated a drug rehabilitation ministry that spread to the Philippines, Thailand, and beyond.[13]

God is using women to do extraordinary things in our time, and he is not seeking anybody's permission to do so. During a visit to Sierra Leone, I learned about Sister Dora Dumbuya – fondly called Mammy Dumbuya – from a taxi driver. Since 1989, Mammy Dumbuya has served as a Christian evangelist, preacher, and senior pastor of Jesus Is Lord Ministries, a church in Freetown that has thousands of followers. In Nigeria, Sarah Omakwu is the senior pastor of Family Worship Centre, Abuja, and president of Family Life Ministries. She has been pastoring this church since the demise of her husband, who was its founding senior pastor. With branches in various parts of Nigeria, this church has over twenty thousand members, one of the largest in the country.

---

13. Pullinger, *Chasing the Dragon*.

According to Marti Wade, "In the mission world, women hold up considerably *more* than half the sky, and have for at least a dozen decades." The report provides illuminating statistics:

> Since the year 1900, missionary women have outnumbered missionary men, sometimes by a 2:1 ratio – especially in the hardest places. Today about two-thirds of missionaries are married couples, and 70–80% of the rest are single women.[14]

In the secular world, too, God is using Christian women as well as men in many nations to lead transformative change in public and private corporations. Women are serving as ministers-at-large, making the sweet aroma of Jesus known with great effect in the non-churched marketplace.

The Spirit vs the Letter: A Liberating Hermeneutic

Both those who support women in ministry and leadership and those who do not have the same desire to be faithful to the biblical text. Similarly, when God commanded Peter to "get up" and to "kill and eat" a variety of meats forbidden to Jews in the Torah, Peter's response shows that he was trying to be faithful to the Old Testament Scriptures (Acts 10:12–14 NLT). God responded to Peter's Scripture-backed protest with these words: "Do not call something unclean if God has made it clean" (10:15). The revelation given to Peter that he "should no longer think of anyone as impure or unclean" (10:28) – that is, to consider them unworthy or unsuitable for use – is valid for all time, revealing a principle of understanding God's liberating and inclusive intent for humanity that is beautifully portrayed by William J. Webb.[15] I explore Webb's ideas in proposing,

> a redemptive-movement hermeneutic that distinguishes culturally-bound dogmas from transcultural timeless truths. In exploring the hermeneutics of cultural analysis, Webb suggests the need for Christians to engage the redemptive spirit of the biblical text to determine its meaning in contemporary contexts. He rejects a static appropriation of Scripture that demeans women's value and social status, and limits their roles in family, church and society by ignoring the underlying spirit of the biblical narrative, interpreting

---

14. Wade, "More Women in Missions: Four Reasons Why," https://pioneers.org/2021/03/19/more-women-in-missions-four-reasons-why.

15. Webb, *Slaves, Women & Homosexuals. Exploring the Hermeneutics of Cultural Analysis*, 30–55.

supposedly difficult texts that seem to prohibit women in certain ministries and in leadership.[16]

This proposal calls for the Body of Christ to consider the cultural context of the text as well as the spirit of the biblical narrative beyond the letter of the text in order to discover the true meaning of the author's (God) intent – and this leads to freedom for the hearer, emanating from revealed truth (John 8:32; 2 Cor 3:6b). Adopting this approach will set women free and elevate them to fulfil God's calling upon their lives in whatever context, capacity, or direction the Holy Spirit moves them in. When women are unfettered to serve in ministry and leadership in both church and society, our world will be a better one.

Bibliography

Adams, Katia. *Equal: What the Bible Says about Women, Men and Authority*. Colorado Springs: David Cook, 2019.

Bevans, Stephen B. *Models of Contextual Theology*. Maryknoll, New York: Orbis Books, 2002.

D & D. "Men and Women in Partnership for the Kingdom of God." Unpublished paper, n.d.

Eklund, K. E., E. S. Barry, and N. E. Grunberg. "Gender and Leadership." In *Gender Differences in Different Contexts*, edited by Aida Alvinius, 129–50. IntechOpen, 2017.

Marx, Karl. "Eleven Theses on Feuerbach" 1845 in *The German Ideology*. Moscow: Marx-Engels-Lenin Institute, 11–15.

Northouse, P. G. *Leadership: Theory and Practice*. 4th ed. Thousand Oaks: Sage, 2007.

Nweze, A., and B. J. Takaya. "Relative Deprivation of the Nigerian Female Personality as Gender Violence: A Nigerian Overview." Paper presented at the workshop on Gender Violence and Poverty organized by the Office of the Special Adviser to the President on Women Affairs. Jos, Nigeria, 11–13 July 2001.

Para-Mallam, O. J. "Theology and Holistic Development in Times of Crisis." Conference paper presented at the Maiden Alumni Reunion of the Alumni Association of Theological College of Northern Nigeria (AATCNN) on "Theology in Times of Crisis: The Nigeria Context." Nigeria, 12 October 2022.

———. "Why Patriarchy Is Still an Issue for Nigerian Feminist Theory and Practice." In *Gender and Development in Nigeria: Concepts, Issues and Strategies, a Reader*, edited by O. J. Para-Mallam and M. O. Okome. Kuru: National Institute for Policy and Strategic Studies.

---

16. Para-Mallam, "Theology and Holistic Development in Times of Crisis," 11.

Payne, Philip B. "The Bible Teaches the Equal Standing of Man and Woman." *Priscilla Papers* 29, no. 1 (Winter 2015): 3–10. https://www.cbeinternational.org/resource/bible-teaches-equal-standing-man-and-woman/.

Pullinger, Jackie, with Andrew Quickie. *Chasing the Dragon*. London: Hodder & Stoughton, 1980.

Reynolds, Kae. "Servant-Leadership as Gender-Integrative Leadership: Paving a Path for More Gender-Integrative Organizations through Leadership Education." *Journal of Leadership Education* 10, no. 2 (2011): 155–71.

Rowlands, Jo. "A Word of the Times, but What Does it Mean? Empowerment in the Discourse and Practice of Development." In *Women and Empowerment: Illustrations from the Third World*, edited by Haleh Afshar, 11–34. London: Macmillan, 1998.

Wade, Marti. "More Women in Missions: Four Reasons Why." *Pioneers*, 2021. https://pioneers.org/2021/03/19/more-women-in-missions-four-reasons-why.

Webb, William J. *Slaves, Women and Homosexuals: Exploring the Hermeneutics of Cultural Analysis*. Downers Grove: InterVarsity Press, 2001.

Wright, N. T. "Women's Service in the Church: The Biblical Basis." Conference Paper for the Symposium "Men, Women and the Church." St. John's College, Durham, 4 September 2004. https://ntwrightpage.com/2016/07/12/womens-service-in-the-church-the-biblical-basis/.

14

Going Deeper in Disciple-Making

Johnson Asare

Leadership development is crucial for the success of any organization, and this is particularly true for Christian missions. The mission of spreading the gospel and serving others requires effective leadership that is grounded in Christian principles and values. However, in order to go deeper in Christian disciple-making, several gaps in leadership development for Christian missions must be addressed.

Gaps in Leadership Development
1. Lack of Emphasis on Servant-Leadership

Servant-leadership is a model of leadership that emphasizes serving others rather than being served. Most important, it is not about being the best but about making everyone else better. This model is particularly relevant for Christian missions, where the focus is on serving others and spreading the gospel. However, many leadership development programmes do not emphasize this model of leadership, focusing instead on more traditional models that may not be as effective in the context of Christian missions.

One example of a programme that emphasizes servant-leadership is the Leadership Development Programme offered by Compassion International. This programme focuses on developing leaders who are committed to serving others and making a positive impact in their communities. The programme includes training in areas such as communication, conflict resolution, and team building, all of which are essential skills for effective servant-leadership.

2. Lack of Diversity in Leadership

Another gap in leadership development for Christian missions is the lack of diversity in leadership. Many mission organizations are led by individuals from a particular demographic – for example, white males from North America or Europe. This lack of diversity can limit the effectiveness of these organizations in reaching diverse communities and can also lead to a lack of understanding and empathy for those from different backgrounds.

One example of an organization that is working to address this gap is World Vision International. This organization has made a commitment to increasing diversity in its leadership positions, with a goal of having at least 50 percent of its senior leaders from outside North America and Europe by 2025. This commitment to diversity is essential for effective leadership in a global context.

3. Lack of Focus on Spiritual Formation

There is a gap in leadership development for Christian missions when it comes to spiritual formation. Many leadership development programmes focus primarily on developing practical skills such as communication and management, without addressing the spiritual aspects of leadership. However, effective leadership in Christian missions requires a deep understanding of and commitment to Christian principles and values.

One example of a programme that addresses this gap is the Leadership in Ministry programme offered by Fuller Theological Seminary. This programme focuses on developing leaders who are grounded in their faith and committed to serving others. The programme includes courses on topics such as biblical studies, theology, and spiritual formation, all of which are essential for effective leadership in Christian missions. This is crucial because actions performed on the outside are a reflection of what is inside a person.

4. Lack of Changeover Guidelines

In most organizations, there are no real mentoring and succession plans. The Elijah-Elisha matrix does not resonate in discipleship today, which results in some leaders overstaying their welcome and their usefulness to their organizations and successors. In spite of the fact that Elijah's time was one of many upheavals, his succession plan paved the way for Elisha to excel in his ministry. In his book *The Changeover Principle*, Brett F. Jones writes, "God commissioned Elijah to find Elisha after he had survived everything that brought him to Horeb. God waited until the mentor had successfully navigated the storms of life before He sent him to the mentee."[1] Our experiences in life should compel us to share our lives with the younger generation who must take over from us.

The gospel should interact with any given culture and transform it to glorify Jesus. Often, many believers do not take the Bible as their final authority. Instead, they seek help from other sources. There is a need to develop systematic theology to meet the pressing day-to-day issues that people face, especially in the Southern Hemisphere. W. Jay Moon puts it so well in his book *Intercultural Discipleship*: "Use the available cultural genres to facilitate the discipleship process, including symbols, rituals, stories, proverbs, dance, drama and music. These genres are needed to transform worldviews, since words alone are often not enough to communicate deep values and emotions."[2] This is true in the light of the high rate of nominalism globally.

By addressing some of these gaps, we can develop leaders who are better equipped to serve others and spread the gospel effectively. And because Christian disciple-making is at the heart of the Christian faith, we need to be proactive in our discipleship development. This will involve helping others grow in their relationship with God and become more like Jesus. However, many Christians struggle to go deeper in disciple-making, often focusing on surface-level interactions rather than truly investing in others. We will now explore some means by which we can go deeper in Christian disciple-making.

Going Deeper in Christian Disciple Making
1. Building Relationships
One of the keys to going deeper in Christian disciple-making is building relationships with others. This involves getting to know people on a deeper level, listening to their stories, and sharing your own story. Jesus modelled this approach in his interactions with people, taking the time to get to know them and to show them love and compassion.

In John 4, Jesus meets a Samaritan woman at a well and engages her in conversation despite the fact that Jews and Samaritans typically did not associate with each other. Through their conversation, Jesus was able to reveal himself as the Messiah and offer the woman living water that would quench her thirst forever. By taking the time to build a relationship with this woman,

---

1. Jones, *Changeover Principle*, 82.
2. Moon, *Intercultural Discipleship*, 209.

Jesus was able to share the gospel with her in a way that was meaningful and transformative. Building lasting relationships does not require agreement. What is needed is alignment. Agreement demands identical opinions. Alignment is having shared values. Alignment is heading in the same direction. Closeness is a matter of commitment, not consensus. So we need to take the time to nurture our relationships and appreciate the people in our lives.

We also need to help the believers whom we disciple to set up healthy boundaries. Lack of boundaries invites lack of respect. To value others and respect their time, we need to intentionally create healthy boundaries in both our personal and professional relationships. Doing so will create a safe and supportive space for mutual respect, trust, self-esteem, open communication, and freedom, making it possible for each other's needs to be met and values and opinions to be expressed freely without fear of criticism or judgment. The lack of healthy boundaries in relationships, however, will create codependent relationships, where individuals become overly dependent on each other, giving rise to resentment, conflict, emotional distress, anxiety, and even depression.

Scripture says, "Let your foot be seldom in your neighbour's house, lest he have his fill of you and hate you" (Prov 25:17 ESV). We must set healthy boundaries in our minds before we disciple people.

2. Investing in Others

Another key to going deeper in Christian disciple-making is investing in others. This involves not only sharing your own faith journey but also helping others to grow in their relationship with God. This can take many forms, such as praying for others, studying the Bible together, and encouraging one another in faith.

Paul's instructions in 2 Timothy 2:2 highlight the importance of investing in others and passing on what we have learned about God to future generations. By investing in others, we can help them grow in their faith and become better equipped to share the gospel with others.

If we intentionally invest in the people around us, our circles of influence will widen. We do not have to be perfect to inspire people. Rather, we can let people be inspired by how we deal with our imperfections. We just need to care genuinely for the success of everyone on our team and seize the opportunities even amid the difficulties.

We also have to help the believers we disciple to break old habits that do not honour God. Changing negative habits is not easy, but with commitment and effort, it is possible to break free from old patterns and create a more positive and fulfilling life as we depend on God's Holy Spirit.

3. Practising Spiritual Disciplines

Going deeper in Christian disciple-making involves practising spiritual disciplines such as prayer, Bible study, and worship. These disciplines help us to stay connected to God and grow in our relationship with him. They also provide a foundation for our interactions with others, allowing us to share our faith in a way that is authentic and meaningful.

In Matthew 6:6, Jesus highlights the importance of prayer as a spiritual discipline and encourages us to seek God in private as well as in public. By practising spiritual disciplines, we can deepen our relationship with God and become more effective in our disciple-making efforts.

We need a divine GPS. People often complain about the lack of time when, in fact, lack of direction is the real problem. For most of us, our lives are not driven by purpose. And the lack of proactive action plans keep us from doing our best. We waste precious time. We push our values aside. May God give us his eyes to see what he sees so that we do what he wants us to do in a timely manner and move in the right direction in making disciples.

In conclusion, going deeper in Christian disciple-making requires building relationships, intentionally investing in others, and practising spiritual disciplines. By following these principles and seeking God's guidance, we can become better equipped to share the gospel with others and help them to grow in their relationship with God.

Bibliography

Jones, Brett F. *The Changeover Principle*. Weston: BG Publishing House, 2023.
Moon, W. Jay. *Intercultural Discipleship*. Grand Rapids: Baker, 2017.
Nouwen, Henri. *Spiritual Formation*. New York: HarperCollins, 2015.

15

Mentoring Next-Generation Leaders

Asia Williamson

History clearly illustrates that if any renewal that God brings to His church is to be sustained, it will be sustained by the effective training of a new generation of leaders to carry it forward.[1]

Therefore, since we are surrounded by such a great cloud of witnesses, let us throw off everything that hinders and the sin that so easily entangles. And let us run with perseverance the race marked out for us, fixing our eyes on Jesus, the pioneer and perfecter of faith. For the joy set before him he endured the cross, scorning its shame, and sat down at the right hand of the throne of God. Consider him who endured such opposition from sinners, so that you will not grow weary and lose heart. (Heb 12:1–3)

Within the Lausanne Movement and beyond, we continue to remember the great kingdom contribution made by its founders – John Stott and Billy Graham. As we read about their lives, we realize that, apart from having a very public ministry, they both committed themselves to mentoring others in one-on-one relationships and stood in the legacy of those who went before.

Lausanne Occasional Paper No. 41 – produced in Pattaya, Thailand, on 29 September 2024 – contains a number of important points that relate to developing leaders through mentoring relationships. This paper begins by casting a vision of some possibilities: "Imagine a worldwide church where every

---

1. Flynn, Tjiong, and West, *Well-Furnished Heart*, xi.

leader is mentoring younger leaders, where leadership is both Christ-like and contextual, where leaders partner together across boundaries, where millions of future leaders are emerging – bringing the whole gospel to the whole world."[2] It also highlights some barriers: "One barrier is a lack of models. There are not sufficient numbers of mature leaders to mentor the rapidly growing churches. There is a lack of open, honest, humble, vulnerable leaders to show the way."[3]

In this chapter, I propose that by pointing young people to the resources locked into the stories of the great cloud of witnesses, we can begin to overcome some of these barriers. Of course, this is not the only solution as one-on-one personal encounters will always be needed both in mentoring and in discipleship, but the biographies of great men and women of God can help us to make sense of our own story and to find meaning and courage in this complex world. As someone whose ministry was "rescued" by someone else's story, I am confident of the enduring possibility of stories to mentor and raise us up to a high level of calling and service.

Personally Speaking

It was a foggy early morning in mid-February, and I was walking around the beautiful campus grounds of my old Bible college. This was where I had spent three years studying for my degree. Looking back, after thirty years of ministry and four more degrees in other colleges and universities, this place, now draughty and empty, had offered by far the most incredible experience and immersion in theological and ministry studies. We had been a small group of eager students, in love with God, ready to change the world. Apart from having some great lecturers, there were meetings which included contemporary and creative worship, dance, arts, healing ministry, and seminars during which we saw God moving in amazing ways. Although we had experienced something of revival, I do not think we recognized it as "revival" then – we just thought of it as "normal" life in the kingdom. We had many resources at our disposal, a lot going for us, and thought we were all set for great ministries – but were we? I suddenly felt the chill of the morning fog and looked up at the beautiful college building standing silently in front of me. Where were these people who had once filled its corridors with chatter about God and thoughts of how they would change the world? What had happened to them, to us? The number of

---

2. "Future Leadership," https://lausanne.org/occasional-paper/future-leadership-lop-41.
3. "Future Leadership."

students was now down by 80 percent, and hardly anyone from my class was running the race any longer. The reality was heartbreaking.

Since then, I have been compelled to look into what it means to run the race and what it is that will sustain us for the long haul in our ministry journey. I found the answer right there in the book of Hebrews – it is the great cloud of witnesses, who are cheering us on. It was fifteen years after I graduated from Bible college that I discovered for myself that this cloud of witnesses is still there and that they are there for me to learn from. I began to see that although leadership is sometimes a lonely task, it does not have to be so. Instead, our lives can be lived out in the community of the faithful that spans ages and cultures.

Now, leading an international ministry, I am reminded that while the need and opportunity for training leaders for today's context is always there, this requires more than just a few cosmetic changes. The reality of the condition of both theological education and leadership development around the world today forces us to consider alternatives. We need to look beyond Western methods and instead look to the global community for educational best practice, and beyond our denominational constraints to find the most effective ways of equipping others. We must focus on and insist on finding and introducing new models of mentoring leaders for missional engagement and sustainable personal spiritual life.

Stories are carriers of meaning in all cultures around the world. This brief chapter is a call to uncover the power of story and biography in the formation of the next generation of leaders.

The Wisdom of the Great Cloud of Witnesses

> For many reasons, the practice and wisdom of mentoring has been weakened in our society. We compensate for this loss with a professionalism that is too often delivered without the "life-giving, caring field once provided by elders." This has contributed to fragmentation and loss of transcendent meaning for which no amount of professional expertise can compensate and has spawned assumptions that tragically widen the gap between generations.[4]

The historical dislocation also manifests itself in leadership development because many do not consider the great leaders of the past worthy of careful and detailed study and attention. None of the theological schools I attended

---

4. Parks, *Big Questions*, 13.

encouraged me to study the lives of great missionaries of the past. If we are seeking to bring transformation in today's world, why not learn from those who have done so before? If we are to persevere through difficulties, raise up other leaders, and finish well, why not look to those who have already done so? These great figures of the past are often considered irrelevant, their books and journals gather dust on the bookshelves of libraries, and the academic world looks down on them. And yet, surely these people should be our mentors. Someone once said that young people follow footprints better then blueprints. The leadership development has overfed its students with blueprints, but what is needed is rediscovery of the footprints of those who have gone ahead of us. We have forgotten the great cloud of witnesses and their wisdom and neglected the opportunity to be mentored by them.

Having written two biographies and working on the third, and having used biographies as a basis for leadership training in my ministry for the last several years, I am convinced that storytelling – and especially, the stories of others (biography) – has an important role to play in any ministry that aims to develop leaders. As I studied the lives of others, especially the lives of Hudson Taylor and Amy Carmichael, I realized how stories connect and keep on providing insights beyond the constraints of time and place. Such stories take us by the hand, so to speak, and help us cross the busy junctions of life.

All of us continue to be influenced by the greatest of all stories – the story of Jesus, written as a form of an ancient biography for the purpose of transformation of character. They, the faithful of the past, understood that they had a role to play in the ongoing story of his redemptive plan to bring the kingdom of God here on earth. Their "story" was written within his "story."

As I read between the lines of their biographies, I can see myself there. I enter their world; I ask the same questions; I identify with their struggles; and I draw courage and hope from their stories.

Metanarratives and Paradoxes of Postmodernity

> The Christian life is one in which we live in the biblical story as part of the community whose story it is. We find in the story the clues to knowing God as his character becomes manifest in the story, and from within that indwelling we try to understand and cope with the events of our time and the world about us and so carry the story forward. At the heart of the story, as the key to the

whole, is the incarnation of the Word, the life, ministry, death, and resurrection of Jesus.[5]

However, the postmodern mindset – which is also, therefore, pluralistic – rejects any notions of metanarratives. Paradoxically, there is also a hunger and curiosity in society for more personal stories, for knowing individuals as individuals, immersing ourselves in their journey, understanding people's moral choices, and even learning about their weaknesses. According to Nigel Hamilton: "Such curiosity fuels our biographical interest in past figures, and gives us a clue to the second great function of biography – namely, its insight into human character, experience of life, and human emotion, as guides to our own complex self-understanding, as individuals"[6]

Jean-Francois Lyotard defines postmodernity as "incredulity towards metanarratives."[7] This, together with what N. T. Wright calls "collapsing reality, deconstructing selfhood, and the death of the metanarrative"[8] is the context of my ministry, maybe your ministry also. "The postmodernism challenges Christian faith in a dramatic way, since it appears to go against every grain of sense of tradition, communion and commitment."[9] What we are left with is "liquid life" that cannot stay on course and is a life lived under conditions of constant uncertainty.[10]

In the global context, young people struggle with the multiplicity of values and world views on offer for their consumption. They have lost trust in what a true story is and in how it makes a difference in their lives. Mentoring is a great way to help them deal with these complexities and find meaning.

Affected by the postmodern context and afraid of the metanarratives to be used as a means of controlling and manipulating, the world and church have lost the anchor of making sense of their own existence; identity has become blurred and character development become fuzzy, and this also translates itself both to formal and informal education experience.

---

5. Newbigin, *Pluralist Society*, 99.

6. Hamilton, *Biography*, 10.

7. Lyotard. https://iep.utm.edu/lyotard/#:~:text=Lyotard%20famously%20defines%20the%20postmodern,legitimise%20knowledges%20and%20cultural%20practises.

8. Wright, "Resurrection," https://ntwrightpage.com/2016/04/05/the-resurrection-and-the-postmodern-dilemma/.

9. Lascaris and van Erp, *Who Is Afraid?*, 5.

10. Bauman, *Postmodern Ethics*, 5.

Mentoring, Meaning Making, and Spiritual Life

Human beings are hermeneutical beings. In other words, they are interpretive beings, meaning making beings.[11] We all, no matter what our background is, are unable to survive, and certainly cannot thrive, unless we can make meaning. If life is perceived as utterly random, fragmented, chaotic, and meaningless, we suffer confusion, distress, stagnation, and despair. "The meaning we make orients our posture in the world and determines our sense of self and purpose. We need to be able to make some sort of sense out of things; we seek pattern, order, and coherence in the dynamic and disparate elements of our experience."[12]

Spiritual mentoring allows us to stick more closely to God's plot than might otherwise have been possible. According to Anderson and Reese, mentoring can be seen as "autobiographical" or the story of our lives. This view is supported by Eugene Peterson, who argues that spiritual mentoring is part of the aspect of Christianity that "specialises in the ordinary."[13] Reese and Loan expand by saying

> Mentoring is all about the mundane, as God cares for us in every aspect of our lives. It is the role of the mentor to slow the pace of our frantic lives down by creating a space, and by asking pertinent questions, which allows and stimulates reflection. The curriculum of mentoring cannot be laid down but is rather, "the unfolding story of life as the mentoree lives it." Where it will lead and develop cannot be predicted or predetermined. Rather the mentor must always stimulate reflection on life.[14]

"Spiritual mentoring, as a reflective process, is thus the exercise that helps us recognize, through our life stories, the already present action of God."[15] Anderson argues that the mentor understands that

> truth is embodied in the sacred story of the mentoree's life. It is through discernment that both see the themes and meanings of this present action. The mentor *facilitates* or *enables* the mentoree to see more deeply the development of this action and story and discern the meaning for their life.[16]

---

11. Randal, *Stories We Are*, 36.
12. Parks, *Big Questions*, 9.
13. Peterson, *Contemplative Pastor*, 10.
14. Reese and Loane, *Deep Mentoring*, 12.
15. Reese and Loane, 12.
16. Reese and Loane, 12.

Conclusion

Sharon Daloz Parks in *Big Questions, Worthy Dreams: Mentoring Emerging Adults in Their Search for Meaning, Purpose, and Faith* states:

> Emerging adults now move in not only a religiously variegated world in which faith and religion have become problematized and polarized, but also a world in which hybrid and atheistic claims have gained currency along with various forms of fundamentalism. This is the context in which all who would mentor emerging adults must respect that today's young adults need to find their way to a place of integrity and commitment in a manner that does not dodge the big questions and can, indeed, forge worthy dreams that honor the potential of their lives in a globalized world.[17]

Young people often seek out authentic mentors at the point of an adaptive need, a challenge, a transition, or a crisis. They seek out advice, discernment, and direction and, most of all, loving presence. "The quality of presence is a vital element in the practice of the art of adaptive leadership. It calls for a centred, responsive, and committed self, and levels of consciousness and competence that cannot be cultivated by mere techniques."[18]

In this complex and chaotic world, it is easy to lose heart, and it is possible for all of us to be implicated in the dysfunctions of leadership training; but we can all heal these dysfunctions and become companions on the journey. So much of what passes for leadership development today lacks interpersonal investment, life upon life. Simply telling others where they must go will not cut it. The journey must be shared.[19] We can learn from the great cloud of witnesses who have gone before us. These people were practitioners, they were in the field, they were missionaries, pastors, theologians – just as the Lausanne family is a group of practitioners from all walks of life. With Lausanne's YLGen commitment to building connections across generations, we are on our way to ensure that the testimonies and stories of the great cloud of witnesses are preserved and that the next chapters of this story are written by the leaders who are rising among us and who live by faith. "If the place where we look for ultimate truth is in a story and if (as is the case) we are still in the middle of the story, then it follows that we walk by faith and not by sight."[20]

---

17. Parks, *Big Questions*, 33.
18. Parks, 110.
19. Reese and Loane, *Deep Mentoring*, 32.
20. Newbigin, *Proper Confidence*, 43.

Bibliography

Bauman, Zygmunt. *Postmodern Ethics*. Torquay, Devon: Blackwell, 1998.

Flynn, James Thomas, Wie Liang Tjiong, and Russell Wade West. *A Well-Furnished Heart: Restoring the Spirit's Place in the Leadership Classroom*. United States: Xulon, 2002.

"Future Leadership." Lausanne Occasional Paper No. 41, presented by the Leadership Development Issue Group at the 2004 Forum for World Evangelization hosted by the Lausanne Committee for World Evangelization, Pattaya, Thailand, 29 September to 5 October 2004. https://lausanne.org/occasional-paper/future-leadership-lop-41.

Hamilton, Nigel. *Biography: A Brief History*. Cambridge: Harvard University Press, 2007.

Lascaris, André, and Stephan van Erp, eds. *Who Is Afraid of Postmodernism? Challenging Theology for a Society in Search of Identity*. Berlin: LIT, 2005.

Newbigin, Leslie. *The Gospel in a Pluralist Society*. London: SPCK, 2004.

———. *Proper Confidence: Faith, Doubt, and Certainty in Christian Discipleship*. Grand Rapids: Eerdmans, 1995.

Nouwen, Henri. *Creative Ministry*. New York Image Books, 2003.

———. *Reaching Out*. **Grand Rapids:** Zondervan, 1998.

Parks, Sharon Daloz. *Big Questions, Worthy Dreams: Mentoring Emerging Adults in Their Search for Meaning, Purpose, and Faith*. New York: Wiley & Sons, 2000.

Peterson, Eugene. *The Contemplative Pastor: Returning to the Art of Spiritual Direction*. Grand Rapids: Eerdmans, 1993.

Randal, William. *Stories We Are: An Essay on Self Creation*. Toronto: University of Toronto Press, 2014.

Reese, Randy D., and Robert Loane. *Deep Mentoring: Guiding Others on Their Leadership Journey*. Downers Grove: InterVarsity Press, 2012.

Wright, N. T. "The Resurrection and the Postmodern Dilemma." https://ntwrightpage.com/2016/04/05/the-resurrection-and-the-postmodern-dilemma/.

Section IV

Christlike Leaders for Every Church and Sector

16

Collaboration in Theological Education: The Church Strengthened for Mission

Michael A. Ortiz

Introduction

While it is essential that believers everywhere proclaim the gospel, it is equally crucial that church leaders demonstrate the gospel through their biblically grounded lives. Failure to do so may mean that even though the church may grow in numbers, it lacks the leadership foundation for sustainable missional impact.

To adequately accompany and strengthen a missionally minded church, an increased collaborative posture in relation to theological education must be the call of the day. Globally, we have an abundance of theological education programmes, ranging from the more formal to the more nonformal types. Dr. Manfred Kohl, a respected global leader in theological education, has often commented that there are over forty thousand nonformal training programmes in the world today.[1] The International Council for Evangelical Theological Education (ICETE) has at least 850 Bible colleges and seminaries within its global hub.[2] No doubt, there are leadership training programmes throughout the world that are unaccounted for that would augment these numbers. We do not lack training opportunities, but we do lack the needed collaboration in training. As long as the global breadth of theological education leans towards

---

1. Manfred Kohl, personal conversation with author, 2022.
2. "ICETE Constituents," https://icete.info/constituents/overview/.

inward rather than outward postures, collaboration will remain merely a nice buzz word with minimal consequence. In the meantime, the church's missional impact is limited and restricted because of inadequately prepared leaders.

In this chapter, I will review the growing demand for theological education that adequately supports the church in its mission. The church is growing, and its leadership development must be accelerated, but this can only be accomplished through genuine postures of collaboration in training. The chapter will also remind us of the missionally centred purpose of theological education. Greater collaboration might be encouraged by recognizing a common biblical aim – a common ground for those involved in leadership development to equip the church in its mission. Finally, although there remains more work to be done, there have been some promising signs of collaboration in theological education in recent times. This chapter will conclude by outlining this recent progress, as well as some ways to carry forward that momentum for increased global collaboration.

Fortifying Church Growth

In 2010, *The Cape Town Commitment* from Lausanne articulated several points relative to the role of theological education and training to support the church to stay on mission. For example, it states, "Theological education stands in partnership with all forms of missional engagement. We will encourage and support all who provide biblically-faithful theological education, formal and nonformal, at local, national, regional and international levels."[3] *The Cape Town Commitment* correctly positions theological education as a missional endeavour, and the next portion of this chapter will deal more specifically with elevating a missional emphasis for the whole of theological education. The statement also upholds the importance of training that produces biblically faithful leaders and doing so through both formal and nonformal means. It is not about who gets it done but about getting it done.

Elsewhere, *The Cape Town Commitment* laments the state of the church and leadership development, declaring that the "rapid growth of the Church in so many places remains shallow and vulnerable,"[4] mainly due to leaders who themselves have not been discipled and so lack the "ability to teach God's Word to God's people."[5] Even back in 2010, there was concern over leadership

---

3. "Cape Town Commitment," IIF-4B.
4. "Cape Town Commitment," IID-3.
5. "Cape Town Commitment," IID-3.

training not producing enough believers who were well discipled and equipped to rightly pass on the truth of the Scriptures to others and, in so doing, fortify the growing global church. Today, the church fortified, deep, strong, and on mission, still depends upon credible leaders who are able to faithfully lead and multiply themselves. Craig Ott, a missiologist and professor, warns of the church's vulnerability even in the present time:

> If current leaders do not develop new leaders who will spiritually shepherd and further guide the movement, it will become susceptible to conflict, false teaching, syncretism, and other problems. The churches will neither be transformational at a deep level nor be sustainable over time.[6]

This is precisely what theological education must guard against by equipping leaders who are prepared to disciple and teach God's word for a transformational and sustainable church on mission. But apart from more outward, collaborate postures in theological education, the church will remain "shallow and vulnerable."[7]

The demand for church leadership today is too monumental to be met through fragmented and inward-looking theological education postures. The magnitude of this challenge is highlighted by a contrast with the United States, where there is one trained pastor for every 230 people. In comparison, Majority World churches have one trained pastor for every 450,000 people.[8] This colossal leadership training imbalance will only become more pronounced. Just as Lausanne, in 2010, noted the "rapid growth of the church in so many places,"[9] today, Majority World churches continue to surge and spread. According to the Global Alliance for Church Multiplication (GACX), the church in Asia, Africa, and Latin America has grown from 30 percent of the world's churches in 1970 to 70 percent in 2022.[10] In addition, the World Evangelical Alliance (WEA), representing churches in over 130 countries, estimates that there are fifty thousand new baptized believers each day.[11] Taking into consideration the data and our anecdotal awareness of church growth, we need hundreds of new

---

6. Ott, *Church on Mission*, 115.
7. "Cape Town Commitment," IID-3.
8. "Need," https://bobinthebush.com/training-leaders-international/the-desperate-need-for-theological-education/.
9. "Cape Town Commitment," IID-3.
10. "GACX Framework," https://gacx.io/about/framework.
11. Thomas Schirrmacher, virtual meeting with author, 4 August 2022.

trained church leaders every single day – a task too great for any one teacher, any one programme, any one school, or any one form of theological education.

Stereotypes about formal and nonformal modes have historically fuelled educational polarities handed down to us. We have known for some time that we must work together to reverse this tide. During Cape Town 2010, another declaration, which had no connection to *The Cape Town Commitment*, was also issued. This document – the "Pastoral Trainers Declaration" (2010) – was formulated by a group of pastoral training leaders, who affirmed the following:

> Since the formal and non-formal sectors of pastoral training have knowingly and unknowingly allowed ourselves to be divided in heart and efforts, we declare together that we shall endeavor to build trust, involve each other, and leverage the strengths of each sector to prepare maturing shepherds for the proclamation of God's Word and the building up of Christ's Church in all the nations of the world.[12]

I asked Ramesh Richard – the chief draftsman of the Pastoral Trainers Declaration – how much progress he thought had been made since 2010 to "build trust, involve each other, and leverage the strengths of each sector." He noted that while some progress had been made, this was not anywhere near enough.[13]

So many years later, more has to happen to increase collaborative postures in the whole of theological education. In order to meet the growing global demands for church leadership that will fortify the church in its mission, leadership training must be collaboratively accelerated. But what still seems lacking is the articulation and embracing of common ground that would spur this type of meaningful collaboration. The next section examines this common ground through one common aim of theological education.

Collaboration Centred on a Common Aim

A recalibration of theological education is in order through a deepened recognition of its collective common aim. The biblical aim for all theological education, regardless of form and structure, is missiological for the sake of the church. We cannot look at theological education in a silo, removed from

---

12. "Pastoral Trainers Declaration," https://rreach.org/wp-content/uploads/2017/05/Pastoral-Trainers-Declaration-Cape-Town-2010.pdf.

13. Ramesh Richard, personal conversation with author, 16 November 2022.

its grand function within God's plan as revealed within the fullness of the Scriptures. Christopher Wright puts it plainly in *The Mission of God: Unlocking the Bible's Grand Narrative*: "The writings that now comprise our Bible are themselves the product of and witness to the ultimate mission of God . . . The Bible renders to us the story of God's mission through God's world for the sake of the whole of God's creation."[14] *The Cape Town Commitment* (2010) most clearly states the common missional aim of theological education in relation to the biblical mission of the church: "The mission of the Church on earth is to serve the mission of God, and the mission of theological education is to strengthen and accompany the mission of the Church."[15]

Jessy Jaison is a theological education leader from India who also understands the vital aim of leadership development for the church's mission. In her book *Building the Whole Church: Collaborating Theological Education Practices in the Ecclesial Context of South Asia*, she calls for a "critical reenvisioning of our philosophy and practice of theological education" by pointing to its one common aim: "The church is not a competitor to any other institution . . . The urgent task, therefore, is to enable the church theologically and spiritually to move from the margins to assume its central space in theological and missional formation."[16] Indeed, the common aim of all theological education, regardless of its form, is to enable the church to assume its space as biblically mandated by God through the whole of the Scriptures. ICETE further reinforces the church's mission as the missional aim for theological education. Soon after being founded in 1980, ICETE developed the *ICETE Manifesto on the Renewal of Evangelical Theological Education* in 1983. In November 2022, during its global consultation in Izmir, Turkey (ICETE C-22), ICETE issued a second global declaration about theological education – the *ICETE Manifesto II: Call and Commitment to the Renewal of Theological Education*, which was developed over the course of two years with input from theological education leaders from every sector of training and

---

14. Wright, *Mission of God*, 48, 51. It is worth noting Craig Ott's words: "Mission is not ours, mission is God's. Certainly, the mission of God is the prior reality out of which flows a mission that we get involved in . . . Mission was not made for the church; the church was made for mission – God's mission." Ott, *Church on Mission*, 62.

15. "Cape Town Commitment," IIF-4. The rest of this statement says, "Theological education serves *first* to train those who lead the Church as pastor-teachers, equipping them to teach the truth of God's Word with faithfulness, relevance and clarity; and *second*, to equip all God's people for the missional task of understanding and relevantly communicating God's truth in every cultural context."

16. Jaison, *Building the Whole Church*, 149–50.

each region of the world. Relative to the aim of theological education, *ICETE Manifesto II* states:

> Perhaps the most formative insight of recent decades is the call for the integration of mission and theological education: Theology and theological education need to become missional in their very essence and orientation. The purpose of theological education must be defined within the framework of the *missio Dei* and a missional self-understanding of the Church.[17]

ICETE and Lausanne stand together on theological education's common aim. They each call on those involved in designing and running training programmes to understand the biblical mission of the church and have as their aim the task of equipping leaders to fortify that mission. This aim is not unique to one form of theological education but common to all forms of theological education. *ICETE Manifesto II* justly asserts that "we understand theological education in a broad sense including formal and non-formal education and learning"[18] and that "formal and non-formal theological education are equally important for church and mission. They should be offered in mutual respect and partnership."[19]

Jaison referred to a critical reenvisioning of the philosophy and practice of theological education. No doubt, this will require that theological education be collectively recalibrated by more fully embracing its actual and certain common aim. I do understand that there are all sorts of pressures on theological education in every part of the world; but rather than walk in humility, generosity, and unity, we tend to retreat and go inwards, thereby creating greater distance between one another and greater distance from our aim, the equipping of the church. We need to recalibrate to lessen our innate harmful tendencies.

Many years have elapsed since 2010, and it is time that each leadership training programme – no matter the size, location, geographical scope, reputation, finances, capacity, or accreditation – come to sincere terms with the very essence of the purpose for which God allowed it to be initiated. Each such programme ought to do what *The Cape Town Commitment* charged such programmes to do: "conduct a 'missional audit' of their curricula, structures and ethos, to ensure that they truly serve the needs and opportunities facing the

---

17. "ICETE Manifesto II," 8.
18. "ICETE Manifesto II," 9.
19. "ICETE Manifesto II," 8.

church in their cultures."[20] As programmes recalibrate towards their common true aim, a common ground across the whole of theological education may become more readily recognizable, leading to more dialogue and candid conversations across programmes, trust and community building, mutuality, and meaningful collaboration in faithful leadership development for the sake of the growing church in its mission.

On the opening night of ICETE C-22 in Izmir, I led the gathering of five hundred people from eighty countries to recite with me the following prayer: "Lord, may our consultation not be measured by our numbers, but by our mutuality in one common aim – to strengthen Christ's Church."[21] May this be our ongoing prayer.

Promise of Collaboration

The ICETE C-22 prayer does indeed seem to be ongoing, and the Lord is listening. There are some encouraging signs that collaboration in theological education across the sectors for the sake of the church in mission is gaining traction. Even before C-22 there had been a history that sought to advance collaboration, even dating back to Lausanne Cape Town in 2010 as has already been noted. In his article, Joseph W. Handley, Jr. explains that

> the conversation between formal and non-formal training organizations began with some significant tension. Groups on either side of the continuum would often point fingers at the other suggesting they were not qualified, or they were antiquated and out of touch with the church and mission. Over time, as we have met with one another, and intentionally set forth space for conversations, relationship and idea sharing, the walls have diminished, and the conversations are beginning to blossom.[22]

In that same article, Handley briefly catalogues developments leading up to ICETE C-22, including prior ICETE global gatherings.

Globally, it is worth noting that regional member associations of ICETE, particularly those found in Asia – Asia Theological Association (ATA) – and Africa – Association for Christian Theological Education in Africa (ACTEA) – had taken the lead in collaboration even before ICETE C-22. Both ATA and

---

20. "Cape Town Commitment," IIF-4C.
21. Ortiz, ICETE Gathering, Izmir, November 2022.
22. Handley, "Collaboration."

ACTEA had developed and instituted standards and guidelines for nonformal training programmes within their regions and had initiated gatherings to explore greater communication and relationship building across theological education sectors. ICETE C-22 simply catalyzed various efforts that had already been initiated.

ICETE C-22 was also instrumental in including various voices in the collaboration dialogue. Esther Ayandokun from Nigeria, who serves as a key leader in church leadership development both at the formal and nonformal levels, says this about her experience at ICETE C-22:

> ICETE has shown us that everyone is very important. The dialogue has shown us to value one another and look for how each group could be their best in the different options of training. These dialogues have shown that those trained for ministry should be handled seriously and not just anyhow.[23]

Esther represents the sentiment of many worldwide who today have an invigorated attitude about theological education, seeking more and more to collectively pursue their common aim in theological education – namely, fortifying the church in its mission. But ICETE is not alone in showing promise for greater collaboration. Since ICETE C-22, there have been other gatherings to further greater collaborative postures in theological education. The following events hold out promise that theological education worldwide might be more focused than previously on its common aim – the church on mission:

- ATA India General Assembly – September 2023: Focus on interactions across India related to seminaries and Bible colleges working more closely with nonformal programmes.
- AEA and ACTEA Consultation – October 2023: This was a continental-wide gathering in Africa, hosted by the Association of Evangelicals in Africa (AEA) and ICETE's ACTEA to specifically consider how to scale up nonformal training for churches in Africa through collaboration between nonformal and formal theological education.
- WEA Future of the Gospel – October 2023: Not only did this include a plenary session on the future collaborative expectations for theological education but also a working track that met daily,

---

23. Ayandokun, "Formal and Non-formal," https://icete.academy/mod/forum/discuss.php?d=1501.

made up of key leaders across the training spectrum and from varied countries.
- Asia Evangelical Alliance 40th Anniversary – October 2023: At this gathering, there was a track established to address the relationships between formal and nonformal programmes within Asian contexts.
- GProCongress II – November 2023: A global gathering of leaders, led by Ramesh Richard and his ministry RREACH, from all sectors of theological education to dialogue, build community, and explore collaborative opportunities to multiply the trainers of pastors worldwide.

In addition to these events, there have been other global virtual meetings and ongoing communications since ICETE C-22 concerning ways to make progress in theological education collaboration. Often, the organizations involved in those conversations have included ministries like Trainers of Pastors International Coalition (TOPIC), Re-Forma, The Galilean Movement, RREACH, Increase Association, United World Mission, and MentorLink International. Finally, there are also certain alliances taking shape that include various ministries involved in theological education from all sectors, most of which adopt a collective impact alliance model. Although this brief overview has demonstrated that there is reason for hope, far more needs to be done to accelerate theological education collaboration.

ICETE's Manifesto II (2022) also recognizes this global need for today:

> In an increasingly globalized and polycentric world, partnerships in theological education will become more and more important and significant. Consequently, we are committed to the development of partnerships in theological education which are shaped by mutual respect and interdependence.[24]

As part of that commitment, ICETE seeks to further advance collaboration through its upcoming global gathering in March 2025. ICETE C-25 – which will likely be its largest gathering in its forty plus years – will embed the formal and nonformal conversation throughout all the elements leading up to and during the in-person gathering. Momentum has been building, and there may be ways to capitalize on that momentum and continue to make meaningful progress in global theological education collaboration.

---

24. "ICETE Manifesto II," 13.

Conclusion

Recently, there seems to be an encouraging improvement in the collaborative posture of theological education. But we do not know how this trend might shift in the months and years to come. This present moment must be captured, appreciated, and propelled towards accelerated and ongoing collaboration.

As noted earlier, while the church continues to grow – especially in Majority World settings – theological education and leadership development simply cannot keep up with the demand to produce biblically faithful leaders. We cannot continue in silos and expect to make significant progress in serving the church in its mission. We know the challenge, we know the urgency, and we know the risk of not having sound leaders who will lead sustainable communities of believers for decades to come. While it is essential that believers everywhere proclaim the gospel, it is equally crucial that church leaders live biblically grounded lives.

At present, there is no reason to believe that church growth will come to a halt any time soon. In fact, most people believe that the church will grow exponentially and that many even from Majority World settings will end up as missionaries – not only in their own homelands but across the globe. If this is true, then there is even more reason to develop leaders who will multiply themselves and effectively teach God's word to God's people.

In the past, there have been challenges of overcoming barriers and inward looking postures within theological education. Lately, however, there have been promising signs that those barriers are slightly lower and those postures are inclining a tad more outward. In God's merciful sovereignty, he might be entrusting us with a unique collaboration stewardship moment. Let us be good stewards, who embrace what is before us, look ahead, and move ahead to accelerate collaboration within the whole of theological education so that the church, in its mission, would stay on course until the Lord Christ returns.

Bibliography

Ayandokun, Esther. 2022. "Formal and Non-formal Theological Education in Dialogue – C22." *ICETE Academy*, 23 September 2022. https://icete.academy/mod/forum/discuss.php?d=1501.

"The Cape Town Commitment." *Lausanne Movement*, 2010. https://lausanne.org/statement/ctcommitment#capetown.

"GACX Framework." *GACX*, accessed 21 January 2024. https://gacx.io/about/framework.

Handley, Joseph. "Collaboration: Accelerating Formal and Non-formal Pastor Training." In *Educating for Contemporary Mission* (EMS 32), edited by Linda Saunders, Edward L. Smither, and Greg Mathias. Littleton: William Carey, forthcoming.

"ICETE Constituents." The International Council for Evangelical Theological Education, 21 July 2023. https://icete.info/constituents/overview/.

ICETE. 2022. "ICETE Manifesto II: Call and Commitment to the Renewal of Theological Education." The International Council for Evangelical Theological Education, updated November 2022. https://icete.info/wp-content/uploads/2023/07/ICETE-Manifesto-II_FinalDraft18Jul2023.pdf.

Jaison, Jessy. *Building the Whole Church: Collaborating Theological Education Practices in the Ecclesial Context of South Asia.* Carlisle: Langham Global Library, 2023.

"The Need." *Training Pastors Worldwide.* https://bobinthebush.com/training-leaders-international/the-desperate-need-for-theological-education/.

Ortiz, Michael. ICETE Presentation, 14 November 2022.

Ott, Craig. *The Church on Mission: A Biblical Vision for Transformation among All People.* Grand Rapids: Baker Academic, 2019.

"Pastoral Trainers Declaration." Cape Town, 2010. https://rreach.org/wp-content/uploads/2017/05/Pastoral-Trainers-Declaration-Cape-Town-2010.pdf.

Wright, Christopher J. H. *The Mission of God: Unlocking the Bible's Grand Narrative.* Downers Grove: InterVarsity Press, 2006.

17

Platforming Women in Missions

Pearl Ganta

Christian mission often portrays men as dominant leaders and women as playing a supporting role. But women have been an integral part in the world of missions since the time of Jesus. From equipping themselves with knowledge of the word to evangelism and discipleship, from providing financial support to extending hospitality and modelling faith, women continue to play an important role both in spreading the gospel and in humanitarian efforts.

In the beginning, God had a mandate for humankind; and he continues to reach out to every male and female he created so that he can bring all humankind to himself and reveal his glory to everyone. God sends us all and we – the sent – need to be obedient to his call, remembering that there is "no male and female, for [we] are all one."[1] This brings up an important discussion about the role of women in missions. Baker's *Evangelical Dictionary of Biblical Theology* describes mission as

> the divine activity of sending intermediaries, whether supernatural or human, to speak or do God's will so that his purposes for judgment or redemption are furthered. . . . The biblical concept of "mission" comprehends the authority of the one who sends; the obedience of the one sent; a task to be accomplished; the power to accomplish the task; and a purpose within the moral framework of God's covenantal working of judgment or redemption.[2]

---

1. Galatians 3:28: "There is neither Jew nor Gentile, neither slave nor free, nor is there male and female, for you are all one in Christ Jesus."

2. William J. Larkin, "Mission," *Baker's Evangelical Dictionary of Biblical Theology*. https://www.biblestudytools.com/dictionary/mission/.

To realize Lausanne's vision of raising Christlike leaders in every sector and society, we need mission-minded women in every sector and society. This involves a process whereby women can fulfil their God-given destiny. The Lausanne Movement's commitment to recognizing both men and women as equal partners and co-workers in God's mission is a foundational aspect of this document.

The Lausanne Movement, in *The Cape Town Commitment*[3] (CTC), states,

> Scripture affirms that God created men and women in his image and gave them dominion over the earth together. Sin entered human life and history through man and woman acting together in rebellion against God. Through the cross of Christ, God brought salvation, acceptance and unity to men and women equally. At Pentecost, God poured out his Spirit of prophecy on all flesh, sons and daughters alike. Women and men are thus equal in creation, in sin, in salvation, and in the Spirit.[4]

The world is talking about progress being achieved only when there is gender equality. According to *UN Women*, gender equality is a right of every woman. According to *UN Women*'s recent report, at the current rate of progress, it will take 286 years to achieve gender equality.[5]

To close the gaps in the Great Commission, we need to achieve gender equality in missions and accelerate our efforts to release women for their calling.

UN Women has identified seventeen areas[6] of sustainable development that affect the lives of women and girls everywhere. These same factors hinder women from being fully released for missions. There must be changes in the laws that govern women, the environment they live in, the way their families treat them, how the church equips them, and how the society and Christian missions empower women.

---

3. *The Cape Town Commitment*, written as a roadmap for the Lausanne Movement, presents a statement of shared Biblical convictions and calls Christians all over the world to action. https://lausanne.org/content/ctc/ctcommitment.

4. "Cape Town Commitment," IIF-3.

5. "Gender Snapshot," https://www.unwomen.org/en/digital-library/publications/2022/09/progress-on-the-sustainable-development-goals-the-gender-snapshot-2022.

6. 1. No Poverty 2. Zero Hunger 3. Good Health and Well Being 4. Quality Education 5. Gender Equality 6. Clean Water and Sanitation 7. Affordable and Clean Energy 8. Decent Work and Economic Growth 9. Industry, Innovation and Infrastructure 10. Reduced Inequalities 11. Sustainable Cities and Communities 12. Responsible Consumption and Production 13. Climate Action 14. Life Below Water 15. Life on Land 16. Peace, Justice and Strong Institutions 17. Partnerships for the Goals. "Sustainable Development Goals," https://www.unwomen.org/en/news/in-focus/women-and-the-sdgs.

Platforming Women in Mission based on Jesus's Model of Missions

Jesus's mission was holistic – it included both theory and practicals. It included everyone and everything around him. Each person fulfilled a different role – for example, some provided finances, some took care of administration, some coordinated the logistics – but all of them walked with Jesus and did all that he commanded. This shows us that no matter what our background or circumstances, which part of the world we belong to, or what our profession is, we can all follow Jesus, abide in God, and serve him wherever he places us.

The lives of women who earned the title "Bible woman" is one of the untold examples of women in missions.[7] These women, while assisting a missionary, were taught practical theology and sent out with Bibles and tracts to reach out to other women – and sometimes even men. They were also taught some basic skills in healthcare and domestic work so that they could help communities. Many people became followers of Christ and became disciple-makers because of the missionary work of these "Bible women." This demonstrates that women can be effective leaders, partners, and practitioners in mission when they are enlightened, equipped, empowered and engaged in missions.

Enlighten

Jesus instructed his disciples to follow him, to abide in him, to obey him, and to teach others to obey him.

> Biblical mission demands that those who claim Christ's name should be like him, by taking up their cross, denying themselves, and following him in the paths of humility, love, integrity, generosity, and servanthood. To fail in discipleship and disciple-making, is to fail at the most basic level of our mission. The call of Christ to his Church comes to us afresh from the pages of the gospels: "Come and follow me"; "Go and make disciples."[8]

Joanna, Susanna, and many other women supported Jesus financially.[9]

Paul acknowledges the intergenerational ministry of Lois and Eunice – the women in Timothy's family – in passing on their faith to the next generation (2 Tim 1:5; 3:14–15). These enlightened women modelled mission because

---

7. Wikipedia, "Bible Woman," last edited 28 November 2023, 20:04. https://en.wikipedia.org/wiki/Bible_woman.

8. "Cape Town Commitment," Conclusion.

9. Luke 8:1–3: "Joanna the wife of Chuza, the manager of Herod's household; Susanna; and many others. These women were helping to support them out of their own means."

they learned, they practised their faith, and they transferred their knowledge and experience to others. We need to help women understand their role in the kingdom – as equal contributors in every area of ministry – and their crucial part in establishing God's kingdom of righteousness, peace, and joy on earth.

> We affirm that evangelism and socio-political involvement are both part of our Christian duty. For both are necessary expressions of our doctrines of God and humankind, our love for our neighbour and our obedience to Jesus Christ . . . The salvation we proclaim should be transforming us in the totality of our personal and social responsibilities. Faith without works is dead.[10]

Pearl, a fourth-generation Christian from Asia, who shares that her upbringing helped her to rise above societal expectations despite facing opposition, exemplifies an empowered woman in missions. She says, "A paradigm shift is necessary for engaging women in ministry, and this involves moving beyond the traditional roles of women in the church and the society." From humble beginnings as a cross-cultural international missionary, a church planter, and a nurturer of orphan children, Pearl became a filmmaker and global catalyst in empowering leaders in both Christian and secular sectors. She says that apart from her family and a few exceptional leaders, not many leaders offered her encouragement or opportunities in her ministry journey.

Pearl also observed that while various movements and gatherings invited women for organizational tasks, to lead intercession, or to speak on occasions related to women and children, there was a barrier when it came to invitations to lead plenary sessions, teach, preach, conduct workshops, or lead networks and movements. On most occasions, women were paired with men to gain acceptance from people. On global platforms, women from Western countries were often given priority over their Asian counterparts. To close such gaps, we need a continual paradigm shift.

> All of us, women and men, married and single, are responsible to employ God's gifts for the benefit of others, as stewards of God's grace, and for the praise and glory of Christ. All of us, therefore, are also responsible to enable all God's people to exercise all the gifts that God has given for all the areas of service to which God calls the Church. We should not quench the Spirit by despising the ministry of any. Further, we are determined to see ministry within

---

10. "Cape Town Commitment," I-10-B.

the body of Christ as a gifting and a responsibility in which we are called to serve, and not as a status and a right that we demand.[11]

May the ministry go forth in an attitude that seeks to serve and reveal God rather than the agendas of our own selfish desires. May our King and his principles be honoured.

Equip

Equip all God's people for the missional task of understanding and relevantly communicating God's Truth in every cultural context.[12]

Jesus affirmed Mary's choice to learn.[13] She was a young girl who was eager to learn about the ways of the Lord. We also see Anna,[14] an older woman who knew the prophecies about the Messiah and understood the kingdom ways, receiving conviction when she saw Jesus and declaring this at the opportune time.

All women need to be equipped to fulfil their mission effectively. No matter how equipped they are to perform in their vocation, to be able to think and act wisely in missions, women need to be educated.

Dr. Seblewongel from the Evangelical Theological College in Addis Ababa, Ethiopia, says that theological schools around the globe adopt diverse approaches when addressing the issues of women studying theology. In many theological institutions, women are generally accepted both to study theology and to teach in the classroom. When it comes to participation in leadership, however, their acceptance is low. It is important for women to recognize and accept that they need to be well equipped for their mission:

> We recognize that there are different views sincerely held by those who seek to be faithful and obedient to Scripture. Some interpret apostolic teaching to imply that women should not teach or preach, or that they may do so but not in sole authority over men. Others interpret the spiritual equality of women, the exercise of the edifying gift of prophecy by women in the New Testament

---

11. "Cape Town Commitment," IIF-3.

12. "Cape Town Commitment," IIF-4.

13. Luke 10:39: "She had a sister called Mary, who sat at the Lord's feet listening to what he said."

14. Luke 2:38: "Coming up to them at that very moment, she gave thanks to God and spoke about the child to all who were looking forward to the redemption of Jerusalem."

church and their hosting of churches in their homes, as implying that the spiritual gifts of leading and teaching may be received and exercised in ministry by both women and men.[15]

Ephesians 4:12 says that we need to equip the saints for the work of ministry. So, let us equip women with both knowledge and skills:

1. Theological knowledge is essential so that they can defend their faith, share their faith, and guard against false teachings and false world views.

2. Skills are necessary so that they can earn their livelihood and also connect with people from the marketplace. This also opens up opportunities for them to find solutions to global problems and creative ways to minister the gospel and serve those around them in various areas such as hospitality, education, social work, medical, civil, mechanical, culinary, counselling, soft skills, media, agricultural, and entrepreneurship.

In India, in 2021, when COVID-19 was at its peak, several Christian professionals came up with solutions for migrant workers who were returning to their villages. Specialists in the areas of agriculture, entrepreneurship, and skill development came up with sustainable solutions to help people. Even those from media and law backgrounds identified issues that needed attention and came forward to be the voice that raised awareness and put in place practices to protect people. All these efforts opened doors to minister holistically to people from various sectors, economic backgrounds, and communities. These men and women were able to do all this because they understood the call of God and also had practical and professional skills.

Empower

Jesus encouraged women to be part of God's kingdom's work in their own unique way. He empowered them by giving them both confidence and a sense of purpose. An empowered woman need not wait for anyone; with God on her side, she is capable of charting her destiny.

The Samaritan woman[16] became an evangelist after her conversation with Jesus. She came from a different background and circumstances, and while her

---

15. "Cape Town Commitment," IIF-3-B.
16. John 4:1–42.

encounter with Jesus was unusual, it was what she needed to be enlightened, equipped, and empowered to immediately become a missionary to her entire village. Susanna and her female friends were involved in the ministry in a different way, supporting Jesus's ministry financially. These women found their purpose and were able to serve in unique ways.

Abbie Desloges, a missionary with Africa Inland Mission, serving in the Democratic Republic of Congo, speaks warmly of missionaries Helen Roseveare, Margaret Hayes, and Maud Kells, who served in remote parts of the country and impacted people in many ways. She says that these missionary heroines inspired her in her own missionary journey. Desloges also observes that one finds in the history of the Protestant church in Eastern Congo, the names of countless women, many of them single, who served as professionals – often as nurses, teachers, or administrators.[17]

Following the most recent war in the Congo – the Second Congo War (1998–2003) – in the north east it was mainly single women who returned to carry on the ministry following the evacuations of the 1990s. Unfortunately – despite Paul's exhortations in 1 Corinthians 7 – singleness is often spoken of in the same breath as disease, poverty, and unemployment, as something from which one must pray to be delivered.

In the contemporary Congolese Protestant church, although many women are active in ministry and evangelism in their churches, leadership and the pastoral collar are reserved, in most denominations, for men alone. These barriers to participation that women face inhibit the use of their gifts and discourage their ministry in the church.

The way forward is to equip female leaders for ministry, allow them space to discern their call, and empower them to live out this call, whether alongside their husbands or in their singleness. If the resilience and commitment of the missionaries – especially the single women – helped bring about a great change in the country, how much more can be accomplished if local women are also empowered and join forces in missions?

> We encourage churches to acknowledge godly women who teach and model what is good, as Paul commanded, and to open wider doors of opportunity for women in education, service, and leadership, particularly in contexts where the gospel challenges unjust cultural traditions. We long that women should not be

---

17. See, for example, the accounts in Anderson, *We Felt Like Grasshoppers: The Story of Africa Inland Mission*.

hindered from exercising God's gifts or following God's call on their lives.[18]

Engage

The women in Jesus's life who supported him in their own unique way and fulfilled their destiny in the kingdom serve as examples of diversified styles of ministry:

- Mary, the mother of Jesus, accepted the role of a mother, nurtured Jesus, and stood by him and his ministry even after his resurrection (Luke 1:26; 2:20). She faced troubles and heartbreak for answering her call; yet she never gave up.
- Martha hosted Jesus and his disciples, fed them, looked after them, and opened her home for Jesus to teach and minister to people (John 12:1–2).
- Mary Magdalene was a devout disciple, who followed Jesus everywhere (Matt 28:1–10; John 20:1–18). She had unwavering faith and was the first person to interact with Jesus after his resurrection and carry the news of the risen Jesus Christ to the disciples.

Julie, a full-time missionary to Asia, belonged to an organization that believed that God anoints and calls women for leadership positions and valued the contributions of women. However, those ministering were predominantly men, with the women who served being mainly their spouses or married women. As a single woman and a Westerner, Julie faced many challenges. She encountered disrespect from some of her male colleagues at the organizational level, which she attributed to cultural biases against single women, Westerners, and ladies in their thirties and forties.

Julie's methods as a Westerner sometimes created challenges but, eventually, the people around her learned to respect and accept each other's calling, culture, and unique giftings and styles in leadership. Her professional experience, combined with her mission experience, has helped Julie, as part of mission, to start a business that has helped her to reach the unreached in the marketplace.

Women are resilient and adaptive. We need to engage them in ways in which they can flourish and bring transformative change in all sectors

---

18. "Cape Town Commitment," IIF-3.

of society; doing so is directly linked to their spiritual journey and their participation in missions.

How Can Women Flourish in Their Personal Lives and in Missions?

The world around us is changing at an alarming rate. Women are being empowered and becoming increasingly active, and we must continue to encourage them to grow through continuous learning, education, and pursuing diversified careers and leadership roles. Some of the ways in which we can do this are described below:

1. **Education and constant learning**
   Provide practical theology training, academic theology, regular school and university education, specialized skill training, and vocational training. Education brings knowledge, awareness, and the strength to break cycles of bondage brought about by social, cultural, economic, and political influences.

2. **Women's leadership and participation**
   Enable women to become directors, administrators, strategists, teachers, preachers, board members, entrepreneurs, and professionals.

3. **Holistic approach**
   Get involved in advocacy and community development, address social and domestic issues, provide healthcare and economic empowerment, and offer moral, mental, emotional, and spiritual support for women. Help women to become mentors and disciple-makers as they grow in their journey with God.

4. **Innovation**
   Create and use technology, social media, AI, and other tools – those available now and those that will be available in the future – to support and inspire others by sharing the word, as well as their own experiences, insights, successes, failures, challenges, breakthroughs, solutions, and prayers.

5. **Alleviate poverty**
   Help to break cultural barriers, superstitions, non-progressive societal expectations, and gender discrimination that place limitations on productivity and the pursuit of career opportunities. Encourage entrepreneurship, skill building, and investment. Create

> infrastructure to help women with the care of the elderly and children in their families so that they can pursue career goals.
>
> 6. **Mutual respect**
>   Create an environment in which men and woman can work together with mutual respect and equality without abusing each other.

By the year 2033, it will be two thousand years since Jesus gave us the Great Commission. Let us enlighten women to understand God, God's word, God's world, and their own role. Let us equip them with the knowledge they need to share their faith and develop the skills they need to address the challenges around them and build their capacity to create solutions. Let us empower them so that they can see their potential and continue developing themselves and impacting the lives of others. Let us engage them so that they remain motivated, focused, and relevant. By doing this, we honour Jesus, who repeatedly reminded his followers that God's kingdom was at hand, invited people to follow him, sent out his disciples to make disciples, and promised to be with us always.

Bibliography

Anderson, Richard J. D. *We Felt Like Grasshoppers: The Story of Africa Inland Mission*. United Kingdom: Crossway Books, 1994.

"The Cape Town Commitment." *Lausanne Movement*, 2010. https://lausanne.org/content/ctc/ctcommitment.

Elwell, Walter A., ed. *Baker's Evangelical Dictionary of Biblical Theology*. Grand Rapids: Baker Books, 1996. https://www.biblestudytools.com/dictionary/mission/.

"Progress on the Sustainable Development Goals: The Gender Snapshot 2022." *UN Women*, 2022. https://www.unwomen.org/en/digital-library/publications/2022/09/progress-on-the-sustainable-development-goals-the-gender-snapshot-2022.

"Women and the Sustainable Development Goals (SDGs)." *UN Women*. https://www.unwomen.org/en/news/in-focus/women-and-the-sdgs.

18

Magnifying Unheard Voices

Darío López, Jocabed Soliano Miselis, Jose L. Cruz,
Laura B. Macias, Paul Turner, and Brenda Darke

By listening to the many unheard voices in the Latin American church, we foster a rich harmony that unveils significant stories and profound insights, enriching our shared narrative with new perspectives. This compilation comprises the diverse voices of six authors, collectively examining the current state and prospective impact of the Latin American church across all facets of society.

Hidden Voices
Women and Leadership by Darío López

A panoramic view of the Gospels is sufficient to understand the unusual and unexpected way – that went against the grain of the social and cultural prejudices of the first century – in which Jesus valued, treated, and related to women, placing them at the centre of his itinerant ministry. The Galilean women who served and followed Jesus – among them, Mary Magdalene – are sufficient evidence of the prominence women enjoyed in the community of Jesus.

These women, and others whose life stories the Gospels record, speak not only with their words but also with their gestures, their silence, the movement of their bodies, and their actions of solidarity. Several of them, including Martha and Mary – the sisters of Lazarus – the Syrophenician woman, the very poor widow, and the sinful woman, do theology from a position of vulnerability, defencelessness, and stigmatization. They never keep quiet. They always have a message to communicate with their words and gestures. And this was so because the liberating practice of Jesus made them visible and gave them a voice in a patriarchal society that had accustomed them to silence and anonymity.

The Acts of the Apostles and the Pauline letters also make women visible as disciples and leaders in the Christian community of the first century. The mother of John Mark, Rhoda, Priscilla, Lydia, Dorcas, the daughters of Philip, and the noble women of Thessaloniki are clear examples of this reality; in addition, we have the examples of Euodia and Syntyche, Phoebe, Mary, Tryphena and Tryphosa, Persis, and even Junia – if it is accepted that she was a woman. Paul had female travelling companions who were directly involved in the mission. Women like Lydia, Priscilla, and Phoebe – in addition to giving up their homes for the disciples to meet – exercised leadership tasks within the churches. Dorcas is an exceptional case because her missionary action went beyond the Christian community and extended to serving widowed women with her financial resources, knowledge, skills, and experience.

Just as in the New Testament, today, too, in various contexts, Christian women are active not only in leadership activities in churches – as deaconesses, women's leaders, teaching children, serving the poor, in charge of planting churches, or generating funds for the construction of church buildings – but also as leaders in popular women's organizations that focus on the fight against poverty or violence against women, the defence of human rights, or equal opportunities for all. In situations of violence, poverty, and death, these evangelical women have gone from being neighbours to citizens because they have understood that the Christian faith is not limited to the religious dimension of life but also requires the full exercise of citizenship made visible in loving service of their defenceless, vulnerable, or stigmatized neighbour.

Just as in the patriarchal society of the first century, Christian women today, too, face social and cultural prejudices that result in their being treated as dependent, subordinate, and less important. Although the prevailing machismo visible in the various forms of violence that women suffer – physical, verbal, emotional, economic, and online – both in society and in churches is a daily challenge, this does not impede their love for life and justice. Despite this reality of visible or covert violence, women today follow in the footsteps of the Galilean women disciples of Jesus and the example of the women who, in the first Christian communities, played a visible role in the communication and extension of the gospel. For these women, the church is a space of service to God and their neighbour and, simultaneously, so is the neighbourhood because, for them, "the world is their parish." In this way, with their example and commitment, they generate new avenues for Christian witness in nontraditional mission frontiers for churches: social movements, women's organizations, and initiatives to fight poverty, marginalization, and exclusion.

Indigenous Communities by Jocabed Soliano Miselis

The gospel of Jesus dignifies and amplifies the voices of so many people in the world. This gospel of this Nazarene carpenter – who walked through towns and villages transforming the lives, faith, and ministry of humble people through his encounters with them – shows us the importance of the mustard seed as one of the symbols and dreams of the kingdom of God.

In this journey that he undertook two thousand years ago, as he travelled through towns and villages, Jesus was knitted with the indigenous peoples of the ancient world, dignifying and bringing hope of life to every culture that embraces the fullness of God and embodies his values. The voices of indigenous peoples in the world are among the least heard, and this has usually been due to structural discrimination, systemic violence, and epistemic injustice.

However, the Gospels show us that Jesus has a special relationship with the vulnerable. The Gospel shows a Jesus who walks with those who are violated and minimized, and his proposal of faith offers full life for all creation, including human beings.

The voices of indigenous Christian communities have much to say to the global church. Their world views – which are centred on a life practice of reciprocity,[1] complementarity,[2] and a deep relationship with the earth – contribute to a deep view of salvation in a holistic way. And the presence of the *ruach* of God in the daily living together with these aspects of experience and wisdom draws back the curtain and opens us to other ways of knowing and recognizing how God is manifesting himself in the world and how Jesus is being illuminated in the world. These communities are living testimonies of the fervent faith that illuminates indigenous peoples. Telling and listening to these memories of the indigenous church is a path to reconciliation, but it is also a prayer that sings and tells of the work that these leaders have done in their

---

1. Reciprocity: Value system of indigenous peoples, which implies gratuity in receiving. We give with joy since we recognize that to sustain life in community, giving and receiving is a natural part of life. We receive life from the Creator, we receive the fruits of the earth, and we take care of the earth.

2. Complementarity: Fundamental value for community life, the importance of all relationships and the role of each person in the community. Woman and man working together. How the role of children, youth, and the elderly is also recognized. Even the names of the rivers in the Gunadule people, for example, have masculine and feminine names due to this system of complementarity.

contexts, which brings us closer to knowing and recognizing the indigenous face of God. The manifestation of how the Spirit of life has manifested himself and continues to manifest itself in the indigenous territories should be a reason for celebration and an invitation to join the dance of the Spirit with the indigenous peoples.

Without the indigenous church, we are not complete as the body of Christ. That is why we believe that listening, knowing, and recognizing the memories of indigenous churches is essential to counteract the epistemic violence that comes from sin, allowing us to see the glory and manifestation of the presence of God in the people of the world whenever these stories are told. Listening to these voices is also telling the good news of Jesus in the world, it is learning from other brothers and sisters, and it is living a faith that humbly embraces the recognition of the powerful work of the action of the Spirit of God in the world and among indigenous peoples.

Unsung Stories
Bi-Vocational Evangelist by Jose L. Cruz[3]

Hilda Gertrudis Sierra de Choriego, known as hermana[4] Tulita, was born to a poor family in El Salvador in 1930. She was the granddaughter of Claudio Anaya, who was married to Erlinda Echegoyén. Her grandfather was the first Salvadorian "call-porter" – which meant travelling the country selling Bibles and Christian literature while evangelizing. In those pioneer days of gospel preaching in El Salvador, this was a dangerous profession since it exposed a person to verbal abuse, physical violence, and even jail.

Education and ministry: Tulita was called by God as a child to teach the Bible to children. Her inspiration came from her grandmother, Erlinda, and a couple of American missionary ladies at Iglesia Central MCA. The source of her love for children was Jesus, her Saviour and Lord.

Tulita graduated as a primary school teacher and served children – both formally and informally – for over seventy years. She founded one of the first Christian schools in the country – "Colegio Evangélico" – in Santa Tecla, El Salvador, in 1960, and this school is still thriving sixty years later.

---

3. This article was compiled from my personal memories of interacting with hermana Tulita for forty-six years and from an interview with Dioneli Melara, one of Tulita's close relatives.

4. "Hermana" is the Spanish equivalent of Christian sister and is used in Spanish-speaking Christian evangelical churches.

Tulita worked as a full-time schoolteacher during the week and served in the church on weekends and holidays, teaching children through Sunday school, kids' clubs, and vacation Bible schools. She seized every opportunity to mingle with children and emphasized Bible stories, Christian values, financial support for God's work worldwide, and praying for missionaries.

Even after retiring, Tulita worked tirelessly to continue her ministry among children. She carried a purse and a bag filled with children's crafts, colouring pencils, crayons, books, notebooks, knitting materials, and other such items. Wherever she went, she busied herself in observing nature (she loved plants), praying, preparing a class, reading, or knitting. Her handcrafted creations usually ended up as a gift for a newborn, an older child, or a family in need. She was a generous woman – truly a Salvadorian Tabitha or Dorcas as in Acts 9:36.

Legacy: Tulita's life motto was "Never stop learning" – and she never did. She and her husband were active in church leadership, conducted seminars, and participated actively in church programmes as long as they were physically able to do so. Even though her husband was a top executive in a multinational corporation, Tulita dressed modestly and hardly ever wore jewellery. She was quiet, observant, transparent, honest, down to earth, and unassuming. Her home, which was always open to people, was a true refuge, especially for younger women in need. Her one weakness was that she struggled to make decisions, a trait that threw her into deeper dependence on Jesus. She read devotional booklets like *Streams in the Desert* and *Our Daily Bread* and enjoyed sharing her findings with others.

Tulita died in her own home at the age of ninety, crippled with osteoporosis but with a sharp mind. Her husband had passed away a month earlier. At her funeral, which took place during the COVID-19 era in 2020, a young professional man stood up to give thanks to God for Tulita's life. He witnessed publicly that it was her life and teaching, when he was a child, that had led him to become a follower of Jesus. His is just one voice among the hundreds of people, from different generations, whom Tulita touched with Jesus's love and words through her faithful ministry to children.

Life lessons: These were some of the life lessons Tulita taught, through her words and her life: never stop learning; follow Jesus's calling through the ups and downs of life; do not underestimate the calling in the life of a child but nurture it; be generous with your possessions as you invest in eternity; promote God's worldwide work; be genuine, and God will use you; and, above all, let Jesus be your inspiration for life and ministry.

Bi-Vocational Pastor by Laura B. Macias

A bi-vocational church leader is someone who fulfils the role of pastoral leadership within a church while also assuming one or more additional forms of employment to ensure financial stability.

The onset of the global COVID-19 pandemic caused a heightened sense of urgency and resolve in Pastor Elgin's ministry. Serving as a bi-vocational pastor in Costa Rica, he has committed over a decade to shepherding a congregation of forty to fifty members at an interdenominational theological centre. His weekly activities include leading worship services and Bible study sessions. Beyond these formal duties, Pastor Elgin extends his pastoral care to visiting the sick, offering counsel to married couples, and investing a significant amount of time in preparing sermons for the Sunday morning services.

Amid these spiritual responsibilities, Pastor Elgin also maintains a delicate balance between his ministry and his secular employment. He works thirty hours a week as a sales manager, a role he undertook to ensure financial stability for his family. Previously trained as an architect, he made a vocational shift to pursue his calling to ministry together with his wife, Rita. His ordination – held in 2010 at the Comunidad Cristiana de Amor in Moravia – marked a significant milestone in his journey. Despite a demanding schedule that offers little room for rest and personal leisure, Pastor Elgin is on the cusp of achieving a longstanding goal: the completion of a master's degree in Biblical studies, reflecting his deep-seated commitment to church leadership.

During the COVID-19 crisis, the resilience demonstrated by Pastor Elgin and his fellow bi-vocational church leaders in Central America has been nothing short of commendable. Confronted with the suspension of in-person worship and Bible studies, Pastor Elgin showed both innovation and resourcefulness in adapting to this new situation. His congregation quickly transitioned to digital platforms, using Facebook Live for services and Zoom for weekly Bible studies. These initiatives were crucial in sustaining community bonds and providing continuous hope and encouragement to counter the pervasive fear and anxiety of the times. Measures such as these have bonded church members in profound ways. After gathering in-person for the first time this year, baptisms have increased, demonstrating a deeper commitment to God and one another. An increased awareness of the devastating toll of COVID-19 in the region fostered a missional step towards providing humanitarian aid to vulnerable communities in Nicaragua, where many churches are encountering significant challenges due to skyrocketing inflation and high unemployment rates. Thanks to prayer and acts of benevolence from congregations outside of Nicaragua, a network of churches inside Nicaragua including Pastor Elgin's congregation are able to work on burgeoning new projects that provide vital assistance. Hence, mutual collaboration and missional engagement are furthering discipleship that is similar to what took place in the early church as described in the book of Acts. Rather than focusing on reclaiming pre-COVID-19 church growth, Pastor Elgin encourages the congregation to think beyond its borders as they fulfil the Great Commission of Jesus Christ with grace and hope.

The coming years will offer additional opportunities and challenges for bi-vocational church leaders like Pastor Elgin and others to lead with love and humility while assuming varied roles that are equally significant and germane to societal transformation.

Muted Realities
Emerging Leaders by Paul Turner

With so many young Christians thrust into the limelight of leadership at a tender age, it may seem strange to consider emerging leaders as a marginalized group in Christian mission. Sadly, those who are given opportunities to lead often crash and burn due to lack of proper support and mentoring, inadequate resources, and having to juggle ministry responsibilities with family life and making ends meet.

In a Latin American context, where the charisma and external qualities of a leader are often emphasized over a leader's character, there is a need to return to the biblical principle of identifying those who are daily being transformed by the work of the Spirit in their lives. In the Gospels, we see how Jesus called, prepared, and sent out the disciples (Mark 3:13–19). In Acts, we catch a glimpse of how the early church selected future leaders. In Acts 6:1–6, the apostles ask the church in Jerusalem to choose seven men who are full of the Spirit and wisdom to oversee the daily distribution of food. In Acts 13:2–3, the Holy Spirit speaks, asking the church in Antioch to set aside Paul and Barnabas for mission. Acts 15:36–41 describes Paul and Barnabas's disagreement over who should accompany them. Barnabas wanted to take John Mark but Paul preferred Silas, and they each went in a different direction. All these people were willing to serve and were used for the extension of God's kingdom.

Despite the opportunities some emerging leaders are given, there is still a tendency for established leaders to cling to power, to fail to prioritize developing leaders, and to feel indispensable. A Latin American female leader comments on the challenges of being a young leader in Latin America:

You must deal with seasoned leaders who might see you as their potential assistant, treat you as their daughter or in the worst case choose not to recognize you as a potential or current leader. A "macho culture" is still prevalent, in denominations, churches and even more so in the mission field. It's hard for young women to find mentors, to grow in their calling and to learn from others.

The continued separation of faith and work – that is, the divergence of church life from everyday life – does not help either. Omar Viazcán, a young Mexican leader, put it like this:

> Balancing my role as a Latin-American Christian CFO in a family-owned company with family and personal projects is a solitary journey. The absence of tailored resources and supportive communities within the Global Church is disheartening. Despite the church's remarkable achievements, the oversight of our unique challenges leaves us feeling unheard and unsupported in our quest for a harmonious intersection of faith and business.

A recent gathering of Arrow Peru leaders identified the following qualities as being necessary for nurturing healthy relationships that include and develop others: trust, humility, empathy, listening more than talking, valuing people, recognizing mistakes, communicating clearly, and being accessible. All these qualities are embodied in our Lord Jesus. May we be led more and more by him as we seek to make room for and develop those whom the Spirit has called but we might have overlooked for various reasons.

People with Disabilities by Brenda Darke

Historically, voices that should have been heard have been silenced. People who have lived with the experience of disability in Latin America have been ignored and discriminated against. Even if they have been able to participate in a church, their contributions have usually been seen as irrelevant and even as untrue because of the widely held myth that disability is God's punishment. Those churches which espouse a doctrine of prosperity have problems hearing the voices of those who do not seem to have found health through God's miraculous intervention. For many years, people living with disabilities have been hidden away in back rooms for fear of what their neighbours would think.

In our twenty-first-century society that sets great store on physical perfection, there is often a fundamental and deep-seated antagonism towards those who are seen as not fully formed or beautiful. In Latin American countries, it is only more recently – following the signing of an international convention on the rights of people with disabilities – that national laws have been introduced and equal access to education, health services, and social interaction become a norm. There is still a huge question mark about the place and purpose of people with disabilities in churches. How can we welcome these people into our congregations? What might their full participation look like?

A biblical perspective – present, their voices invited by God

The Old Testament gives examples of people with disabilities being used by God. The most obvious example is probably Moses, although some would contest whether he actually had a disability or not. But this debate is less important than God's response to Moses. God seems to declare that having a disability is no limitation to working with and for God: "Now go; I will help you speak and will teach you what to say" (Exod 4:12).[5]

Jesus himself showed compassion for many people with different disabilities, offering them abundant life through his healing touch. We also read in the epistles that God values those who are considered "less worthy" (see 1 Cor 12:21–23, 27). Paul, a man of great faith, may have had a visual disability (2 Cor 12:7–9) but had to live with this hardship.

Changes are coming – some voices are beginning to be heard

These are a few examples from Latin America of people living with disabilities who are working in our churches and in mission:

Rolando Verdecia (Cuba): theologian and coordinator for PwD in churches in Cuba.

Lourdes Cordero: staff worker for many years with the IFES-related Bolivian student movement, as well as being a poet and editor.

Pastor Poblete (Chile): pastor and promotor of inclusion for PwD in society.

Rev. Noel Fernández (Cuba): a pastor for many years, a writer, and coordinator of the Ecumenical Disability Advocacy Network in Latin America.

Mainor Jokson Mora: a missionary from Costa Rica, working with SIL in Mexico.

Let us not forget those who are not gifted to be great leaders. They may not have the intellect of a Moses or a Paul, but they have faith and love Jesus in spite of the many struggles they live with. Some of my friends with cognitive disabilities may not be able to explain their faith, but they have an infectious delight in praising God, often with music. One of these, a young man with

---

5. For more examples, see Darke, *Un Camino Compartido*, and Yong, *Disability*.

Down's syndrome, plays bongo drums as he praises God. We all need to hear his voice, and other voices like his, in our churches today. Our churches will be better and more welcoming places when these voices are heard.

How can we hear these voices better?

We can begin to hear these voices by taking time to listen to these people, coming alongside them, and making it easier for them to speak to us. We may need to make some adjustments and put in place arrangements to facilitate their communication. Whatever needs to be done will be truly worth doing as many of these people have a deep faith borne out of their suffering and their exclusion.

Bibliography

Darke, Brenda. *Un Camino Compartido*. 2nd ed. Lima: Ediciones Puma, 2020.
Yong, Amos. *The Bible, Disability, and the Church*. Grand Rapids: Eerdmans, 2011.

19

The Christian Response to Persecution: An Integrated Examination of Faithfulness amid Trial

Patrick Fung and Hwa Yung

Introduction

Throughout history, Christian communities have grappled with the reality of persecution – a reality that presses upon the faithful to this day. In one of Dietrich Bonhoeffer's best-known works, *The Cost of Discipleship*, he poignantly asserts, "Discipleship means allegiance to the suffering Christ, and it is therefore not at all surprising that Christians should be called upon to suffer."[1] Bonhoeffer's allegiance to his faith led to his execution at the hands of the Nazi regime, embodying the highest cost of discipleship: martyrdom. He was hanged on 9 April 1945. These were thirty-nine-year-old Bonhoeffer's last words: "This is the end – for me, the beginning of life."[2]

The church has faced varying seasons of prosperity and adversity. The reality of persecution echoes the suffering of Christ and his call to his disciples to bear their crosses. From the accounts of the early church in the New Testament to contemporary contexts globally, Christians have grappled – and

---

1. Bonhoeffer, *Cost of Discipleship*, 45.
2. History.com Editors, "Anti-Nazi Theologian Dietrich Bonhoeffer Is Hanged," *History*, last updated 7 April 2021. https://www.history.com/this-day-in-history/defiant-theologian-dietrich-bonhoeffer-is-hanged.

continue to grapple – with the theological, historical, and ethical dimensions of persecution.[3]

The Early Church: Luke-Acts and the Paradigm of Persecution

The Gospel of Luke, together with Acts, frames the Christian response to persecution within the sovereignty of God and the promises of Christ. Jesus himself, predicting that his disciples would face persecution, assured them of divine guidance (Luke 12:11–12). The early church, forged in this crucible, held to the principles of unity in prayer, bold proclamation of truth, and perseverance. Although they encountered opposition from both Jewish and Gentile sources, this did not deter them from their mission. Even when persecuted, they responded with wisdom, choosing whether to stay and face the danger or to leave for safety based on divine guidance and practical considerations.

Luke and Acts: A Continuum of Response and Maturity

The response to persecution in Luke and Acts reveals a mature and contextually sensitive church. Whether through wisdom in defence, negotiation, or evasion, the early Christians exemplified dynamic engagement with persecution rather than a static endurance of suffering.

Luke is very clear that the disciples rejoiced in being counted worthy to suffer disgrace for the sake of Jesus's name (Acts 5:41). At Lystra, Iconium, and Antioch, Paul and Barnabas explained to the disciples there that "we must go through many hardships to enter the kingdom of God" (Acts 14:22). Twice, Peter asserted that they would rather obey God than human beings – that is, the opposing authorities (Acts 4:19; 5:29). When Peter was in prison, the church prayed earnestly for him (Acts 12:5). Paul testified about the pain he had to endure because of persecution. He told the Ephesian elders that he had "served the Lord with great humility and with tears and in the midst of severe testing by the plots of my Jewish opponents" (Acts 20:19). Peter, Stephen, and Paul all witnessed for Jesus before the Sanhedrin (Acts 4:8–12; 5:29–32; 7:1–53; 23:1–9), and Paul also witnessed before the governors Felix and Festus, as well as King Agrippa (Acts 24:10–21; 25:6–11; 26:1–23). What happened in the book of Acts was a fulfilment of what Jesus had already predicted: "They will

---

3. For a very helpful explanation on the meaning of persecution, see Lee, *When Christians Face Persecution*, 3.

seize you and persecute you. They will hand you over to synagogues and put you in prison, and you will be brought before kings and governors, and all on account of my name" (Luke 21:12).

Keener notes that Peter's defence before the Sanhedrin displays amazing wisdom and the use of the rhetorical technique of irony. It is ironic that Peter and John were charged for their benefaction in healing the paralytic. As Keener points out, "One benefaction should weight the burden of proof in favour of the speakers' positive character, and hence one's innocence."[4] Although the authorities viewed Peter as "unschooled," they were astonished by Peter's ability to present such a wise defence (Acts 4:13).

The various Christian responses to persecution under the different circumstances that are reflected in Acts demonstrate resistance – resilience, and perseverance in the midst of persecution. However, this does not mean that the disciples responded in the same way every time there was persecution. There were times the believers chose to flee and avoid danger. At other times, the disciples decided to stay or even confront danger directly, as in the case of Paul going up to Jerusalem. External circumstances, personal experience, and, in particular, the prompting of the Holy Spirit are all important factors that affect our decisions. It would be wrong or overly simplistic to judge a person's obedience to God based on the decision to stay or leave.

The work of the Holy Spirit is evident throughout the book of Acts. While the disciples faced opposition and persecution, the Spirit remained at work. The Spirit enabled the believers to speak with power and wisdom, as in the case of Peter, Stephen, and Paul (Acts 4:8; 6:10; 17:22–31). In addition, many signs and wonders also testified to the message proclaimed by the disciples (Acts 2:22; 5:12; 6:8; 14:3; 15:12; 28:5).

Many of the stories recorded in Acts do not depict the disciples as passive recipients of persecution. On the contrary, they are portrayed as persevering in their initiatives and enduring to the end. They proclaimed Christ courageously, forgave their persecutors – as in the case of Stephen – and entrusted themselves to God. They were victors, not victims of persecution. Through all this, the mission and the church continued to advance.

---

4. Keener, *Acts*, 2:1145–48, quoted in Lee, *When Christians Face Persecution*, 65.

The Historical Perspective
The Boxer Uprising and the Shaping of an Indigenous Church

The Boxer Uprising (1900) marked one of the darkest periods for Christians in China. Amid the chaos and violence, the China Inland Mission (CIM) – led by Dixon E. Hoste, who was appointed by CIM founder Hudson Taylor – opted for a revolutionary stance in refusing compensation for their martyred.[5] Instead, CIM shifted its focus to support local Christians and strengthen the church's resolve, thereby fostering a significant leap towards indigenous leadership and autonomy, in the spirit of the earliest Christians who saw value in adversity and grew stronger through it.

Hoste believed that the crisis caused by the Boxer Uprising might, in the end, provide an opportunity for the native church to take on leadership in the absence of missionaries. Greater changes would certainly take place with the absence of missionaries "in whom the centre of gravity of power, influence, and initiative had rested."[6] This would lead to a period of greater rearrangement in the relationship between the missionaries and the native leaders. Hoste observed that those local Chinese leaders who were used to being only in the background "under the old regime would come to the front; and proving themselves equal to the facing of danger and bearing of responsibility, grow into leadership."[7]

Post-Uprising: Resolution and Reconstruction

In the aftermath of the Boxer Uprising, the CIM, while facing financial challenges, reinforced their commitment to denying compensation. This choice led to an unexpected outcome: the growth of the Chinese church's independence, demonstrating an alignment with the spirit of the New Testament church's response to trial – strength through suffering, endurance, and growth beyond adversity. The CIM saw this as a pivotal moment for the Chinese church's emergence as an autonomous entity that was capable of leadership and resilience. The Boxer crisis, while a time of immense loss, sparked a transformative change in the understanding of indigenization and the urgency of empowering local leadership.

---

5. Hoste, "Possible Changes," 511.
6. Broomhall, *Martyred Missionaries*, 280.
7. Broomhall, 281.

Roman and European Eras

During times of Roman persecution, the Christian response was characterized by endurance and martyrdom. Luther's Reformation and the subsequent defence of Protestantism by sympathetic German princes modelled a form of resistance grounded in state authority or, in rare cases, justifiable revolution as in Dietrich Bonhoeffer's plot against Hitler. The contemporary conflicts in the Middle East and Africa highlight the urgent need to differentiate between enduring persecution and resisting genocide when the very existence of Christian communities is at stake, especially in contexts where law and order have broken down.

The Contemporary Context
The Global Perspective on Persecution

Today's church is witnessing an unprecedented level of persecution globally. Scholars like Todd Johnson have highlighted shifts in the geography and intensity of persecution, with a significant rise of persecution in the Global South. The Pew Research Center reported that one-third of the world's population is facing increased religious restriction, highlighting the stark reality that 75 percent of religious persecution is against Christians.[8] The total number of countries with "high" or "very high" levels of government restrictions has been mounting as well. Most recently, that number climbed from fifty-two countries (26 percent of the 198 countries and territories included in the study) in 2017 to fifty-six countries (28 percent) in 2018.[9] As of 2018, most of the fifty-six countries with high or very high levels of government restrictions on religion are in the Asia Pacific region (twenty-five countries, which is half of all countries in that region) or the Middle East-North Africa region (eighteen countries, which is 90 percent of all countries in the region). The Asia Pacific region also saw several instances of widespread use of government force against religious groups.[10]

Studies have shown that persecution against peoples of all faiths has been on the rise and, today, is widespread globally, with Christians being the most targeted group. Paul Marshall, Lela Gilbert, and Nina Shea assert:

---

8. Katayoun, "Key Findings," https://www.pewresearch.org/fact-tank/2018/06/21/key-findings-on-the-global-rise-in-religious-restrictions/.
9. Katayoun.
10. Katayoun.

Christians are the single most widely persecuted religious group in the world today. This is confirmed in studies by sources as diverse as the Vatican, Open Doors, the Pew Research Center, *Commentary*, *Newsweek*, and *The Economist*. According to one estimate, by the Catholic Bishops' Conferences of the European Community, seventy-five percent of acts of religious intolerance are directed against Christians.[11]

Similarly, Pope Francis has repeatedly spoken out against widespread persecutions, especially in the Middle East, where the continuing existence of historic Christian communities is being threatened among Armenians, Assyrians, Chaldeans, Maronites, Melkites, and Syriac Catholics. "Where is the conscience of the world?" he asks.[12] Regretfully – for reasons too complex to discuss here – various observers have noted that Western political leaders have often been reluctant to act or failed to act.[13]

Estimates of the numbers of Christians killed vary. Todd M. Johnson – from the Center for the Study of Global Christianity – using a broad definition of martyrdom, suggests that some one hundred thousand Christians were killed annually from 2000 to 2010.[14] But others are more conservative and speak of figures between seven and eight thousand.[15] Nevertheless, these figures do not tell us the gravity of the problem, especially in relation to the massive displacement of whole communities and their exile from ancestral lands where they have lived for centuries, if not millennia. For example, of some one and a half million Christians living in Iraq before 2003, less than a quarter of a million are left today.[16] Another example, from a very different context, is the displacement of minority Christian tribal groups by the government in Burma.

Persecution in the Modern Secular West

Even in Western countries, which are often considered bastions of freedom and tolerance, Christians experience nuanced forms of persecution. Legislation and societal shifts have resulted in restrictions on religious expression and

---

11. Marshall, Gilbert, and Shea, *Persecuted*, 4; Allen, *Global War*.
12. Marshall, Gilbert, and Shea, 4.
13. For example, see Marshall, Gilbert, and Shea, 292–300.
14. Johnson, "Christian Martyrs," http://www.gordonconwell.edu/resources/documents/csgc_Christian_martyrs.pdf.
15. Alexander, "New Christian Martyrs," http://www.bbc.com/news/magazine-24864587.
16. "Iraq," *Open Doors*. https://www.opendoorsuk.org/persecution/world-watch-list/iraq/.

practice, challenging the church to respond with wisdom and engagement, reminiscent of both the early church's dynamic response and the CIM's contextually sensitive approach during the Boxer Uprising.

A Living Example: Wang Ming Dao

People like Wang Ming Dao stand as emblematic figures of enduring faithfulness. Wang's unwavering stance and poignant ministry, despite severe persecution under Maoist China, reflects the deep-seated conviction of both the New Testament paradigm and CIM missionaries who placed commitment to Christ above societal favour.

Wright Doyle and Yading Li wrote a moving article on the life of Wang Ming Dao, a man "in trouble."[17] Wang, born in 1900 – the year of the Boxer Uprising – is widely recognized as one of the most influential and respected Chinese Christian leaders who worked to build the indigenous Chinese church. He became a pastor in Beijing. His church, the Christian Tabernacle, grew steadily and, by 1949, "had a membership of about 570, making it one of the largest evangelical churches in Beijing at that time."[18] "Wang took a firm stand against any form of political involvement. . . . Under the guidance of, and supported by, the Communist Party, the Three-Self Patriotic Movement (TSPM) was organized to direct the nationwide Christian church." However, Wang refused to join the TSPM.[19]

Doyle and Li tell how in September 1954, the authorities called an accusation meeting, which all churches in the city had to attend and where, "many people were incited to criticize Wang and make up ugly charges against him. . . . In the summer of 1955, on August 7, he preached his last sermon at the tabernacle, with "The Son of man is betrayed into the hands of sinners" (Matt 25:45 KJV) as his text."[20]

Wang and his wife were then arrested and imprisoned. Despite Wang's long years of imprisonment, "he never criticized communism as an ideology, as some have averred, and he never opposed the government or called for it to

---

17. *Biographical Dictionary of Chinese Christianity*. http://bdcconline.net/en/stories/wang-mingdao, accessed 7 October 2022.

18. *Biographical Dictionary of Chinese Christianity*. http://bdcconline.net/en/stories/wang-mingdao, accessed 7 October 2022.

19. *Biographical Dictionary of Chinese Christianity*, http://bdcconline.net/en/stories/wang-mingdao, accessed 7 October 2022.

20. *Biographical Dictionary of Chinese Christianity*, http://bdcconline.net/en/stories/wang-mingdao, accessed 7 October 2022.

be overthrown even though he was accused of being a 'counter-revolutionary.'"[21] While Wang took a clear stand on the separation of church and state, he strongly opposed evil or injustice in society, and he taught firmly the need for Chinese Christians to live holy lives.[22]

Wang's life shows us what it means to adopt an uncompromising stance in preaching the gospel of Jesus Christ even under persecution. The hallmarks of his preaching were repentance, holiness, purity, and truth.[23] He spoke strongly against a false gospel or a compromised gospel: "We must exert all our strength to oppose the false gospel . . . For the sake of the commission that God has entrusted to me, for the protection of the church, for the good of mankind, and for the glory of God."[24]

A Call to Action: Prayer, Information, Advocacy

Given the global scale of persecution, the church today needs accurate information, diligent prayer, and thoughtful advocacy. The plight of persecuted Christians should compel us to respond – as the New Testament believers and the early church did – by showing solidarity through intercession and active engagement in the face of the world's opposition.

If history and contemporary experiences teach us anything, it is that the faithful are called to a paradox of life where joy and grief intermingle. Persecution, though diverse in its expression – whether in government crackdowns, societal alienation, or overt violence – remains a persistent challenge to the global church. Yet it is met with an array of responses, from faithful endurance to active defence. The spectrum of actions, ranging from spiritual wisdom to legal recourse, exemplify the church's dynamic engagement with the world in the face of suffering. As Christians worldwide confront trials, it is the amalgamation of prayer, unity, and a deep-seated reliance on the promises and power of Christ that galvanizes believers to stand and persevere.

Jesus, in his discourse on the parousia (Matt 24), gave his disciples stern warnings about the end of the world's history. God's kingdom has come with the first coming of Jesus. It has been inaugurated, but it has not yet been

---

21. *Biographical Dictionary of Chinese Christianity*. http://bdcconline.net/en/stories/wang-mingdao, accessed 7 October 2022.

22. *Biographical Dictionary of Chinese Christianity*, http://bdcconline.net/en/stories/wang-mingdao, accessed 7 October 2022.

23. *Biographical Dictionary of Chinese Christianity*. http://bdcconline.net/en/stories/wang-mingdao, accessed 7 October 2022.

24. Wang, *Spiritual Food*, 127.

consummated. Disciples are citizens of two countries. They belong both to this age and to the age to come. They live at the intersection of the ages, hence the glory and the shame of the Christian life and the Christian church. As Michael Green points out, "Hence the ambiguity of Christian experience. We are not what we were, but equally, we are not yet what we shall be. The kingdom inaugurated at the first coming of Jesus will be consummated by his return at the end of history."[25]

Jesus warned his disciples about the sufferings to come. They will, as he had already predicted, be persecuted and hated (Matt 24:9, 21). The persecution will come from all nations, and the disciples will be handed over to be persecuted and put to death because of their association with Jesus (24:9). This persecution will take its toll, in that many will fall away and lawlessness will lead to the cooling off of love.[26] Yet the gospel of the kingdom will be preached to the whole world, and then the end will come.

As global Christians, we share the pain, scars, and bruises, and hear the cries of distress of our persecuted brothers and sisters. We may be living in a comfortable and safe environment, but we cannot pretend to be ignorant about their suffering.

First, there is a need for accurate and comprehensive information. Too often, exaggerated or false reports are available on the internet. What starts off as a rumour slowly becomes an accepted fact. Stories should be confirmed from multiple sources. As Miriam Adeney rightly points out, good stories or biographies need to give the proper context, including sin and failure as well as honour and dignity.[27] Stories of persecution should not be motivated by sensationalism but should drive us to prayer.

Second, accurate and comprehensive information should drive us to urgent prayer for persecuted Christians. All stories should begin, end, and be infused with prayer. Diane Knippers, the late president of the Institute on Religion and Democracy, said,

> pray not only for a broken heart, but a big heart. Your heart will be broken. You will weep. Sometimes you will be tempted to pull away. You will feel guilty because you have so much – materially and freedom. Pray for a heart big enough to obey the God of the nations. Big enough to embrace a child sold into slavery. Big

---

25. Green, *Matthew*, 250.
26. France, *Matthew*, 341–42.
27. Adeney, "How Saintly," 159–66.

enough to remember Chinese Church leaders. Big enough to play your part in the household of faith.[28]

Third, there needs to be thoughtful advocacy and prayerful action. No matter where we stand in our understanding of the question of separation of church and state, Jesus encouraged his disciples to be the light of the world (Matt 5:14). Light exposes darkness. Effective advocacy demands courage, creativity, and wise communication through various means, including social network, arts, music, drama, and film. In this way, God's people will be well informed and governments made aware of the situations.

Conclusion

The church, in its diverse history, has always confronted persecution with a blend of acknowledgement, wisdom, and courage. Drawing from the theological richness of the New Testament narratives, the historical resolve of missions like CIM, and the enduring legacy of leaders like Wang Ming Dao, Christians today are called to uphold a nuanced, informed, and action-oriented response to persecution. In the midst of persecution, the church is compelled to navigate the tension between the spiritual kingdom they embody and the empirical realities they confront – a tension residing at the very core of Christian existence. As the kingdom of God advances during hostility and adversity, the mandate for Christ's followers to embody the dichotomy of being "in the world but not of it" gains ever sharper focus.

The disciples in the early church are not depicted as being passive recipients of persecution. They endured to the end. They proclaimed Christ courageously and entrusted themselves to God. They were victors and not victims of persecution.

The CIM missionaries understood and accepted the cost of sacrifice. The CIM's decision not to accept compensation "even if offered" in the aftermath of the Boxer crisis was most unexpected. Yet out of the Boxer crisis, the church began to grow. As Hoste had indicated, the Chinese church ultimately came to the forefront, proving themselves equal to facing danger, bearing responsibilities, and growing into leadership.

Finally, there is no evidence that persecution is on the decline. Jesus warned his disciples about the sufferings to come (Matt 24). As global Christians, we must help to disseminate accurate and comprehensive information, encourage

---

28. McDonnell "Accurate Information," 482–85.

urgent prayer, and take courageous and thoughtful steps to help both Christians and the authorities be well informed so that they can take appropriate action.

Let me conclude by referring to the Celtic Christians' "tricolored theology of martyrdom." White martyrdom spoke of the costly pain of leaving behind family, clan, and tribe to spread the gospel of Christ. Green martyrdom spoke of self-denial and penitential acts that led to personal holiness. But red martyrdom spoke of persecution, bloodshed, or death.[29]

As Jesus told his disciples, "If anyone would come after me, let him deny himself and take up his cross and follow me. For whoever would save his life will lose it, but whoever loses his life for my sake will find it" (Matt 16:24–25 ESV).

We are to be beacons of hope and strength, affirming our identity in Christ even as we navigate the complexities of a world that often stands in opposition to the gospel. Faithfulness remains the indelible mark of the church – a faithfulness that reveals the depth of our allegiance to the suffering yet triumphant Christ and to his call to disciple-making regardless of cost or consequence.

Bibliography

Adeney, Miriam. "How Saintly Should Biographies Be?" In *Sorrow and Blood*, edited by William D. Taylor, Antonia Van Der Meer, and Reg Reimer, 159–66. Pasadena: William Carey, 2012.

Alexander, Ruth. "Are There Really 100,000 New Christian Martyrs Every Year?" *BBC*, 12 November 2013. https://www.bbc.com/news/magazine-24864587.

Allen, John L., Jr. *The Global War on Christians*. New York: Image, 2013.

Bennett-Jones, Owen. "The Christian Militia Fighting IS." *BBC Magazine*, 11 April 2016. http://www.bbc.com/news/magazine-35998716.

Bonhoeffer, Dietrich. *The Cost of Discipleship*. London: SCM, 2001.

Boyd-MacMillan, Ronald. *Faith That Endures: The Essential Guide to the Persecuted Church*. Ellel Grange: Sovereign World, 2006.

Broomhall, Marshall. *Martyred Missionaries of the China Inland Mission: Perils and Sufferings of Some Who Escaped*. London: Morgan & Scott, 1901.

Doyle, G. Wright, and Yading Li. *Biographical Dictionary of Chinese Christianity*. Translated by Laura Mason. Charlottesville: Global China Centre, 2005–24. http://bdcconline.net/en/stories/wang-mingdao.

France, Richard. *Matthew: An Introduction and Commentary*. TNTC 1. Leicester: Inter-Varsity Press, 1985.

---

29. See Taylor and Taylor, "Final Themes," 475–76.

Fung, Patrick. *Live to Be Forgotten: Dixon Edward Hoste, China Inland Mission, and the Indigenous Chinese Church in Early Twentieth-Century China*. Carlisle: Langham, 2024.

Green, Michael M. *The Message of Matthew: The Kingdom of Heaven*. Leicester: Inter-Varsity Press, 2000.

Hays, Richard B. *The Moral Vision of the New Testament: A Contemporary Introduction to New Testament Ethics*. Edinburgh: T&T Clark, 1996.

Hoste, D. E. "Possible Changes and Developments in the Native Churches arising out of the Present Crisis." *Chinese Recorder* (October 1900): 511.

Johnson, Todd M. "The Case for Higher Numbers of Christian Martyrs." Gordon-Conwell Seminary Resources. https://www.academia.edu/36470014/The_case_for_higher_numbers_of_Christian_martyrs.

Johnstone, Patrick. *The Future of the Global Church: History, Trends and Possibilities*. Colorado Springs: Biblica, 2011.

Kishi, Katayoun. "Key Findings on the Global Rise in Religious Restrictions." *Pew Research Center*, 21 June 2018. https://www.pewresearch.org/short-reads/2018/06/21/key-findings-on-the-global-rise-in-religious-restrictions/.

Lee, Chee-Chiew. *When Christians Face Persecution: Theological Perspectives from the New Testament*. London: Apollos, 2022.

Marshall, Paul, Lela Gilbert, and Nina Shea. *Persecuted: The Global Assault on Christians*. Nashville: Thomas Nelson, 2013.

McDonnell, Faith J. H. "Accurate Information, Urgent Intercession, Thoughtful Advocacy, and Courageous Action." In *Sorrow and Blood*, edited by William D. Taylor, Antonia Van Der Meer, and Reg Reimer, 482–85. Pasadena: William Carey, 2012.

Metaxas, Eric. *Bonhoeffer: Pastor, Martyr, Prophet, Spy*. Nashville: Thomas Nelson, 2010.

Moffett, Samuel H. *A History of Christianity in Asia. Vol. 1: Beginnings to 1500*. New York: Harper Collins, 1992.

Stark, Rodney. *The Rise of Christianity: How the Obscure, Marginal Jesus Movement Became the Dominant Religious Force in the Western World in a Few Centuries*. New York: HarperCollins, 1997.

Stott, John. *Issues Facing Christians Today*. 4th ed. rev. by Roy McCloughry. Grand Rapids: Zondervan, 2006.

Taylor, Yvonne, and William D. Taylor. "Final Themes: Lessons from Celtic Christianity." In *Sorrow and Blood*, edited by William D. Taylor, Antonia Van Der Meer, and Reg Reimer, 475–76. Pasadena: William Carey, 2012.

Wooden, Cindy. "Pope Francis: 'International Community Must Act to Stop Anti-Christian Persecution.'" *Catholic Herald*, 1 September 2015. https://catholicherald.co.uk/pope-francis-begs-international-community-to-act-to-stop-anti-christian-persecution/.

Section V

Kingdom Impact in Every Sphere of Society

20

Peacebuilding as Christian Mission

Gideon Para-Mallam

Introduction

Ethno-religious tensions, cross-border conflicts, wars and general insecurity are today the new normal on the global stage. The Russia-Ukraine war lingers on, and the Israeli-Hamas-Gaza war of 7 October 2023 rages on. In Africa, almost every country is currently grappling with conflicts of varying dimensions and proportions. The multi-faceted wars in DR Congo[1,] the Islamic inspired ideological wars of Boko Haram in Nigeria, Ansaru Deen in Mali, Burkina Faso and other countries in the Sahel (West Africa), continue unabated. Countries like Sudan[2] and Somali[3] are also currently grappling with conflicts of varying dimensions and proportions. In the continent of Asia, there is a civil War in Myanmar[4] and skirmishes between Afghanistan vs Pakistan.[5] Colombia in

---

1. The New Humanitarian, "How DR Congo's M23 conflict is impacting Goma." https://www.thenewhumanitarian.org/news-feature/2024/04/04/crowded-camps-and-local-aid-how-dr-congos-m23-conflict-impacting-goma.

2. Magdy, "Looting and Fighting Reported in a Central Sudan City as Paramilitary Group Attacks Military Troops." https://apnews.com/article/sudan-war-military-rsf-new-front-0652f8cdca14a17195ec3d593292a4c1.

3. IRC, "Crisis in Somalia." https://www.rescue.org/article/crisis-somalia-what-you-need-know-and-how-help.

4. Conflict Tracker, "Civil War in Myanmar." https://www.cfr.org/global-conflict-tracker/conflict/rohingya-crisis-myanmar.

5. Javed, "Pakistan Will Continue Attacks on Afghanistan." https://www.bbc.com/news/articles/c7289yvl84po.

South America is also experiencing violence.[6] Peace and development have taken a back seat while insecurity and chaos have taken a front row, threatening to reverse the economic growth opportunities of the 2000s especially in Africa. Globally, many people currently face untold hardships, hunger, sufferings, and other deprivations. Nations of the world are troubled and in dire straits – religiously, socially, and politically. For example, in Nigeria, Christian communities have come under sustained violent attacks for over a decade – food terrorism is manifesting in strange ways as farm crops and livestock are targeted and intentionally destroyed or what human beings should eat after harvesting their crops are destroyed by armed herders and eaten by their cows. The Sahel groans under the effects of climate change, religious extremism, and radicalization leading to intense ideological contestations with deadly consequences. All these social combustibles have combined to make peace elusive and Christian mission a casualty. In the midst of the present global chaos, carrying out missionary activities becomes almost suicidal.

The church's response to this global reality appears unsure and uncoordinated. Christians lack a clear perspective on how best to respond to all the conflicts, killings induced by insecurity and on-going wars around the world. Some bemoan the situation, others raise their hands in resignation, insisting that the events are a demonstration of eschatological realities and that there is nothing to be done. Others are agitated and would prefer to fight back: violence for violence as a deterrent. Others think a pacifist approach is needed. What then should we do about this precarious situation? Without doubt, the body of Christ worldwide needs clear direction in responding to conflictual contradictions. In such times, church and mission leaders need to take responsibility by being intentional in seeking to provide much-needed guidance to believers. To do so, Christian leaders need a clear understanding of the relationship between peacebuilding and Christian mission. This entails crafting a response that honours the integrity of Scripture and offers hope in situations of despair, hopelessness and extreme anger. As John Maxwell, a leadership expert, says, "A leader is one who knows the way, goes the way, and shows the way."[7]B

---

6. The New Humanitarian, "Deadly attacks intensify violence in southwest Colombia. https://www.thenewhumanitarian.org/news/2024/05/22/deadly-attacks-intensify-violence-southwest-colombia.

7. Kruse, "100 Best Quotes on Leadership." https://www.forbes.com/sites/kevinkruse/2012/10/16/quotes-on-leadership/.

Conceptual Framework

Conflicts creates emotional trauma and also destroys lives and properties, but peace saves lives and creates social harmony among human beings. Since we are all created in God's image, peace upholds human dignity. Peacemakers are called "sons and [daughters] of God" (Matt 5:9). Christian mission cannot flourish in the context of conflicts, insecurity and wars. Yet, Jesus commanded us to take the gospel to the ends of the earth (Matt 28:18–20 and Matt 24:14).

Peace

Peace is viewed as the absence of war or conflict. Pragmatically, peace goes beyond the mere absence of war. A country or community may experience the absence of war and yet not be peaceful. Ronald Reagan, former US President says, "Peace is not the absence of conflict, it is the ability to handle conflict by peaceful means."[8] Jean Guy Vaillancourt (1991), quoting Anatol Rapoport (1972), defines positive peace as "the unification of mankind in a cooperative enterprise on a large scale."[9] Anita Kemp (1985), also quoted in Vaillancourt (1991) views positive peace as "the creation of justice and development without structural violence."[10] The ancient Hebrew word for peace is "shalom," which demonstrates that the concept of positive peace is not a recent one. Timothy Keller suggests that "in the New Testament, *shalom* is revealed as the reconciliation of all things to God through the work of Christ . . . *Shalom* experienced is multidimensional, complete well-being: physical, psychological, social, and spiritual; it flows from all of one's relationship being put right with God, within oneself, and with others."[11] Therefore, peace is not a destination arrived at in a day. A contemporary musician Bono says: "Peace is the opposite of dreaming. It's built slowly and surely through brutal compromises and tiny victories that you don't even see. It's a messy business, bringing peace into the world."[12]

---

8. West, "Handling Conflict by Peaceful Means." https://www.usip.org/publications/2011/11/handling-conflict-peaceful-means.

9. Vaillancourt, "Peace: A Socialist's View." http://www.jstor.org/stable/23609922.

10. Vaillancourt, "Peace: A Socialist's View."

11. Keller, "Shalom," *NIV Biblical Theology Bible*.

12. Bono, "Bono on Paris." https://www.rollingstone.com/music/music-news/bono-on-paris-peace-is-a-messy-business-but-it-can-be-done-68606/.

Peacebuilding

> Peace building involves those activities which are designed to displace the felt need for destructive confrontation with an increased sense of supportive, mutual interdependence. Peace building is aimed at developing a sense of mutual hope and trust upon which peace can grow.[13]

Peacebuilding focuses on acknowledging and addressing injustices done to every human being, regardless of race, religion, who they are or where they come from. Just like building any structure, building peace is done brick by brick – with intentionality and hard labour – and it takes time. Peacekeeping is concerned merely with deterring confrontation between opposing parties, but peacebuilding is concerned with building bridges – it is about rebuilding trust when trust has broken down. You may wonder if world peace is ever going to be a reality. Should such doubts tempt us to give up in despair? Albert Camus, French novelist, essayist, and playwright once said, "Peace is the only battle worth waging."[14]

Christian Mission

The term "Christian mission" presupposes that an assignment has been given to Christians, as indeed it has. The assignment Christ gave his followers after his resurrection and before his ascension is generally called the "Great Commission." "Go and make disciples of all nations" (Matt 28:19). This missional assignment is given to all believers in Christ. Therefore, Christian mission is a call and mandate for believers to live Christlike lives in a way that draws people to Christ. This is also done alongside the proclamation of the gospel as good news to humankind. Just like Christ, the believer and church's mission should align with God's mission. This should be anchored to the task of reconciling God's humanity to him as revealed in Scripture.

God's mission is the realization of his ultimate peace: humanity's reconciliation to God and to one another. Christian mission is expressed through the Great Commission. The Great Commission should never be reduced to a task but seen as a process of reaching all of God's humanity for the transformation of relationships. Context is hugely important in understanding

---

13. Crossman, "Creative Justice in a Nuclear World." http://scholars.wlu.ca/consensus/vol11/iss1/2.

14. Oxford Essential Quotations (5 ed.). https://www.oxfordreference.com/display/10.1093/acref/9780191843730.001.0001/q-oro-ed5-00002544.

and shaping our mission theology. Our God is a missionary God. Ultimately, God's mission in Christ is the renewal of relationships in a world that is broken and lost to its creator. Christians are called to love God and love their neighbours – including their enemies – as themselves (Mark 12:30–31). The church is also called to a mission of peacemaking (Matt 5:9). We discover who God is in mission as we witness to, serve, and love others. The believers' mission is ultimately God's mission and this is rooted in Christian identity.

Connecting Peace Building and Christian Mission

Peacebuilding and Christian mission are not mutually exclusive. The Scriptures describe Christ as the "Prince of Peace" (Isa 9:6), which makes a compelling case for peacebuilding as Christian mission. If Jesus Christ is the "Prince of Peace," this suggests, therefore, that whoever follows Jesus should be an effective advocate for peace. What intersections are there between peacebuilding and Christian mission? Why should Christians care?

The answer lies, to a great extent, in what Jesus Christ did during his earthly ministry. Jesus advocated for peace and justice. He reached out to those on the margins of society – those who were experiencing the poisonous toxins of pain due to the social injustice meted out to them. The church likewise is called to reach such unreached people groups. When a segment of people is neglected and oppressed, they lose faith in society. This results in the violence and lack of peace we see in our communities. Peacebuilding as Christian mission is therefore anchored on truth, mercy, justice, and forgiveness. These are virtues associated with Christlikeness, the qualities that we should embrace, incarnate, and model on a daily basis. In the words of Jean Vanier, "Peace is the fruit of love, a love that is also justice."[15]

Conversations around the role of the church in peacebuilding easily split Christians into separate camps. While some Christians advocate for warfare, using just war theories, others are pacifists, and do not see the need for warfare. Some see peacebuilding as an activity that should be separated from Christian mission as it is perceived sometimes as a distraction to the "real deal" which to them is direct evangelism and mission through preaching. Some Christians still see a dichotomy between the sacred and the secular when in actual fact there should be none. Indeed, such dichotomized thinking and action should be rejected because a critical study of Scripture reveals that

---

15. Social Justice Resource Center, "Peace Quotes." https://socialjusticeresourcecenter.org/quotes/peace/.

peacebuilding is also Christian mission. Christians should care deeply about the conflicts and wars in the world and see how they too can be part of the peacebuilding process as this is an integral part of God's mission. Peacemaking is a core component of living out the power of the gospel in demonstrative love, forgiveness and proactiveness in making *the peace* in a world that is troubled and in need of the power of the Holy Spirit who transforms conflict situations. Believers are ministers and peace ambassadors of reconciliation in their peacemaking mission of mending broken relationships and caring for the vulnerable. "A socially disengaged [spirituality] or Christianity is inconceivable and inexcusable."[16] We ought to practise peacebuilding because it is rooted in the self-giving nature of God, who in Christ, revealed his willingness to become vulnerable before his enemies and reconcile the world to himself. In the death of Christ, the cross became a symbol for the church's kerygmatic [compassion] peacemaking.[17]

Christians are God's ambassadors on earth, charged with spreading a kingdom message of righteousness, justice, and peace. Redemption – as instituted by God from Genesis to Revelation – is rooted in an unrelenting peacebuilding mission. God reached out to his estranged creation. We, then, who are God's children, have been called to a ministry of reconciliation (2 Cor 5:18, 20). God is interested in redeeming the whole world. "Love your neighbour as yourself" (Mark 12:31). This biblical concept of neighbour is non-restrictive. Muslims, Hindus, Buddhists, Confucianists, African Traditional Religionists (ATRs), and Atheists are all, in a redemptive sense, our neighbours, deserving of reconciliation and peace with God. Our Christian witness shines through when we promote peaceful coexistence between different faiths in our communities. In a place like Nigeria, where ethno-religious tensions are a daily occurrence, it is imperative for Christians to show the love of Christ in practical ways in such a contextual reality. As an individual, this is something I have tried to imbibe and model as a Christian leader, and there is evidence that God's love makes a difference. About a decade ago, when ethno-religious tensions broke out in a cascade of violence, with fireball flashes all over the city of Jos for days, lives were lost and properties destroyed. It did not stop there. Balkanized living set in almost immediately because Christians felt unsafe with their Muslim neighbours and vice versa. This resulted in a mass

---

16. Gushee, "Spiritual Formation," in *Life in the Spirit: Spiritual Formation in Theological Perspective*, 213.

17. Martin Accad, *Kerygmatic Peacebuilding as the Practice of Biblical Salam*. https://fullerstudio.fuller.edu/kerygmatic-peacebuilding-as-the-practice-of-biblical-salam/.

movement of people during the attacks and the killings. Christians sold their homes and moved to Christian-dominated areas of the city, and Muslims sold their homes in Christian-dominated areas and did exactly the same. In some cases, Muslims in Christian-dominated areas exchanged their homes with Christians in Muslim-dominated areas and vice versa. Worse still, silent killings commenced – if Christians strayed into a Muslim-dominated area, they were killed, and the same thing happened to Muslims who entered Christian-dominated areas. How can Christians engage in evangelism and engage in missions activities in balkanized settlements?

During this time, the Lord led me to initiate peace gatherings between Muslim and Christian leaders in Mai-Adiko, a suburb of Rayfield, Jos, Plateau State, Nigeria. This suburb has a minority Muslim community. After meeting with the Muslim leaders, including their imam, I was able to secure their consent to meet Christian leaders with a view to promoting peaceful coexistence. These Muslim leaders said in Hausa "mun baka amana" – *we have given you our trust*. The Christian leaders, on their part, were very suspicious of the peace initiative I was proposing but reluctantly agreed to meet. Eventually, a joint meeting, at which four hundred people turned up, was held. On that day, both the Christian and Muslim leaders made a commitment to stay together and keep the peace. An elderly pastor stepped forward and held the hand of the imam, who was also an elderly man. Raising the imam's hand, he declared, "Since my coming here on posting I have never cared to make contact with you or visited your home but from today, I have decided in my heart that I will not only visit your home but I will like to eat a meal." That was how the tension in Mai-Adiko was eased. From that time, to date, this community has an enduring testimony of Christians and Muslims living peacefully side by side. This is a clear testimony of how peacebuilding supports Christian mission.

The message of redemption is comprehensive; peacebuilding is part of God's redemptive mission for humankind. Global peace continues to be threatened on a daily basis. The church – whether local or global – does not live on an island and must engage with the realities of our time. The global mission context right now is hostile and not church-friendly. Peacebuilding as Christian mission holds a strategic key to unlocking some locked doors.

Biblical Basis for Peacebuilding

In the previous sections, I identified Bible verses that suggest that peacebuilding has biblical foundations. In this section, I highlight some passages that support the idea of peacebuilding as Christian mission:

Jesus as the "Prince of Peace." Isaiah 9:6 declares that Jesus is the "Prince of Peace." Christians are heirs with Christ, and they also share in his nature.

1. ***Jesus as our Peace:*** Micah 5:2–5 and Ephesians 2:13–14. Christ is not only our source of peace, but it is he who keeps the peace. The secret of living without conflicts in personal and community life is rooted in Christ. Christ mends and heals hostile relationships.

2. ***Jesus's instruction:*** In Matthew 5:9, Jesus enjoined believers to be peacemakers; in Matthew 5:24, he commanded them to be reconcilers; in Luke 17:3–4, he called believers to forgive those who sin against them; and in Matthew 5:44, Jesus called them to love their enemies. It is imperative to note that in Matthew 5:9, Jesus spoke about peacemaking. To "make" means that peace does not happen by chance but is an intentional act of kingdom service. Peacemaking is not passive – it requires intentional peacebuilding proactiveness. Christians are to take the initiative in building and maintaining the peace.

3. ***Seeking and pursuing peace:*** Psalm 34:12–14 instructs us to seek and pursue peace; Proverbs 12:20 challenges us to promote peace; Galatians 5:22–23 caps it by classifying peace as a fruit of the Holy Spirit; and, finally, James 3:17–18 says that to be peace-loving is synonymous with possessing the wisdom that comes from above. "Jesus came to establish peace; his message explained peace; his death purchased peace; and his resurrected presence enables peace."[18] Believers, following in the footsteps of Christ, are called to be peacebuilders and conflict transformers. The work of peacebuilding is sometimes difficult, messy, and emotionally draining. But it is worth it. Peacebuilding work provides unbelievers with a glimpse of what life in Christ is like, and this draws them to him. I have personally experienced this in my peacebuilding journey as a missionary and peace practitioner.

Promoting Peacebuilding in Ministries

Christians are called to be the salt and light of the world (Matt 5:13–14). Light guides people, salt preserves food and makes meals tastier. There are

---

18. Ezell, "Being a Peacemaker," https://www.lifeway.com/en/articles/sermon-blessed-peacemakers-sons-god-matthew-5.

historical examples of Christian leaders championing peace and justice causes. In Northern Ireland, the church played a major role in bringing an end to conflicts that had lasted for nearly thirty years: "Throughout the troubles, the leaders of the churches organized joint workshops and marches, denounced violence, and advised prominent politicians behind the scenes."[19] Their efforts culminated in the signing of the *Good Friday Agreement* on Good Friday, April 1998. The church worked to bring peace to Northern Ireland. The same can be said about the struggle to promote peace in Sudan in 2005 and independence for South Sudan in July 2011. Local and global churches also played leading roles that went beyond the traditional roles of praying and involved active engagement until peace and independence were restored in South Africa.

Believers are called to champion the causes of peace on earth. Jeremiah 29:7 encourages Christians to seek the peace and prosperity of the land they find themselves in because if that land prospers, so would they. What does this mean to church and mission leaders? The church can achieve such prosperity by promoting independent initiatives for peace. This does not in any way undermine the church's calling to lead men and women to Christ. We can promote peace initiatives in our ministries in any of the following ways:

- Constantly awaken the consciences of our followers to the importance of peaceful living.
- Support people and organizations that work for peace.
- Raise our voices, without fear, against injustice.
- Promote Christ as the Prince of Peace, who was a social crusader for justice.
- Work with government and civil society organizations to promote peace and denounce the injustices that create the conditions for violence in the first place.
- Engage in advocacy for the less privileged and those on the margins of society without religious bias or identity profiling.
- Promote peacebuilding as Christian mission through theological education and reflection in our seminaries and Christian schools by designing a curriculum that promotes peacebuilding as Christian mission.

---

19. Sandal, "Religious Leaders and the Northern Ireland Peace Process." https://berkleycenter.georgetown.edu/responses/religious-leaders-and-the-northern-ireland-peace-process.

Church and mission leaders should show by example what it means to love not just our neighbour but also our enemy. As Dietrich Bonhoeffer reminds us, Christian love draws no distinction between one enemy and another, except that the more bitter our enemy's hatred, the greater his need of love. Be his enmity political or religious, he has nothing to expect from a follower of Jesus but unqualified love. In such love there is not inner discord between the private person and official capacity. In both we are disciples of Christ, or we are not Christians at all.[20]

To live up to this standard, Christians must learn to love and practise forgiveness towards those opposed to the faith. When we are able to let go of the hurt caused by our offenders, we have peace in our hearts and, with this peace, are able to extend a hand of love and peace to people around us. The Rwandan author Célestin Musekura – in the book *Forgiving as We've Been Forgiven: Community Practices for Making Peace*, co-authored with Greg Jones – narrates how God spoke to him, telling him to forgive the killers who had killed his father and family members.[21] Forgiveness has a healing power; as Célestin healed, he was inspired to work for forgiveness and reconciliation across Africa. Church and mission leaders can learn from the Catholic Church's Catholic Relief Services (CRS). The CRS has engaged leaders – bishops and priests – in conflict zones around the world. These leaders play key roles in peacebuilding, including facilitating peace agreements and providing safe spaces for conversations between contending parties. They have also reached rebel groups and worked with the victims of war.

Youth Mentoring

Jesus's call to his followers to be peacemakers has already been emphasized. Mentoring youth is one impactful way in which the church can advance Christ's mission of peace and reconciliation. By walking alongside young people, listening to their perspectives, and nurturing their gifts, mentors can equip the next generation to become ambitious and catalytic peacebuilders. Mentors help youth to develop a sense of morality, resilience, empathy, and skills to non-violently transform conflicts in their relationships and communities. With patient investment, the message of peace can be planted in the hearts and minds of young people. Our broken world cries for healing. Therefore, the church must actively work to raise impassioned peacemakers in Christ-

---

20. Bonhoeffer, *Cost of Discipleship*, 164.
21. Jones and Musekura, *Forgiving as We've Been Forgiven*, 12.

followers who are devoted to the restorative ways of Christ. Through youth mentoring, we can advance Christ's mission across generations, training and inspiring young peacebuilders to help write a new restorative story for our wounded world.

Conclusion

Peacebuilding should be an integral part of Christian mission in the twenty-first century. As conflicts continue to rage and cascade around the world, church and mission organizations must promote peace, justice, and reconciliation issues as part of living out the gospel as good news. Doing so will serve as a continuation of the church's historic concern for the marginalized and oppressed, as well as a greater focus on peacebuilding as a key component of Christian mission. How can we claim to be children of God if we do not work for peace? Christians are supposed to be transformational agents of peace in the world. Living harmoniously with our fellow human beings inspires respect not only for the sanctity of life but also for our shared humanity, regardless of religious or ethnic identities. No matter how long we pray for peace, we will not have peace unless we work to make peace happen, and this has great rewards. Peacebuilding as Christian mission is about saving lives in this world for eternity. "The will of God, to which the law gives expression, is that men [and women] should defeat their enemies by loving them."[22]

Bibliography

Accad, Martin. *Kerygmatic Peacebuilding as the Practice of Biblical Salam.* https://fullerstudio.fuller.edu/kerygmatic-peacebuilding-as-the-practice-of-biblical-salam/.

Berger, Brett A. "Theology Thursday: Blessed Are the Peacemakers." Grand Canyon University, 11 March 2021. https://www.gcu.edu/blog/theology-ministry/theology-thursday-blessed-are-peacemakers.

Bonhoeffer, Dietrich. *The Cost of Discipleship.* London: SCM, 2015.

Bourne, Richard. *Seek the Peace of the City: Christian Political Criticism as Public, Realist, and Transformative.* Eugene: Cascade Books, 2009.

Center for Preventive Action, "Civil War in Myanmar," *Global Conflict Tracker*, 23 March 2024. https://www.cfr.org/global-conflict-tracker/conflict/rohingya-crisis-myanmar.

---

22. Bonhoeffer, *Cost of Discipleship*, 163.

Crossman, Richard C. "Creative Justice in a Nuclear World." *Consensus* 11, no. 1 (1985). http://scholars.wlu.ca/consensus/vol11/iss1/2.

Escobar, Samuel. *A Time for Mission: The Challenge for Global Christianity*. Leicester: Inter-Varsity Press, 2003.

Ezell, Rick. "Sermon: Being a Peacemaker – Matthew 5." *Lifeway*, 1 January 2014. https://www.lifeway.com/en/articles/sermon-blessed-peacemakers-sons-god-matthew-5.

Gushee, David. "Spiritual Formation and the Sanctity of Life." In *Life in the Spirit: Spiritual Formation in Theological Perspective*, edited by Jeffery P. Greenman and George Kalantzis, 213–26. Leicester: Inter-Varsity Press, 2010.

International Rescue Committee. "Crisis in Somalia: What You Need to Know and How to Help," The IRC, 29 April 2024. https://www.rescue.org/article/crisis-somalia-what-you-need-know-and-how-help.

Javed, Farhat. "Pakistan Will Continue Attacks on Afghanistan – Minister," 2 July 2024. https://www.bbc.com/news/articles/c7289yvl84po.

Jones, L. Gregory, and Célestin Musekura. *Forgiving as We've Been Forgiven: Community Practices for Making Peace*. Downers Grove: InterVarsity Press, 2010.

Katongole, Emmanuel, and Chris Rice. *Reconciling All Things: A Christian Vision for Justice, Peace and Healing*. Downers Grove: InterVarsity Press, 2008.

Keller, Timothy. *Generous Justice: How God's Grace Makes Us Just*. London: Penguin Books, 2012.

Kelly, Michael. "The Good Friday Agreement Brought Peace in Northern Ireland, but Empty Pews Followed." *Our Sunday Visitor*, 5 April 2023. https://www.oursundayvisitor.com/the-good-friday-agreement-brought-peace-in-northern-ireland-but-empty-pews-followed/.

Magdy, Samy. "Looting and Fighting Reported in a Central Sudan City as Paramilitary Group Attacks Military Troops | AP News." *AP News*, 30 June 2024. https://apnews.com/article/sudan-war-military-rsf-new-front-0652f8cdca14a17195ec3d593292a4c1.

"The Meaning of Shalom in the Bible." *The NIV Bible*. Accessed on 11 May 2023. https://www.thenivbible.com/blog/meaning-shalom-bible/.

The New Humanitarian. "Deadly attacks intensify violence in southwest Colombia", 22 May 2024. https://www.thenewhumanitarian.org/news/2024/05/22/deadly-attacks-intensify-violence-southwest-colombia.

———. "Crowded camps and local aid: How DR Congo's M23 conflict is impacting Goma," 4 April 2024. https://www.thenewhumanitarian.org/news-feature/2024/04/04/crowded-camps-and-local-aid-how-dr-congos-m23-conflict-impacting-goma.

Peace Catalyst International. "FAQ 3: Why Should We Bother with Peacemaking?" Peace Catalyst International. https://www.peacecatalyst.org/blog/2015/9/2/faq-3-why-should-we-bother-with-peacemaking?rq=faq.

Penaskovic, Richard, and Mustafa Şahin, eds. *Peacebuilding in a Fractious World: On Hoping against All Hope*. Eugene: Pickwick, 2017.

Ratcliffe, Susan. *Oxford Essential Book of Quotations*. 5th ed. Oxford University Press. 2017. https://www.oxfordreference.com/display/10.1093/acref/9780191843730.001.0001/q-oro-ed5-00002544.

Roberts, Mark D. "Christ Is Our Peace." *The High Calling*. https://www.theologyofwork.org/the-high-calling/daily-reflection/christ-our-peace.

Sandal, Nukhet. "Religious Leaders and the Northern Ireland Peace Process," 2018. https://berkleycenter.georgetown.edu/responses/religious-leaders-and-the-northern-ireland-peace-process.

Social Justice Resource Center. "Peace Quotes." https://socialjusticeresourcecenter.org/quotes/peace/.

Vaillancourt, Jean-Guy. "Peace: A Sociologist's View." *Peace Research* 23, no. 2/3 (1991): 65–74. http://www.jstor.org/stable/23609922.

West, Robinson. "Handling Conflict by Peaceful Means." 2011. https://www.usip.org/publications/2011/11/handling-conflict-peaceful-means.

Yoder, Perry. *Shalom: The Bible's Word for Salvation, Justice, and Peace*. Eugene: Wipf & Stock, 2017.

21

Leading with Love: Jesus's Incarnational Ministry

Eraston Kighoma and C. J. Davison

The Word Became Flesh

> The Word became flesh and made his dwelling among us. We have seen his glory, the glory of the one and only Son, who came from the Father, full of grace and truth. (John 1:14)

When God took on human flesh and came to earth, the world changed forever through one of the greatest acts of leadership the world has ever seen. Jesus's mission revealed God's heart to step into a situation himself. Jesus's birth and life demonstrated a radical and incarnational approach to ministry, service, and leadership that has much to teach us in our complex and changing world.

With the birth of Christ, God fulfilled his promise to send a son who would identify as "Immanuel," God with us (Isa 7:14). The incarnation proved how far God was willing to go to make salvation possible. It is hard to imagine the magnitude of God becoming a man, leaving the greater reality of heaven and stepping into our limited world. What we do know is that God's loving agenda is to move towards people.

Scripture says that the Father sent the Son out of love for the world (John 3:16). That same love compelled the Creator to surrender the comforts of heaven to dwell in a broken world. And when God came, he did not come to judge in anger but to save (John 12:47), humbling himself even to death on a cross (Phil 2:8) for the sake of rebellious humanity.

It is important to note that the Word came in cooperation with the Father. He did not come alone on his own initiative to please the Father but in partnership with the Father. Since Christ was involved in creation, he understood the context and situation perfectly. If anyone could have done it alone, it was Christ, yet he did not separate himself from the Father. Since he did not leave the fellowship of heaven, he never lost connection with his identity and purpose. And it was precisely this intimate relationship with the Father that allowed Jesus to bear the great burden of incarnational leadership.

Jesus came with grace and truth (John 1:14), which are not two arbitrary traits. Grace and truth, which uniquely reveal the glory and nature of the Word made flesh, were pillars of Christ's model incarnational ministry. Grace and truth operate like guardrails that keep ministry both missional and merciful, effective and relatable, purposeful and personal. God could have come in any fashion, but humanity needed grace and truth. We must not pursue one without the other. They are the two arms of a loving parent wanting to mature their children, which is exactly what God wants for us.

Truth requires walking and talking in accordance with reality. Sin had greatly distorted the world's view of reality, and rebellion had separated humankind from a proper understanding of God's design and intent. Jesus had to confront the world with truth because transformation and a better future cannot happen without dealing with offence and wrongdoing. Our reality before salvation was death, and that is why a foundational part of Jesus's message was "Repent!"

Grace was also needed. Truth alone could not restore broken human hearts that had rebelled in distrust. Undeserved favour softens hard hearts and offers gifts instead of punishment. Humanity had spent so much time separated from God that it scarcely knew God's tender and generous nature. God knew that his love and forgiveness would draw people – who were slaves to sin and hence naturally distrustful – to repentance (Rom 2:4).

Incarnational Leadership

Christian leaders today should lead in the same way that Jesus did. If Christ was willing to come from heaven to earth, should we not be willing and able to move from our comfortable context into the missional context that God sends us?

The heart of God compels us to move intentionally towards those in need so that we may serve them. This requires contextualization, and each decision we make must balance grace and truth. There needs to be conviction of truth and values must be maintained, but there must also be a willingness to listen, understand, and have mercy to win hearts towards God.

Incarnational leadership shapes people through grace and truth. Christ showed that a grace and truth approach means putting people first. Like Christ, leaders will be remembered for their impact on people, not their positions and status, as they bear fruit in the most difficult situations and win over the hardest hearts.

Incarnational leaders do not enter into situations so that people can remain as they are. Therefore, part of a leader's calling is to cast God's vision for a better future – that is, God dwelling with humankind in his kingdom. It is this very kingdom vision that motivated God to step into our world and lead us out of darkness and forward through hope and faith.

Godly leaders live out the vision they proclaim. They put into practice the ideals of God's future in the here and now. That is why merely sharing information is not enough. Screaming and shouting a message from a mountaintop will not produce life change. Life change happens when incarnational leaders actually enter into the situation of those whom they serve so that people can taste and feel what God has done for them.

Take Moses, for example. He did not send letters to Egypt. He went back to Egypt to lead the people out of Egypt. Moses did not simply cast a vision of freedom for the Israelites but returned to Egypt as a free man – neither slave nor royalty. Moses lived out the values of the future reality God wanted for Israel through humble, sacrificial, and incarnational leadership. He demonstrated the power of God through truth and miracles.

Jesus asked us to do the same through our loving engagement with the world. He said, "Everyone will know that you are my disciples, if you love one another" (John 13:35). Not only that, Jesus defined what great love looks like: "Greater love has no one than this: to lay down one's life for one's friends" (John 15:13). Jesus wanted his disciples to be known for their sacrificial actions for the sake of others, especially those around them, with whom they are in close relationships.

Spending time with the hurting, the poor, and the vulnerable was part of Christ's leadership strategy. He said that people will be divided according to their actions towards Christ's brothers and sisters who are hungry, thirsty, strangers, without clothes, sick, or imprisoned (Matt 25:31–46). These categories present us with leadership opportunities to pursue, as we love and serve those in need. In doing so, we demonstrate, in the here and now, the vision of the kingdom that we proclaim.

This kind of leadership and ministry changes lives because it puts reconciliation with God at the centre, with grace and truth as our tools. Leaders do not need to build grand structures and organizations to begin to have an eternal impact. Drawing people to God simply requires intentional influence that moves towards people in love. We see this simple and profound leadership demonstrated by Christ's dealings with the Samaritan woman at the well (John 4). In this encounter, we find four key aspects of incarnational ministry to L.E.A.D. like Jesus: Love, Engagement, Affirmation, and Direction.

Love

The story of Jesus and the woman at the well (John 4) teaches several key leadership lessons. The primary principle is that leadership begins with love. Despite the stigma attached to Samaria, Jesus intentionally travelled through this village and intentionally began a conversation with this outcast woman, moving the conversation towards a redemptive ending. That kind of love is risky, yet Jesus crossed barriers of gender and culture to talk with the Samaritan woman. Leadership today requires leaders to cross boundaries and barriers, whether these are geographic, political, or ethnic. The more a leader moves across boundaries and makes sacrifices, the more love is demonstrated to those who are pursued, opening doors to receive the message they bring.

Engagement

Coming to people where they are at is the starting point for incarnational leadership, but it does not complete God's work. Jesus engaged the Samaritan woman in an intentional dialogue and masterfully moved the conversation towards trust in God. He began the dialogue by connecting with what was in her hands and then moved the conversation to what was on her heart – living water. Jesus showed that he was willing to associate with the woman despite her past. Leaders today must engage with people by living and speaking with those we hope to serve. This requires interaction at a personal level and listening at a heart level to understand their needs and build trust for when it is time to share God's truth.

Affirmation

Actions speak, but words clarify. Leaders need to speak God's truth. After listening to people's needs and discerning the gaps, truth needs to be administered like mortar to a broken wall. Jesus taught the Samaritan woman about living water, leading her to a deeper spiritual truth. He spoke prophetically into her life and revealed her past and her adulterous situation.

By doing so, he lovingly built credibility that he was a prophet who knew what he was talking about. But Jesus also spoke truth about the nature of God's heart, saying that "true worshippers will worship the Father in the Spirit and in truth, for they are the kind of worshippers the Father seeks" (John 4:23). This was not an irrelevant fact but something crucial for this woman, as an outcast and as a Samaritan – since Samaritans were considered outcasts by the Jews – to understand. You could say that she was an outcast of outcasts. This truth of "in the Spirit and in truth" touched a hard place in her heart and softened her towards God. This prepared the woman to receive the truth about the identity of Christ as the Messiah.

Direction

Christlike leaders move people from truth to trust in God. This requires leaders to direct the lost to God through repentance, reconciliation, and a right relationship with God. It is the love, listening, and truth that prepare the way to know the God who truly changes hearts. Jesus rebuked the Pharisees for knowing the Scriptures but failing to come to him, about whom the Scriptures testified (John 5:39). Providing people with physical food and spiritual truth is beneficial in this life, but "what will it profit a man if he gains the whole world and forfeits his soul?" (Matt 16:26 ESV). If we follow Jesus's pattern, we will earn the right to direct people to salvation in Christ and the redemption of their soul. Jesus directed the Samaritan woman to faith in him. He said, "I who speak to you am he" (John 4:26 ESV). What greater aim for our leadership than to bring salvation to the lost?

Transformational Impact

Incarnational leadership, when filled with grace and truth, results in transformation. Notice how the Samaritan woman left behind her water jar – even though she had come for water – and went back to the villagers she had been afraid of interacting with. Having encountered Jesus, she was transformed by living water, new hope, and evangelistic courage.

The Samaritan woman copied Jesus's pattern. She became an incarnational leader who loved the lost in her village. She surrendered her reputation and went to her village to engage her peers and affirm the truth of the Messiah, directing people to find out for themselves. Our story is similar to that of the Samaritan woman – we were lost in the world until we met Christ.

The story of incarnational leadership continued with the early church. One of the "incarnational challenges" was that the believing Jews were not fellowshipping with the Gentiles. In Acts 10, God stepped into the situation and brought Peter and Cornelius to the same place to witness the outpouring of the Holy Spirit on the Gentiles. Although the Holy Spirit could have done this alone, he chose to orchestrate events so that both sides met in a dramatic encounter. This required Peter to go against tradition and stereotypes. But once the Holy Spirit fell on those in Cornelius's household, the early church better understood God's missional heart to reach the Gentiles; not long after, Paul and Barnabas were sent out, changing the nature of missions forever.

We have the same calling to go into the world and be heralds of Christ's good news. For example, the CIMR – a ministry in the Democratic Republic of Congo (DRC) – is living out incarnational leadership and seeing incredible fruit. The CIMR works in the war zones of the DRC to extend the love of God to all, including the rebel forces who exercise violence against the people. Years ago, Adam was being trained in ministry and decided to go back to his hometown to share the gospel. As he was preaching at a church, rebel forces came in, kidnapped him, and took him into the jungle. Along the way, Adam volunteered to nurse a rebel soldier who had been shot.

When the hostages arrived at the rebel base, Adam led them to thank God for their safety and pray for forgiveness for their captors. When Adam was brought before the commander, he witnessed the murder of innocent hostages. In boldness and desperation, expecting to die, Adam shared the gospel with the commander and called the commander to repent of his sin. The rebel captain decided to test Adam. More hostages were brought, and the commander gave Adam the choice to die or watch the hostages be killed. Adam bravely asked to be the one killed to save the other hostages. The watching rebels were moved and declared, "We have seen the face of Jesus."

The rebels released the hostages, and the commander took Adam to share the gospel with nine other rebel camps. The commander and sixty-three others were saved. Six months later, the commander and ten of his men decided to leave their lives of war and surrender their guns. Subsequently, the entire rebel force was dismantled after the commander turned himself over to UN forces. Adam is still witnessing to rebels today.

The reason incarnational leadership has the ability to transform is because it engages people holistically. When leaders like Adam step into situations with grace and truth, there is a tendency to care for people spiritually and physically through God's love that compels us to care in both deed and truth

(1 John 3:17–18). This builds trust and credibility for the precious message that we bring.

Trust is essential to transformation because it is foundational to the gospel. Though the world may have an abundance of information, people are confused by the competing narratives. Incarnational leaders break through this confusion and build trust by listening, engaging, and caring for people as humans created in God's image – not as projects or consumers – sharing God's truth, and offering forgiveness. We see this same desire in the apostle Paul, who cared so much for the Thessalonian church that he brought them more than just the gospel and shared his very self (1 Thess 2:8). This tender approach builds trust and transformation in a confused and sceptical world. Grace becomes the "knock" on the door that causes people to open their hearts, and when that door is opened, truth can be spoken in love.

Holistic Leadership Development

If we want a new generation of incarnational leaders, this will require a shift in thinking, organizing, and funding. Continuing along an old path will not result in new incarnational leaders. Raising up incarnational leaders requires holistic leadership development. Classrooms alone will not equip leaders to live out the gospel and transform lives. Programmes and ministries should consider balancing informational teaching and practical training for head, heart, and hands.

When travel and gathering was prohibited during COVID-19, some ministries began to think of new ways to serve. Ministries like Leadership International used their training centres as food distribution points. They built service into their leadership training programme, and they are now funding projects that allow students to put leadership into action to show and share the gospel. One example is a class in the Himalayas that decided to buy school supplies in order to reach remote villages with the gospel. Another example is two students in the DRC who, moved by the training they received about God's compassion, decided to use their own funds to start a prison ministry.

In the same way that truth needs training, service needs practice. Remember, Jesus came full of grace and truth. He equipped his disciples through teaching the truth and living out grace in loving service. He commanded us to do the same in the Great Commission and the Great Commandment – and this requires knowledge and action. Jesus's teachings must be obeyed (Matt 28:20), and loving God requires heart, soul, *mind* and strength (Mark 12:30).

These mutually reinforcing commands are inseparable from one another. Christians must teach believers to obey, and obedience requires teaching. This has important implications, not just for leadership development but in our leadership of ministries.

Will we lead with love like Jesus? The world is certainly watching church leaders, and Jesus said that leaders are validated by the fruit that they bear (Matt 7:16). Remember that our primary fruit is love (John 13:35; Gal 5:22). So, for leaders who want to impact the world with the gospel of Christ, this is a call to examine Christ's path of incarnational leadership and demonstrate God's abundant love. The question is, are you willing to follow in Jesus's steps by leading with love?

22

Developing Leaders for Every Sphere

Francis Tsui

Writing over half a century ago, missiologist Hendrick Kraemer said, "We stand at the definite end of a specific period or era of mission, and the clearer we see this and accept this with all our heart, the better." We are called to a "pioneer task which will be more demanding and less romantic than the heroic deeds of the past missionary era."[1] This attitude and perspective seem applicable today as we navigate deeper into the new millennium.

Today's globalized world is no longer the unipolar world of the previous centuries that was dominated by the Christian-West. Western theology and missiological concepts are struggling for relevance in a world that has become increasingly alienated from a Western world view and ecclesiastic order. This is about how we can continue to fulfil *missio Dei* in a transforming global context.

In the old Christendom, professional clergy were part of the institutional spiritual order, missionaries were in "full-time" vocational ministry, and then there was the laity. There was a clear clergy-lay or spiritual-secular divide. This understanding saw laity as those who are not trained, qualified, or experienced in ministry. The clergy and those in full-time vocational ministries were considered the "professionals," those "called" to the ministries. The laity were the flock to be shepherded.

This sacred-secular divide has been a key expression of church life for centuries. The secular is always less desirable than the sacred, especially if the secular is associated with mundane work or business. Augustine is reported

---

1. Kraemer, *Uit de nalatenschap*, 70.

to have said, "Business is in itself evil."[2] Over many centuries of philosophical and theological developments, it seems that the institutional ecclesiastic and professionalized clerical order has further entrenched the conviction of a spiritual-secular divide.

The Call of *Missio Dei* in the New Millennium

Tim Keller's biblical teaching on the theology of work offers an alternative to the Augustinian view. More important, it has called for a recommitment of every believer to not only "live out the gospel in all spheres of culture" but also to "seek to draw others into a redeeming and renewing faith."[3] Keller does not trivialize the ordained ministry; instead, he encourages "ordinary" Christians to be extraordinary in their workplaces and in their culture.

While the Christendom paradigm customarily used the word "calling" to refer to those who sacrificially responded to the call to ordained ministry or vocational mission work, Keller suggests that "our daily work can be a calling . . . (and) reconceived as God's assignment to serve others."[4] Keller asserts that "the purpose of work is to create a culture that honors God and enables people to thrive."[5] Believers not only need to unshackle themselves from the sacred-secular divide and understand their identity as lying beyond this divide, they should also assume a distinct role in their own sphere in their contemporaneous cultural setting.

This is indeed a missional "calling" for Christ followers to mend the perceived cultural chasm between church and contemporary culture. Most churchgoers are struggling to bridge the gap at work or in their social lives. Many know that their friends find church incomprehensible, irrelevant, and archaic. It is a reality in the "Christian" West that unitary Christendom culture has already given way to the pluralistic subcultures of the postmodern world. This ambivalence is even more prevalent in Global South regions where Christendom never existed.

This church-culture tension has fed into the age-old sacred-secular dichotomy, where "sacred" involves all things church – such as worship, Bible studies, and mission work – and the rest of life in the contemporary culture – such as work and social life – are all "secular." Furthermore, the church has

---

2. Chewning, Eby, and Roels, *Business*, 4.
3. Keller, *Every Good Endeavor*, loc. 242, Kindle.
4. Keller, loc. 66.
5. Keller, loc. 21.

so domesticated and institutionalized its "membership" that it has resulted in many believer-members being totally consumed with the mechanics of the "organized church" and finding themselves peripheral both to the kingdom calling and to the contemporary contexts. This sacred-secular divide reduces the church's capacity to do mission in the world. Restrained within such a paradigm, and sometimes complacent about this, many believers fail to comprehend their own relevance in the Great Commission.

The post-Christendom postmodern reality offers new opportunities. Christ-followers need a new paradigm that goes beyond the Christendom sacred-secular dichotomy, from theology to missiology, and from world view to the understanding of church or *ecclesia*. As Hendrick Kraemer pronounces,

> This is indeed a new era for mission. The call of *missio Dei* is no longer just for the "sacred/spiritual" vocational or ecclesiastic order. It is a call for every believer from all spheres, being placed in all sorts of circumstances and workplace environments.[6]

Believers are being placed in all walks of life to live out their callings. They are also being challenged to excel in their earthly roles and to become leaders who reclaim God's original intent. They are to be proactive to usher in God's kingdom on earth, thereby bringing transformation to individuals and communities. This is about *missio Dei* being reimagined and reaffirmed. This requires the mobilization of all believers to preach the totality of the gospel for holistic transformation until Christ comes again.

Mobilizing the Whole Church

In June 2019, the Lausanne Movement held a Global Workplace Forum in Manila. Almost nine hundred people attended this unprecedented gathering, where the majority (65 percent) of the participants from 110 countries were believers whose vocations lay outside of churches or ministry organizations. This Global Workplace Forum brought together a wide spectrum of Christians from the global workforce – from labourers to CEOs, and including blue-collar, white-collar, as well as the "no collar" workers. In an article in *Christianity Today*, Michael Oh, global executive director and CEO of the Lausanne Movement, says,

> I want to repent, on behalf of the 1%, for viewing the 99% of the church not in professional ministry as existing to support *our*

---

6. Kraemer, *Uit de nalatenschap*, ??

ministry. This couldn't be more wrong," and adds that "the 1% of those who are in professional ministry will never reach the world with the gospel. The 1% cannot make disciples of all nations.[7]

His message to the 99 percent is this: "You don't exist to help professional ministry leaders fulfil the Great Commission. We exist to help *you* do it."[8] This is about intentionally launching and empowering the 99 percent to reach the unreached who are readily accessible in their communities.

This message has amplified the challenge and the opportunity of the new millennium. For centuries, the history of global mission has been the history of the advance of the church from the West. Mission societies were formed to mobilize and support churches to bring the gospel from the West to the rest of the world. In the nineteenth and twentieth centuries, they represented the main thrust of efforts of the Protestant churches in the West to send missionaries to the non-Christian world. This was definitely the era of mission being "from the West to the rest."

Missionaries of that era would usually leave their homeland, put down roots in faraway places, learn the language, and, in some cases, even willingly endure physical danger. The Great Commission they were fulfilling was grounded in the monotheistic and superior nature of the Christian faith and the assumption of Christianity's acceptability and adaptability to all people, all cultures, and all conditions.[9] However oftentimes churches established in those non-Western contexts would adopt the customs, cultures, and even the apparel of the West in a wholesale manner. From worship, liturgy, music, and theology to church building layouts and church decor, and especially the institutional and organizational structure of the church, these churches were practically replicas of the church in the West, whose intent was ecclesiastic expansionism that sought to bring their own culture and church order to a foreign land.[10]

Although centuries have gone by and there have been changes in some of these trends because of changing times and values, similar practices and values still persist. Often, the benchmark to measure the effectiveness of mission is the number of missionaries sent out or the number of churches planted. The majority of those in evangelical leadership are those who have come through the conventional pathway of vocational ministry, with a binary mindset of

---

7. Oh, "Apology," https://www.christianitytoday.com/ct/2019/june-web-only/apology-christian-99-1-percent-lausanne-gwf-michael-oh.html.

8. Oh.

9. Bosch, *Transforming Mission*, 302.

10. Wostyn, *Doing Ecclesiology*, 17.

spiritual vs secular. It is time to usher in a fundamental strategy shift that will empower and launch the 99 percent.

Royal Priesthood of All Believers

Martin Luther is usually regarded as the champion of the doctrine of the priesthood of all believers, as set out in his treatises calling for the reform of the Catholic Church. To use his own words, Luther taught of a "general priesthood of all baptized Christians."[11] The doctrine of the priesthood of all believers emphasizes that all who are baptized in Christ are designated priests and share in the royal priesthood in Christ. When every believer has equal access to the Father through Christ, they also share the same responsibility to minister to one another as priests.

During the Reformation, Luther's theological teaching was both an attempt to challenge the sole authority of the church and to rectify the misunderstood teaching about the role of ordinary believers. Luther's teaching on the priesthood focused on challenging the hierarchical roles and authorities of the papal office on the basis that both spiritual power and secular authority are divinely sanctioned.[12]

In his writings, Luther argues that there is no spiritual divide between the ordained and lay people and that there is only "one estate" to which all baptized believers belong.[13] There are not separate tiers of those who come before God. Luther's teaching rehabilitated the once desanctified temporal earthly realm and sought to debunk the belief that the spiritual world takes precedence over the temporal realm. British church historian Roland Bainton states, "The repudiation of ordination as a sacrament demolished the caste system of clericalism and provided a sound basis for the priesthood of all believers . . . what the priest does any Christian may do, if commissioned by the congregation, because all Christians are priests."[14]

This is not to say that the church should not ordain people – such as the clergy and the elders – or send out vocational missionaries. Luther maintains that the act of preaching publicly has special status: "Although we are all

---

11. Luther, *Selected Psalms II*, 332.

12. Luther, "Pagan Servitude," 304.

13. Luther differentiates between two estates and one estate. Luther, "Christian Nobility," 129.

14. Bainton, *Here I Stand*, 106.

equally priests, we cannot all publicly minister and teach."[15] However, the focus is on embracing the diversity of spiritual gifts given to the body of Christ. Although not everyone is called to the public ministry of teaching God's word authoritatively, all believers are called to be witnesses for the faith. Paul Althaus makes a fair observation: "Luther recognizes no community which is not a preaching community and no community in which all have not been called to be witnesses."[16] Within the community, each believer should affirm their role and ministry of priesthood, to care and to witness in all circumstances.

Luther was not trying to put down the role of pastoral ministry. Rather, he sought to raise the bar for the "ordinary laity." Luther offers a profound perspective: "A Christian is a perfectly free lord of all, subject to none. A Christian is a perfectly dutiful servant of all, subject to all."[17] Believers are all priests through their faith, which gives them freedom from the bondage of the world. Yet, as priests, believers also become servants and bear responsibility to witness and minister because of their love for humanity and God. They must always be mindful of the priestly functions of praying for and ministering the word to one another, assuring one another of God's promises and forgiveness. The royal priesthood of all believers is a reassertion of balanced biblical teaching. It is a vision of an *ecclesia* with its people ministering to one another and witnessing to the world, with believers bearing one another's burdens and becoming ministers to one another (Gal 6:1–2; Eph 5:19; Col 3:16).

With Luther attributing unprecedented value and dignity to the "earthly vocations" of the laity – encouraging a life of sacrifice and worship among "ordinary" believers – there is no longer a divide between the spiritual and secular realms. Since all believers are called to lead a life of worship and glorify God as priests, the laity must no longer see themselves as being merely engaged in mundane and material earthly pursuits.

Martin Luther's doctrine of the priesthood of all believers remains a core belief in Protestantism today. Yet, with time, the pendulum has once again swung back, and the sacred-secular divide has again became a paradigm that is visibly impacting the way the roles of the clergy and the laity are viewed in the contemporary church and mission movement. It is of utmost importance to rediscover and highlight this important teaching in the Protestant tradition.

---

15. Luther, *Freedom*, 65.
16. Althaus, *Theology of Martin Luther*, 315–16.
17. Luther, *Freedom*, 53.

Thy Kingdom Come: Equipping the Saints for Every Sphere

When work in the "secular" arena is no longer viewed as just an activity offering utilitarian value that is devoid of spiritual meaning but is seen as also meaning worship and witness, this brings about a revolutionary change in missional leadership development. Instead of relying on or delegating to a few "professionals" to achieve a task or setting up a committee to organize "programmes," we may truly mobilize the whole church to share the whole gospel to the whole people.[18]

All believers are charged with obeying the Great Commandment (Matt 22:36–40) and the Great Commission (Matt 28:16–20). We are all called to love our neighbours and to take the good news to the ends of the earth. In their daily living, believers may respond to the call to love their neighbours as they go about their business. In the Bible, the young lawyer asked Jesus who his neighbour was (Luke 10:29). On a daily basis, we already have opportunities to reach those who are in immediate proximity to us: co-workers, customers, suppliers, and even competitors. Both the Great Commandment and the Great Commission should, therefore, be fulfilled through the spiritual ministry of our daily work life. Since gospel transformation should be a natural outworking of the physical presence of the faithful, leadership development planning has to align with such convictions.

The unprecedented pace of urbanization and globalization in the new millennium has offered tremendous opportunity to change the trajectory of the sharing of the gospel. We can truly mobilize the whole church, not through programmes or committees, but through believers-priests to share their witnesses for all spheres daily. The new missional landscape and the renewed understanding of the priesthood of all believers call for the rethinking of leadership development, debunking traditions and prejudices. The fragmented postmodern missional landscape can be better served through new approaches. The new wineskin of the ministry of the laity that trains and releases average believers into the intercultural mission field called the workplace would potentially be more relevant as a strategy and more effective as a process.

Believer-priests are being prepared and called to the fallen world. The postmodern new millennium might be treacherous and challenging to our faith journey in a multireligious and multicultural landscape. It seems like an easier path to keep faith matters private and personal from Monday to Saturday and just enjoying the Christian experience and the fellowship on Sunday. Yet

---

18. Oh, "Apology," https://www.christianitytoday.com/ct/2019/june-web-only/apology-christian-99-1-percent-lausanne-gwf-michael-oh.html.

to do so is an abdication of our identity and our purpose. We are all called to be priests who proclaim the good news to the lost. We are being placed in different spheres and circumstances in this fallen and broken world. When our lives cross paths with others, the Holy Spirit in us will work through us and make us a blessing to many.

Mark Greene, executive director of the London Institute for Contemporary Christianity, suggests that there are basically two different approaches to the evangelization of the world. The first approach is to encourage believers to invest some of their spare time and to be financially generous towards church programmes and mission activities. The second is to capture people with a vision and commitment that seeks to equip and launch them back into their everyday work and activities to be salt and light wherever they are, all the time, to everyone, in everything they do.[19]

If we were to go back to the origin of the global mission movement sparked by the Holy Spirit (Acts 1:8; 2:2–4) even before any ecclesiastic orders or mission societies were founded, we would appreciate the authentic flavour of the *missio Dei*. Cross-cultural mission started not with the church sending out professional evangelists but with the work of the Holy Spirit in the midst of ordinary sociocultural interactions (Acts 2:5–13) and by Christ-followers as witnesses of Christ (Acts 8:1; 11:19) wherever they were. Early missionaries Paul and Barnabas were not full-time missionaries in today's sense of the term. Rather, they were workplace professionals who were engaged in their business practice and actively found opportunities to share the gospel in the marketplace (Acts 17:17; 18:3–4; 1 Cor 9:6).

As the Lausanne Movement has pronounced, the Great Commission needs the active involvement and participation of the 99 percent from the workplace or the marketplace.[20] The marketplace serves as the best wineskin to carry forth the good news. For those raised on the old Christendom spiritual-secular dichotomy mindset, this may seem a novel approach. Yet this is but a return to the biblical understanding of both the early church and the Reformers about our calling into a kingdom lifestyle.

Mobilizing the 99 percent is not a programme to add to or replace the old paradigm. Rather, it is about real, viable, and sustainable missional participation in the workplace, releasing local believers to authentic and genuine Christian

---

19. Greene, "Church's Failure," YouTube video, 11:41.

20. Oh, "Apology," https://www.christianitytoday.com/ct/2019/june-web-only/apology-christian-99-1-percent-lausanne-gwf-michael-oh.html.

witness to share the good news among their neighbours with a kingdom purpose and impact, leading to transformation of people and communities.

God has a purpose in calling believer-priests to live in this world. It would be so sweet to be able to return home to Jesus the moment we become Christians. Yet God tasks us with being salt and light in the world so that other people can come to know him through our witness. Paul, who worked as a tentmaker, puts it succinctly: "For to me, to live is Christ and to die is gain" (Phil 1:21). Paul considered it better to die since this meant no more struggle to survive the daily grind. But to live gives the opportunity for fruitful labour, which is far better for the lost. Paul was not caught between a rock and a hard place but, rather, between two strong desires – to engage in more fruitful ministry or to go and be with Christ in heaven. Although Paul had a burning desire to be with his Lord, he knew that there was still fruitful ministry that needed to be done (Phil 1:21–24).

All who are Christ-followers should claim their identity with a sense of gratitude and stewardship. We are forgiven, blessed, and transformed because of our encounter with Jesus. It is imperative that we make ourselves available as a conduit of forgiveness, blessings, and transformation. We are the instruments through which God's kingdom is revealed whenever we proclaim the good news, heal the sick, and let the Holy Spirit work through us to bring transformation to others.

In fact, whenever we bring forth a Jesus presence in the midst of people, we bring the kingdom on earth. The kingdom of God is not something entirely invisible "out there" but something that we can see at work in the everyday realities of all spheres of our lives. While this might not look spectacular, it is faithfulness in the ordinariness of life. It is ordinary people serving as extraordinary leaders in every sphere. In the calling of *missio Dei*, there should no longer be a difference between the 1 percent and the 99 percent as all are his instruments of grace. Every believer is called to walk in the steps of the incarnate Jesus, in and for all spheres, so that we can truly usher in what we plead for in the Lord's Prayer: "Thy kingdom come."

Bibliography

Althaus, Paul. *The Theology of Martin Luther*. Philadelphia: Fortress, 1966.
Bainton, Roland H. *Here I Stand: A Life of Martin Luther*. New York: Abingdon-Cokesbury, 1950.
Bosch, David. *Transforming Mission: Paradigm Shifts in Theology of Mission*. Maryknoll: Orbis Books, 2011.

Chewning, Richard C., John W. Eby, and Shirley J. Roels. *Business through the Eyes of Faith*. San Francisco: Harper & Row, 1990.

Greene, Mark. "The Church's Failure to Embrace the Workplace." Lausanne Movement. Presented as part of the multiplex "People at Work" at Cape Town 2010: The Third Lausanne Congress on World Evangelization. Uploaded 4 October 2011. YouTube video, 11:41. https://youtu.be/JErZzKBCf5M.

Keller, Timothy. *Every Good Endeavor: Connecting Your Work to God's Work*. New York: Penguin, 2012. Kindle.

Kraemer, Hendrik. *Uit de nalatenschap van Dr. H. Kraemer*. Kampen, Netherlands: Kok ten Have, 1959, 1970.

Luther, Martin. "To the Christian Nobility of the German Nation." In *The Christian in Society*. Volume 44 of *Luther's Works*. Edited by Jaroslav Pelikan and Helmut T. Lehmann. St. Louis: Concordia, 1955–1986.

———. "On the Freedom of the Christian." In *Martin Luther: Selections from His Writings*, edited by John Dillenberger, 42–85. New York: Anchor Books, 1962.

———. "The Pagan Servitude of the Church." In *Martin Luther: Selections from His Writings*, edited by John Dillenberger, 249–359. New York: Anchor Books, 1962.

———. *Selected Psalms II*. In *Luther's Works*. 55 vols. Edited by Jaroslav Pelikan and Helmut T. Lehmann. St. Louis: Concordia, 1955–1986.

Oh, Michael. "An Apology to the Christian 99%, from the 1%." *Christianity Today*, 13 June 2019. https://www.christianitytoday.com/ct/2019/june-web-only/apology-christian-99-1-percent-lausanne-gwf-michael-oh.html.

Wostyn, Lode L. *Doing Ecclesiology*. Quezon City: Claretian, 1995.

23

Public Leadership

Femi B. Adeleye, with an addendum by Prashan De Visser

When leadership is addressed or discussed in Christian circles or contexts, we often think of it in relation to positions of responsibility or service in Christian ministries. However, leadership goes beyond such contexts and must include leadership in public spheres of engagement as well as the necessary lifelong formation process in the life of leaders in any given context. Public leadership is about effective influence and impact in all public spheres of engagement. I suggest that there is a gap that needs to be bridged between the understanding of leadership in Christian ministry and leadership in other spheres of life. What it takes to shape leaders for Christian ministry is needed as much, if not much more, for those serving in other spheres of engagement outside the church. Public leadership requires that all forms of dichotomies related to the sacred-secular divide be broken down for effective transformation. In this way, a holistic understanding and practice of biblical leadership can impact all spheres of life to address some of the pressing challenges in various contexts of our world.

Public Leadership beyond Positions

When speaking about leadership, it is common to think of roles or posts and those who occupy these positions. In relation to this, it is common to think that most of our challenges, particularly in Africa, can be attributed to lack of adequate or effective public leadership. While it takes seasoned leadership to instil discipline, sound judgment, and good governance in corridors of power or to stem the plague of corruption in various spheres of engagement, merely emphasizing posts or positions does not necessarily deliver the desired results.

Furthermore, when leadership related to the public sphere is mentioned, it is common to think primarily of political leadership and those who occupy various positions in the political space. Hence the expectation often is that those turning the political wheel would resolve most of, if not all, our problems. However, their failure to do so has been a frequent source of lament. For example, describing the state of affairs in Africa as far back as 1998, Kofi Annan – a former secretary-general of the UN – said, "For all too many . . . life is a continuous struggle against hunger, malnutrition, polluted drinking water, infectious disease, ignorance, oppression and violent conflict."[1]

This failure in public leadership is what made Stephen Adei conclude that "leadership is cause; everything else is effect." He illustrates by saying,

> Our leaders have failed in most of the areas in which leadership makes the difference; the provision of vision, development of workable strategies, mobilizing our people as one nation, mobilizing national resources for development, managing change internally and responding effectively to outside threats and opportunities, making credible decisions and solving the big problems we face.[2]

This is not just an African problem but one that can also be seen in other parts of the world. Part of the reason for such laments is that more expectation has been placed on leaders related to the position they occupy in the public sphere than attention has been given to the process of leadership formation in the life of those who occupy such positions. It often becomes clear that those who occupy certain leadership positions, especially in the public sphere, are not there on the basis of their character but because of their connections or influence in the sociopolitical machinery. Beyond roles and positions, biblical leadership in any sphere of life cannot ignore the inner life qualities and the process of formation that prepares people for effective service. Where such qualities are lacking, it does not take long for lack of impact to be felt or negative consequence to show up. As J. Robert Clinton rightly says,

> Leadership is a dynamic process in which a man or woman with God-given capacity influences a specific group of God's people toward His purposes for the group. This is contrary to the popular notion that a leader must have a formal position, a formal title or formal training. Many who are called to lead in church or

---

1. See Kofi Annan, cited in https://press.un.org/en/2001/sgsm7801.doc.htm.
2. Adei, *Leadership and Nation Building*, 51.

parachurch organisations may not have formal titles such as pastor or director.[3]

This understanding of leadership is important for re-examination of two predominant lenses through which leadership is viewed. One such lens views leadership as something that is exercised primarily in the sociopolitical sphere to the exclusion of the spiritual realm. To make such an assertion is to see rather dimly through a single lens. Such a view wrongly assumes that leadership in the sociopolitical sphere is secular and that those who occupy a position of such responsibility can get by as long as they have certain qualities of leadership. However, this assumption underestimates the very process of leadership formation that nurtures these leadership qualities. It has become all too clear that there is a vast difference between lists of essential qualities expected in leaders and the formative process that equips them to live out leadership in a way that produces the desired impact.

The other lens through which leadership is viewed is a spiritual one focused within the church and Christian circles. The tendency is to see a disconnect between leadership that is considered spiritual and leadership that is exercised in other so-called secular spheres of life. The sacred-secular approach to leadership formation contributes significantly to the detrimental outcome of leadership in the public sphere and that the flawed perspective of looking through fractured lenses has no place in the Bible.

Leadership in the Public Sphere for the Common Good

The church has produced significant leaders for Christian ministry. But there is a growing sense of urgency for such leadership to be replicated in the public sphere of engagement for the common good of society. This need has been recognized and emphasized in various contexts. In the African context, Osei-Mensah's emphasis in *Wanted: Servant Leaders* looks beyond leadership in the church to leadership in the public sphere. In the last chapter of this book, he says, "The Church in Africa stands at a critical point. A tremendous trust is being placed upon our shoulders by the Lord."[4] This trust that he refers to can be seen as a twofold mandate: first, to build and nurture effective leadership within Christian communities; second, to replicate this process in the larger

---

3. Clinton, *Making of a Leader*, 14.
4. Osei-Mensah, *Wanted: Servant Leaders*, 60.

public sphere of engagement. Tite Tienou, in his foreword in a book on leadership, also challenges Christians:

> Africans have recognized the importance of leadership for their well-being and for the social, economic, political and spiritual vitality of the continent. They have convened conferences on leadership, have produced books and various publications on the subject, and have established organisations such as the Africa Leadership Initiative . . . for the purpose of promoting leadership on the continent.[5]

In the context of Africa's significant church growth, expectations are high for the church to equip leaders from the growing Christian population to influence all spheres of life with the transforming power of the gospel. Since it has become all too clear that our political structures and systems may not necessarily produce the kind of leadership that Africa needs – even if we go through the frequent motions of elections which in themselves are often flawed and marred with violence – the onus is on the church to be more intentional in leadership formation for ministry in the public sphere. This situation does not arise for lack of training facilities for, as Kwame Bediako observes,

> "The crisis of leadership and other crisis related to inadequacy in the whole area of theological education," does not arise "simply because there is a need for more theological training but because those who receive training appear to be ill-informed and ill-equipped to contribute to the renaissance that is needed" in the African context.[6]

The need to overcome being "ill-informed and ill-equipped" calls for a more intentional approach to leadership formation that focuses on the broader needs of discipling nations not only in matters that are considered spiritual or sacred but also in a more holistic way that impacts all facets of life. The commitment and effort it takes to nurture leaders for Christian ministry is equally necessary to equip the saints for works of service – particularly for leadership roles – in the public sphere for the common good of society. There is, however, a gap that must be bridged.

---

5. Tienou, *African Christian Leadership*, xv.
6. Bediako, "African Renaissance," 29.

A Gap to Be Bridged in Leadership Formation

While significant gains have been made in the development of leaders for ministry in church and other Christian ministries, a gap remains when it comes to such leadership development in other public spheres of life. It is important to bear in mind that what is needed in the various nations of the world is an integral or holistic engagement with leadership in all spheres of life and not just in what is considered "Christian ministry." The obvious gap in leadership related to service in the public sphere derives from a flawed Christian mindset.

This flawed mindset creates dichotomies between clergy and laity, as well as between spiritual and so-called secular spheres of life, and makes an unwarranted distinction between clergy, missionaries, and theological educators on the one hand and the rest of God's people on the other, suggesting that while the former are called to ministry, the latter are just "doing jobs." Hence pastors, evangelists, prophets, worship leaders, and missionaries have a "calling," but economists, mechanics, doctors, engineers, politicians, and others who should provide leadership in the public sphere are thought to just have a job or vocation. This mindset, therefore, tends to exclude from Christian engagement matters related to leadership in politics, business, the environment, and art, leading to a deeper dichotomy of fractured lives in which people are Christians on Sundays but live contradictory lives on Monday through Saturday. Most scholars attribute this mindset – and the obvious gap between faith and life in the African context – to inherited flaws in our approach to theological education. Akrong argues that both this dualistic mindset and the resulting gap in the African context are linked to an inherited "structure of the dominant missionary soteriological paradigm of inclusion and exclusion" that "created a definition of salvation in terms of separation, distancing and rejection of African culture because it was deemed to be primitive, devilish and therefore incompatible with the Christian life."[7] This has significant implications for the lack of effective leadership in the public sphere even when there are Christians in leadership positions in the public sphere. Africa is not lacking in professional Christian presidents, prime ministers, members of Parliament, and various other public roles. The expectation is that such leaders – like Daniel and Nehemiah – will serve with integrity in the public sphere for the common good of the citizenry. Often, this is not the case. If the church has been so effective in producing significant leaders, the same fountain of leadership nurture should have significant impact on all other spheres of human engagement – be they political, economic, or social. Time and events

---

7. Akrong, "Challenge of Theological Education," 26.

have proved that good leaders within the Christian arena do not necessarily make the best leaders in other spheres of engagement.

Being Christian and Leading in the Public Sphere

The challenge of leadership in the public sphere and the rigorous preparation such leadership demands is grossly underestimated by many Christians. We do not seem to pay attention when Christians who have dared to step out into such leadership positions report that it is, for all intents and purposes, a battleground that is not for the faint-hearted. The assumption that simply being a Christian is good enough to qualify a person for effective leadership in the public sphere has often proved false. When Christians, under God's guidance, desire to lead in such a space, in addition to their faith and conviction, it is critical that they not only know the rudiments of the space but also have the strength of character and the necessary competencies to fulfil the demands of such a public office. In emphasizing conviction and competency, adequate attention is not always given to competencies, skills of engagement, and expertise related to diverse scope of service. When character is emphasized at the expense of competency, or when both character and competency are lacking, the outcome is often counterproductive. Stephen Adei asserts that "a competent, visionary leader can make quick progress in advancing nation building where national institutional apparatus are weak, while a demagogue can cause incalculable damage under the same conditions."[8] We have since learned that while having significant numbers of Christians in leadership positions in the public sphere or declaring a nation "Christian" might have some benefits, this may not necessarily bring about the transformation that society needs as an outcome of Christian witness.

Biblical World View of Leadership for All Spheres of Life

Leadership as seen in the Scriptures is rooted in the Hebraic world view that all aspects of life are sacred. In Old Testament times, God demonstrated interest in how governance, agriculture, architecture, industry, marketing, and so on should be conducted. There were sacred guidelines for international relations, social engagement, and all other aspects of life, including those that, today, are often categorized as secular. God was, and is, as concerned with how grain was measured in the market as he was with how the tabernacle was to be

---

8. Adei, *Leadership and Nation Building*, 73.

constructed. These guidelines were both for leaders and lay people. Leadership as seen in the Old Testament was not restricted to the political sphere. Besides kings, there were different kinds of leaders for different seasons in the history of the nation. There were patriarchs, priests, judges, prophets, and prophetesses as well, reflecting the diverse giftings God expects his people to exercise for the common good of the nation.

However, leadership is not limited to those who hold such formal positions. There are other layers of leadership that we tend to overlook but which are just as important. These include the various lay leaders described in the Scriptures who had a passion to bring their faith to bear on the things that touched the very heart of God in various contexts. These included ordinary lay people whose hearts were broken by the things that break the heart of God and who were moved to go beyond lament to work to redress or correct those situations. Nehemiah was neither a priest nor a prophet, but his heart was broken by news of the state of Jerusalem. His actions – which included standing up to the nobles and rebuking those who opposed the national rehabilitation – demonstrate leadership at its best.

Scripture gives other examples of people who exercised leadership from a holistic world view and served God's purposes in various spheres of engagement – for example, Joseph as an economic manager under Pharaoh in Egypt during a time of famine; David, as a shepherd boy and, later, king of Israel; Nehemiah, as cupbearer to a king and as governor during a season of national reconstruction; Esther, as queen, did what she had to do to save a whole nation; Daniel, as an administrator while in exile; and Lydia, a dealer in purple cloth, who hosted a church in her home. All these people, in their leadership roles in such diverse spheres of engagement, bore witness to God's saving plan.

These biblical examples are relevant for leadership formation in contemporary times. While some believers will be called to be pastors, teachers, or missionaries who go to other nations, most Christians will remain as teachers in public schools, businesspeople, financial consultants, technicians, administrators, publishers, salespeople, medical doctors, nurses, engineers, university professors, and so on. As people who have been nurtured in the church to develop the mind of Christ, they have significant roles to play in each of these positions.

The Need for the Church to Lead by Example

By its own example of leadership, the church should serve as a model for those who exercise leadership in other areas of life – for example, homes, institutions, governance, and business. People sometimes adopt a "if you can't beat them, join them" mentality. For example, in many parts of the world, it is in the weeks leading up to elections that some churches carry out their most significant fund-raising events, with politicians being invited to serve as chairpersons or chief launchers of such events. The unspoken question seems to be, "Do you really need our vote? Demonstrate it by how much you give to our project." Such practices undermine the role of the church as a prophetic voice speaking truth to power. Is our Christianity deep enough and bold enough to offer countercultural leadership in any and every sphere – the home, the church, the marketplace, society, and the nation?

In conclusion, while emphasizing the lifelong formation process for leaders in all spheres of engagement, we have noted some key "C" words: Conviction, Character, and Competency. Conviction is a fruit of being solidly grounded in God's purposes and understanding the times. Character is shaped internally and demonstrated externally. Competency is having the necessary God-given skills to exercise leadership in relation to particular needs and contexts. Here are some additional Cs that are essential for public leadership:

- Consistent leadership: By some definitions, consistent means "agreeing or accordant; compatible; not self-contradictory." It can also mean unchanging or steady. Consistency begins with an alignment of our beliefs, thoughts, words, and actions. The consistency of leaders is deeply rooted in the core values they have embraced and lived by over time. Hence, consistent leaders do not promise one thing and do something else. They work to keep their election promises and, on tasting power, do not manipulate people for constitutional amendments for longer terms.
- Credible leadership: Credible leaders emerge over time from being consistent in their words and practices. Such leaders do not constantly reverse their decisions or confuse people by shifting the goalposts. Undergirded by deep-rooted values like truth and honesty, they live and act in ways that make people see that they are indeed credible. Credible leaders also hold themselves accountable to colleagues and team members.
- Compassionate leadership: To be compassionate is to identify with and, if necessary, to suffer with another. Compassionate leaders identify not only with the needs of their people but also with their dignity, regardless of status, gender, or ethnic affiliations. Such

- Courageous leadership: When we think of courage, we often think of physical courage in the face of a challenge or adversity. However, a fundamental requirement for any level of leadership is moral courage. Moral courage is a commitment to do what is right in any given circumstance.

All these "C" words should be grounded in the big "C" – the Lord Jesus Christ, concerning whom it is said, "For in him all things were created: things in heaven and on earth, visible and invisible, whether thrones or powers or rulers or authorities; all things have been created through him and for him (Col 1:16).

In conclusion, if, as J. Robert Clinton suggests, "leadership evolves and emerges over a lifetime" of "God's lessons,"[9] all leaders, regardless of the position they occupy, must remain open to ongoing learning and personal renewal, with a view to serving God's purpose in their own generation as David did. When such leaders, nurtured and equipped in the church, serve God faithfully in whatever leadership role they have in society, the lordship of Christ is brought to bear on all spheres of life for the common good of society as a whole.

Mandate for Christians to Engage in the Public Space: Addendum by Prashan De Visser

The Bible unequivocally gives us a clear mandate to serve and contribute towards the redemption of a fallen creation. Christians have clear biblical directives to serve outside the four walls of the church. Jesus calls us to be the world's light and not be limited to being the light of the church. Yet many believers still fail to boldly take the plunge to serve in the public sector, including in government. In many parts of the Majority World, the public sector, politics, and government are some of the darkest and most corrupt places in society. Hence, many faithful Christians hesitate to engage in these spheres. However, we have been called to take Christ's light into these dark realms in our society.

> Neither do people light a lamp and put it under a bowl. Instead they put it on its stand, and it gives light to everyone in the house. In the same way, let your light shine before others, that

---

9. Clinton, *Making of a Leader*, 205.

they may see your good deeds and glorify your Father in heaven. (Matt 5:15–16)

We are not called to remain within the comfort zone of a Christian subculture but, rather, to take a risk and serve wholeheartedly where our nation's greatest needs abound.

Most Majority World nations are overwhelmed by corruption, abuse of power, dictatorial regimes, and various violations of fundamental human rights. As believers in Christ, we cannot ignore these realities and enjoy life in Christian bubbles. Each of these nations are blessed with individuals with a heart for the greater good, a posture of servant-leadership, and wisdom and skill to contribute to meaningful change. There are many people – from various walks of life and different religious communities – fighting the good fight and looking to bring about sustainable change in their societies. Christians who are called to the public sphere have no excuse for standing as well-wishers on the sidelines; instead, they must engage wholeheartedly as active participants and leaders.[10]

Competence and Conviction

As Dr. Femi rightly points out, it is not sufficient to engage merely based on our Christian identity and assume that we will be effective. Our faith and our values convince us to serve. However, we must also gain the understanding, skill, and competence to deliver at a higher level. If one enters into public leadership with the desire to contribute towards societal transformation, there needs to be a level of skill, competence, and a work ethic that is on par with the task at hand.

The realities of serving and leading in the public sector are far from ideal. Transformation does not happen overnight. Although the allure of our values and the vision for change sparks enthusiasm, the harsh reality unfolds as a gruelling and painful journey. We must prepare ourselves for the challenging path, recognizing that engaging in corrupt and broken structures – as highlighted by Dr. Femi – requires resilience. Despite the daunting nature of this task, we hold firm to the belief that our faithful calling from God forbids compromising our values or surrendering our mission.

---

10. See discussion in: Wolters, *Creation Regained*.

Realities of Engaging in the Public Sphere in the Asian Context

Unlike other continents, where Christians form a majority or a significant portion of the population, Asia stands as the sole continent without a predominantly Christian population. This unique circumstance in Asia is a hurdle for Christians seeking involvement in the public sphere. Historical mistrust stemming from colonial legacies, discrimination, and potential persecution loom as probable challenges when Christians venture into the public sector in this region.

In this context, there are considerable challenges for Christians who seek opportunities to serve in the public sector in influential leadership positions or to run for office. This reality deters many Christians from engaging in the public sector. Furthermore, corruption, defamation, and the possibility of persecution intensify the considerable challenges. Nevertheless, the calling and mandate for Christians to serve in the public sector persists. The biblical directive to engage remains unwavering, unaffected by the challenging circumstances. Despite the difficulties, we are called to step up and serve.

However, as Dr. Femi has indicated, it is crucial that we approach such tasks with competence, professionalism, and with an uncompromising commitment to transparency and integrity. Claiming to be a Christian and failing to live out Christian values in the public square does no good for the cause of transforming society or to the testimony of Christ. We are called to serve in humility with like-minded people from all faiths to bring about justice, reconciliation, and a society that paves the way for all people to thrive.

Certainly, formidable barriers exist. Persecution and discrimination pervade various realms, including the political landscape. We step into an arena that often contradicts the values and ideals we uphold. Nevertheless, this should not compel us to retreat.

Even in nations with a significant Christian presence, being a prophetic advocate for justice and change often provokes retaliation, discrimination, and demonization by those in power. Yet, the calling remains unaltered. Here are just three examples of remarkable Christians who, despite many challenges, served in the public sector and effected substantial transformation. Their example is an inspiration for us all.

William Wilberforce (United Kingdom): An influential Christian politician who played a key role in the abolition of the transatlantic slave trade. He had to be countercultural and awaken the conscience of a nation that had turned a blind eye to the cruelty and inhumane nature of the slave trade.

Desmond Tutu (South Africa): An Anglican archbishop and anti-Apartheid activist who later became involved in politics, advocating for reconciliation and human rights. He stepped outside the walls of the church to play a crucial role in reconciliation and accountability and in ensuring that the nation did not spiral into war. Initially, his role was not welcomed by many on either side of the radical divide.

Dietrich Bonhoeffer (Germany): Though not a politician, he was a theologian who resisted the Nazi regime and participated in plots to assassinate Adolf Hitler. God called him to respond and – despite the risks and overwhelming challenges he faced – he had courage to respond by engaging and not walking away.

These Christian leaders guided the public sector even when their advocacy for truth and justice met with resistance. They offered authentic leadership to stir the nation's conscience and guide society towards becoming a just and flourishing nation.

Many other leaders have helped shape their societies towards becoming more just and thriving nations through their leadership while remaining true to their faith and values. Among these were the following: Abraham Kuyper (Netherlands), a Dutch politician and theologian who served as prime minister and contributed significantly to the development of Christian political thought; Angela Merkel (Germany), chancellor of Germany and a pastor's daughter who was known for her leadership in the European Union; Sir John A. Macdonald (Canada), the first prime minister of Canada and a key figure in the country's founding, known for his contributions to the Canadian Confederation; Kim Dae-jung (South Korea), a Christian politician who served as president of South Korea and received the Nobel Prize for peace for his efforts towards reconciliation with North Korea; and Corazon Aquino (Philippines), the first female president of the Philippines, known for her role in the People Power Revolution and for her commitment to democracy. Despite the odds and the overwhelming challenges they faced, these leaders strove to remain faithful and significantly impacted their nations.

Finally, I also wish to underscore Dr. Femi's perspective regarding the significance of Christians not limiting their involvement in the political arena and not seeking titles in society. Instead, engaging across all spheres – including education, healthcare, business, media, and entertainment – is essential. We need individuals who will serve in alignment with their faith and values for the common good, contributing to meaningful and sustainable transformation that fosters healing, justice, and positive change in our societies.

Bibliography

Adei, Stephen. *Leadership and Nation Building*. Accra: Combert Impressions, 2004.

Akrong, Abraham. "The Challenge of Theological Education in Ghana." *Journal of African Christian Thought* 10, no. 2 (December 2007): 24–30.

Annan, Kofi. https://press.un.org/en/2001/sgsm7801.doc.htm.

Bediako, Kwame. "The African Renaissance and Theological Reconstruction: The Challenge of the Twenty-First Century." *Journal of African Christian Thought* 4, no. 2 (December 2001): 29–33.

Clinton, J. Robert. *The Making of a Leader*. Colorado Springs: NavPress, 1988.

Osei-Mensah, Gottfried. *Wanted: Servant Leaders: The Challenge of Christian Leadership in Africa Today*. Ghana: African Christian Press, 1990.

Tienou, Tite. Foreword to *African Christian Leadership, Realities Opportunities, and Impact*, edited by Robert J. Priest and Kirimi Barine. Maryknoll: Orbis Books, 2017.

Wolters, Albert M. *Creation Regained: Biblical Basics for a Reformational Worldview*. Grand Rapids, Eerdmans, 2005.

24

Accelerating Leadership Development for Missions

Mary Ho and Janelle Stoops

We have been thrust into an era of convulsive disruptions. In global missions, these disruptive changes can only be harnessed into a forward momentum by intentionally accelerating leadership development. Since 1981, we celebrate that Christianity is truly global – *not* Western – as the pendulum of the Christian population has swung from the Global North to the Global South.[1] Although a hundred years ago, 82 percent of all Christians lived in the West, over two-thirds of the world's Christians now live in Asia, Africa, Latin America, and Oceania, and this figure is projected to exceed three quarters of the world's population by 2025.[2] In this demographic reversal, the greatest growth is in Africa, followed by Latin America and Asia.[3] Moreover, based on every available national census and Christian denominational data, the majority of people in churches worldwide are now women.[4] In fact, the face of Christianity is now a non-Western woman – specifically, an African woman.[5] Similarly, the global population, especially in Africa, is becoming more youthful. According to the Pew Research Center, 70 percent of sub-Saharan Africa is under the age of thirty, and three out of every ten evangelicals will

---

1. Johnson and Zurlo, *World Christian Encyclopedia*, 4.
2. Johnson and Zurlo, 4.
3. Johnson and Zurlo, 4.
4. Zurlo, *Women in World Christianity*, 13.
5. Gina Zurlo, Co-Director of Center for the Study of Global Christianity, Zoom interview by Mary Ho, 16 May 2023.

be African youth by 2030.⁶ According to the World Economic Forum, Gen Z will make up one-third of the global workforce by 2025.⁷ Therefore, leadership development in missions must reflect the face of Christianity – which is non-Westerners, women, and youth.

These facts are daunting. These same continents where Christianity is growing the fastest are also where the Human Development Index (HDI) – measuring life expectancy, literacy, education, and the gross national product (GNP) – is trailing behind or sometimes the lowest. These underdeveloped regions are characterised by civil unrest and host the world's largest megacities with deafening socioeconomic dissonance.⁸ Yet these same regions are our largest mission field, being home to most of the world's least reached people groups. Leadership development must equip the mission forces in these regions.

Global missions also reflect the same dramatic shift to the Global South. As of 2020, five of the world's six top mission senders (after the United States) are Global South nations – Brazil, South Korea, Philippines, Nigeria, and China, respectively.⁹ Unlike a hundred years ago, today's mission sending emerges largely from the less-stabilized and less-resourced Global South regions. Moreover, we are engaging in missions during a time of heightened persecution – even martyrdom – of Christians. Today's mission landscape is one of disruptive reversals.

We can only accelerate mission leadership development by equipping the majority of the world's Christians who reflect the face of Christianity. These are the non-Westerners, the women, the youth, and the economically underserved. There is a global leadership shortage because most traditional leadership development programmes are Western, individualistic, expensive, conceptual, and task-oriented. Such programmes are incompatible with many of the world's receptor societies, which are collectivistic, oral, concrete, relational, and limited in resources. Mission leadership development must equip the vast majority of the world rather than the elite few.

---

6. Kolo, "Leadership in Missions."
7. Cohen, "Companies are Learning," https://www.cnbc.com/2023/05/26/employers-are-learning-gen-z-isntthe-easiest-generation-to-work-with.html.
8. Johnstone, *Future of the Global Church*, 6, fig. 1.17.
9. Johnson and Zurlo, *World Christian Encyclopedia*, 32.

Democratizing Leadership for the Global Majority

Mission leadership development must be inverted from the bottom of the socioeconomic pyramid "to reach hundreds of millions of people versus the hundreds of thousands who are reached through our usual ways of developing leaders."[10] Leadership development must become more affordable, scalable, accessible, inclusive, and collectivistic.[11] To accelerate leader development for mission, we need to democratize leadership development for the underserved populations:

> Thus democratization of leader development applies to two key groups: people who cannot afford mainstream leadership development inventions (many in the developing world and people from lower socioeconomic strata) and people who are not in formal leadership positions in organizations (the self-employed, entrepreneurs, under employed, or unemployed).[12]

We can only catalyze a wave of emerging leaders through value-based leadership development that is affordable and accessible to those from all walks of life.

Challenging Assignments and Developmental Relationships

While most Western leadership development occurs in classrooms, a survey of over five hundred senior leaders in forty-seven organizations in multiple sectors and countries confirms that the key factors shaping leaders are as follows: first, challenging assignments; second, developmental relationships; third, adverse situations; fourth, personal experience;[13] and the fifth and least influential leadership formation factor is coursework. Challenging assignments include difficult tasks, promotions, job rotations, and working in different cultures. Developmental relationships include coaching, mentoring, feedback, and peer coaching.

A combination of these factors, known as the 70/20/10 development mix, is highly effective: 70 percent on-the-job challenging assignments; 20 percent developmental relationship; and 10 percent formal learning.[14] Formal

---

10. Altman, Rego, and Harrison, "Democratizing Leader Development," 227.
11. Altman, Rego, and Harrison, 223.
12. Altman, Rego, and Harrison, 223.
13. Altman, Rego, and Harrison, 68.
14. Byham and Byham, "Leadership Development Strategy," 163.

training is useful for assisting low- to mid-level leaders in acquiring cognitive knowledge and rudimentary skills, while developmental relationships and challenging assignments are essential for developing senior leaders.[15]

Servant-Leadership Transcends Age and Culture

Research has shown that servant-leadership is ideal for mentoring individuals from multiple generations, transcending age.[16] Servant-leaders model the seven biblical characteristics of *agapao* love, humility, altruism, vision, trust, empowerment, and service.[17] Servant-leaders identify as being "servants first."[18] They do not wait for but actively seek out opportunities to serve their followers, knowing that this will require time, energy, sacrifice, and resources.

There are three key approaches to leadership development: universal, contingent, and normative.[19] While many leadership development programmes adopt a normative approach by equipping people with the requisite skills and competencies, leadership development must first establish servant-leadership as the universal foundational approach to "be directed at the worldview of a people so that it influences each of the subsystems from the very core of the culture."[20] Servant-leadership has proven to be universally applicable, effective, and transformative across all cultures.[21] Second, servant-leadership must be adapted to be contingent to the local culture. The twenty-year GLOBE research on leadership concluded that leaders must "behave in a manner consistent with the desired leadership found in that culture" and that, culturally, "leaders who behave according to expectations are effective."[22] Therefore, the universally effective style of biblical servant-leadership must be adapted to each local culture.

Across all cultures, servant-leaders make excellent mentors who validate others' talents and empower people to grow to their full potential. In the mentoring process, the mentees mature into the mentor role because of experienced leaders who selflessly invest in others and put the learner's needs

---

15. Byham and Byham, 164.
16. Zimmerer, "Generational Perceptions," 157–58.
17. Patterson, "Servant Leadership," 8.
18. Greenleaf, "Servant-Leadership," 21–27.
19. Steers, Sanchez-Runde, and Nardon, "Leadership in a Global Context," 479–82.
20. Hofstede, Hofstede, and Minkov, *Cultures and Organizations*, x.
21. Ho, "Transcendent Culture," https://www.lausanne.org/content/lga/2020-03/transcendent-culture-servant-leadership.
22. Dorfman et al., "GLOBE," 504–18.

above their own.[23] Mentors must provide safe spaces, build trust with their mentees, and intentionally invest in them.[24]

Collectivistic and Contextualized Leadership

Contrary to Western perceptions, leadership is not just about the individual who is in charge. In many global cultures, leadership is a collectivistic process. Jesus trained his leaders in groups of three, twelve, and seventy, and he seized teachable moments to train these individuals. Therefore, to accelerate leadership development, the strategy must be "expanded from an exclusive focus on individuals in leader roles to a focus that also includes the role of collectives in enacting leadership."[25] This collective empowerment resonates with the African philosophy of ubuntu, which says, "I am because you are."[26] This belief system emphasizes that collective leadership is critical to success in "all cultures, traditions, relations, and philosophies."[27]

Rather than taking learners out of their own settings and sending them elsewhere for training, such training should be done within their own contexts. Emerging leaders who are sent outside the community sometimes do not return, or they may return but be unable to adapt their learnings to their own community context. Accelerating leadership development will require learners to integrate and implement their learnings in culturally appropriate ways.

Therefore, leadership development must increase the group's capacity to (1) set a shared direction, (2) align collective communication and coordination, and (3) formulate and build group goals.[28] Leadership training must be offered to grassroots Christian organizations so that all individuals and groups are engaged in leadership development.

Scalable and Accessible

Scalability makes leadership trainings accessible and affordable at the grassroots level. Most traditional leadership assessments and training programmes are patented and expensive. But democratized mission leadership trainings need

---

23. Kowalski, "Mentoring," 540–41.
24. Bell and Goldsmith, *Managers as Mentors*, 33, 69, 91, 212.
25. Altman, Rego, and Harrison, "Democratizing Leader Development," 226.
26. Netshitangani, "Queen Bee Syndrome," 197–203.
27. Netshitangani, 197–203.
28. Altman, Rego, and Harrison, "Democratizing Leader Development," 226.

to be accessible – an open-source sharing of intellectual property that does not require external expertise to impart. Local instructors must be trained to train locals. They must learn to ask simple questions to uncover leadership stories, often without even using the word "leadership."[29] Instead of cookie-cutter, in-a-box curriculums, the trainings need to be adaptable and scalable modular trainings that can easily be selected and transferred from a training menu to meet the felt needs of the learner. This approach fuels the motivation of learners and allows them to implement their new discoveries in their current situations with new solutions. They can then easily transfer these just-in-time training sessions to other people around the world.

These scalable modules empower people to learn in "chunks," building learning upon learning over the course of their lives. These leaders view learning not just as what they *do* but also who they *are*.[30] Leadership development is not a two-year formal degree programme but an ongoing and lifelong journey.[31]

Interactive Immersive Experiences

For mission leadership development to be accessible for the majority, it must be interactive and experiential rather than print- or PowerPoint-based. About 80 percent of the world's population are oral learners, who prefer to learn orally even if they are highly educated.[32] Songs, drawings, stories, drama, group activities, simulations, and interactive writing walls are effective immersive methods of leadership development. Direct interactive experiences – which allow participants to discover, express, observe, and suggest – personalize trainings and significantly enhance the likelihood of retention.[33]

Storying

Because most of the world's population are oral learners, mission leadership development is best communicated through concrete stories rather than abstract principles. The Center for Creative Leadership confirms that "time and again, we found that the elements of our conceptual model of leadership

---

29. Altman, Rego, and Harrison, 234.
30. Mariama-Arthur, "Exceptional Leaders," 3–8.
31. Clark, "Leader Training Challenge," The Church's Leader Training Challenge: More than One Way to Address the Need – *InSights Journal*.
32. "Who Are Oral Communicators?," International Orality Network, last accessed 26 November 2023. https://orality.net/about/who-are-oral-communicators/.
33. Altman, Rego, and Harrison, "Democratizing Leader Development," 234.

development were easier to understand when conveyed through stories."[34] Storying, combined with discussion questions as the group processes their learning together, is a powerful means of teaching and developing others. In missions, we draw our key leadership principles from the Bible, which is made up mainly of narratives – 43 percent of the Bible is narrative, 33 percent poetry, and 24 percent prose discourse.[35] God himself chose to instruct us through stories. We must follow not only biblical leadership principles but also God's instructional methodology through storying.

Multiplication, Train the Trainers, Rapid Prototyping

The ultimate goal of accelerating leadership development is the multiplication of mission leaders. Traditional leadership development often features long trainings, complex assessments, and certified professionals. Instead, leadership development must focus on multiplying leaders by transferring competencies and abilities – not just knowledge – through a train-the-trainer approach, in which newly trained leaders immediately train others in rapid succession. By asking questions of one another – for example, "What are you learning?" and "Who can you share this learning with this week?" – the DNA of multiplication is present from the start.

Applying lessons learned, learning from failures, and timely teaching of others are among the most effective ways to grow as leaders.[36] In Luke 10, Jesus instructed the seventy-two disciples, sent them out to apply the lessons learned, and then provided corrective feedback when they returned. This type of rapid prototyping assumes "that faster learning occurs when you fail early and fail often. . . . (with) permission to learn by doing and to incorporate the lessons learned into subsequent iterations."[37] Training-the-trainers transforms followers into leaders and the underserved into empowered populations. As these leaders share learnings with others and mentor them, leadership development will multiply throughout communities, movements, and nations, with no sector left untouched.

---

34. Altman, Rego, and Harrison, 233.

35. "Literary Styles," Bible Project, last modified 22 June 2017. https://bibleproject.com/explore/video/literary-styles-bible/.

36. Altman, Rego, and Harrison, "Democratizing Leader Development," 245.

37. Altman, Rego, and Harrison, 238.

Developing Women Leaders in All Life Stages

Since the face of Christianity is an African woman, more women must be empowered and equipped to lead. Mentorship programmes and accessible just-in-time training must provide safe spaces for women to learn and receive the input and support they need to flourish at all different life stages. It is vital that mentors equip, impart wisdom, and build confidence in women to lead in all life stages, instead of waiting until women no longer have children at home, which may be too late. While women mentoring women is vital, supportive men in leadership positions also play a crucial role by opening doors, facilitating networking, suggesting other beneficial opportunities, and helping to strengthen women's self-confidence.[38]

Women leaders are pivotal in missions. A survey of ninety-five women mission leaders from thirty-one countries reveals that women lead as "faithful" and "connected" influencers.[39] Another research study confirms that women are especially hardwired to be boundary spanners, transcending the barriers of race, religion, age, and class to lead as cross-cultural influencers.[40]

Developing and Inviting Generation Z Leaders

As previous generations retire, Gen Z is moving quickly into vacant leadership roles. According to generational theory, each generation has its own unique set of "characteristics, interests, styles, and preferred learning environments."[41] Gen Z is unique in that they are (1) diverse and inclusive, (2) purposeful and solution-oriented, (3) ambitious and pragmatic, (4) digitally native and technologically ambivalent, (5) individualistic and identity-oriented, and (6) entrepreneurial and innovative.[42] Gen Z wants to tackle complex problems, advocate for the marginalized, impact their communities, and change the world.[43]

Learning experiences must meet the needs of Gen Z and equip them to excel.[44] In addition to mentoring them in collaboration, leading change, and ethical leadership, other suggested competencies include the following:

---

38. Blaique and Pinnington, "Occupational Commitment," 555–83.
39. Lederleitner, *Women in God's Mission*, 53.
40. Zurlo, personal interview.
41. Prosser, "Future Leaders."
42. Prosser, 39.
43. Prosser, 42, 61.
44. Seemiller and Grace, *Generation Z*, 21, 24, 27.

(1) leveraging the capacity of others; (2) engaging in complex thinking and innovative problem solving; (3) utilizing a collaborative and interdependent approach; (4) communicating effectively; (5) being adaptable; (6) guiding others to greatness; (7) being optimistic; (8) persevering through adversity; and (9) employing honesty and altruism.[45]

Leadership trainings must align with Gen Z's preferred learning style, which is overwhelmingly experiential rather than in a classroom setting.[46] Customized content, just-in-time delivery, and interactive discussions are key to engaging Gen Z. They value learning opportunities and established leaders giving them wisdom.[47] These digital natives also engage in "reverse mentoring" through coaching senior leaders in technology! Challenging assignments and adverse situations combined with developmental relationships are crucial to developing young leaders. Mentors and coaches can effectively design "stretch" assignments for youth while providing invaluable support and feedback.

Many young people view current leaders as unethical and, therefore, hesitate to take up leadership positions. Inviting such youth to be involved in leadership development could be reframed as welcoming them to develop into ethical and caring leaders who pursue their passions to make a desperately needed difference in the world.[48] Such an invitation aligns with Gen Z values and addresses their concerns.

Adaptive Leadership in a VUCA World

As the generations change, leadership theories and styles must evolve. The world today is a VUCA world: Volatile, Uncertain, Complex, and Ambiguous.[49] Today's leaders cannot lead in old ways that were successful in a more stable environment. Styles such as "command and control" – that were effective in the factories of the 1900s – have given way to adaptive leadership, a nimble form of leadership that is ideal for today's rapidly changing world.[50]

Adaptive leaders set themselves apart from other leaders by being open to feedback, ready for inevitable change, and skilled at navigating adaptive challenges. Leaders today face two types of challenges: technical challenges –

---

45. Seemiller and Grace, 22.
46. Prosser, "Future Leaders," 151.
47. Prosser, 61.
48. Prosser, 171.
49. Bennett and Lemoine, "What a Difference," 311–17.
50. Northouse, *Leadership*.

that can be solved with existing knowledge or expertise – and adaptive challenges – for which existing knowledge is insufficient and which can only be navigated by innovation and experimentation. Solutions to adaptive challenges usually require a painstaking culture shift in organizations.[51]

Adaptive leaders anticipate challenges and work to identify their root causes. Such leaders possess high emotional intelligence (EQ) and the capacity to "tolerate distress."[52] Leaders with high EQ provide a non-anxious presence, giving others space to work through conflicts and concerns. Adaptive leaders initiate courageous conversations and practise deep listening with "curiosity rather than judgement."[53] Adaptive leaders can thrive in this volatile, uncertain, complex, and ambiguous world.

Conclusion

Adaptive leadership is the leadership of the future. As Christianity shifts from the North to the South and from the West to the rest, more non-Western women and youth are assuming key leadership roles. These realities must shape our leadership trainings. Just-in-time learnings, combined with mentorship, will accelerate leadership development. Democratizing leadership training will unleash a wave of exemplary Christian leaders. These servant-leaders, fluent in adaptive leadership, will lead us into the uncertainty of tomorrow with humility, wisdom, and skill.

Bibliography

Altman, David, Lyndon Rego, and Steadman Harrison. "Democratizing Leader Development." In *The Center for Creative Leadership: Handbook of Leadership Development*, 3rd ed., edited by Ellen Van Velsor, Cynthia D. McCauley, and Marian N. Ruderman, 221–50. San Francisco: Jossey-Bass, 2010.

Bell, Chip R., and Marshall Goldsmith. *Managers as Mentors*. 3rd ed. San Francisco: Berrett-Koehler, 2013.

Bennett, Nathan, and G. J. Lemoine. "What a Difference a Word Makes: Understanding Threats to Performance in a VUCA World." *Business Horizons* 57, no. 3 (2014): 311–17.

---

51. Heifetz and Laurie, "Adaptive Strategy," 14–15.
52. Heifetz and Laurie, 14–15.
53. Wheatley, "Turning to One Another," 8–19.

Blaique, Lama, and Ashly H. Pinnington. "Occupational Commitment of Women Working in SET: The Impact of Coping Self-Efficacy and Mentoring." *Human Resource Management Journal* 32, no. 3 (2022): 555–83.

Byham, Tacy, and William Byham. "Leadership Development Strategy." In *The ASTD Leadership Handbook*, edited by Elaine Biech, 155–70. Alexandria: ASTD, 2010.

Clark, Paul Allan. "The Church's Leader Training Challenge: More Than One Way to Address the Need." *InSights* 6, no. 2. https://insightsjournal.org/the-churchs-leader-training-challenge-more-than-one-way-to-address-the-need/.

Cohen, Mikaela. "Companies Are Learning That Gen Z Isn't the Easiest Generation to Work With." *CNBC*, last updated 11 July 2023. https://www.cnbc.com/2023/05/26/employers-are-learning-gen-z-isnt-the-easiest-generation-to-work-with.html.

Dorfman, Peter, Mansour Javidan, Paul Hanges, Ali Dastmalchian, and Robert House. "GLOBE: A Twenty Year Journey into the Intriguing World of Culture and Leadership." *Journal of World Business* 47, no. 4 (2012): 504–18.

Greenleaf, Robert K. "Who Is the Servant-Leader?" *The International Journal of Servant-Leadership* 1, no. 1 (2005): 21–27.

Heifetz, Ronald A., and Donald L. Laurie. "Adaptive Strategy." *Leadership Excellence* 15, no. 12 (1998): 14–15.

Ho, Mary. "The Transcendent Culture of Servant Leadership: Principles for 21st Century Global Mission." *Lausanne Global Analysis*, March 2020. https://www.lausanne.org/content/lga/2020-03/transcendent-culture-servant-leadership.

Hofstede, Geert, Gert Jan Hofstede, and Michael Minkov. *Cultures and Organizations: Software of the Mind*. New York: McGraw Hill, 2010.

Johnson, Todd M., and Gina A. Zurlo, eds. *World Christian Encyclopedia*. 3rd ed. Edinburgh: Edinburgh University Press, 2020.

Johnstone, Patrick. *The Future of the Global Church: History, Trends, and Possibilities*. Grand Rapids: Zondervan, 2014.

Kolo, Mark. "Leadership in Missions for the Next Generation." Zoom presentation. Lausanne, 12 October 2013.

Kowalski, Karren. "Mentoring." *The Journal of Continuing Education in Nursing* 50, no. 12 (December 2019): 540–41.

Lederleitner, Mary. *Women in God's Mission: Accepting the Invitation to Serve and Lead*. Downers Grove: InterVarsity Press, 2018.

Mariama-Arthur, Karima. "Exceptional Leaders Are Lifelong Learners," in *Poised for Excellence*, by Karima Mariama-Arthur, 3–8. New York: Springer, 2018.

Netshitangani, Tshilidzi. "Queen Bee Syndrome: Examining Ubuntu Philosophy in Women's Leadership." *Ubuntu: Journal of Conflict Transformation* 8, (2019): 197–203.

Northouse, Peter Guy. *Leadership: Theory and Practice*. Los Angeles: SAGE, 2022.

Patterson, Kathleen A. "Servant Leadership: A Theoretical Model." PhD diss., Regent University, 2003.

Prosser, Michelle Ann Epiphany. "Growing Our Future Leaders: Emerging Leadership Development Curriculum Design for Generation Z." Ed.D. diss Marymount University, 2023.

Seemiller, Corey, and Meghan Grace. *Generation Z Learns: A Guide for Engaging Generation Z Students in Meaningful Learning.* Independently published, 2019.

Steers, Richard, Carlos Sanchez-Runde, and Luciara Nardon. "Leadership in a Global Context: New Directions in Research and Theory Development." *Journal of World Business* 47, no. 4 (2012): 479–82.

Wheatley, Margaret. "Turning to One Another: Simple Conversations to Restore Hope to the Future." *The Journal for Quality and Participation* 25, no. 2 (2002): 8–19.

Zimmerer, Tatiana Ekaterina. "Generational Perceptions of Servant Leadership: A Mixed Methods Study." PhD diss., Capella University ProQuest Dissertations Publishing, 2013.

Zurlo, Gina A. *Women in World Christianity: Building and Sustaining a Global Movement.* Hoboken: Wiley-Blackwell, 2023.

25

Developing Leaders in Unknown Movements

Eurico Buanaissa and Esther Chengo

In his opening remarks at the 2019 Lausanne Global Workplace Forum, João Mordomo gave this paraphrase of Ephesians 2:10: "We are God's masterpieces created to do masterpieces for the glory of the Master."[1] This paraphrase draws attention to the reality of God's intentional design of us in Christ to fulfil his purpose and glorify him through it. A vital part of the good work that God created us to do is expressed in the Great Commission (Matt 28:18–20), one of the most important descriptions of what Jesus wanted from his disciples. It is clear that everything Jesus proclaimed, taught, and demonstrated personally was a preparation for the Great Commission: his command to make disciples of all nations. That said, an obvious reality we must consider is that "we can't make disciples of all nations without making disciples."[2] Therefore, we must view disciple-making as critical in the leadership continuum.

This chapter seeks to delve deeper into this biblical mandate of leader identification and development using a disciple-making model. Since the focus is on unknown movements, we begin by developing a working definition to help us grasp how leaders can be identified and how their capacity can be built.

---

1. Mordomo, "Call to Startups," https://youtu.be/goMt57CE2kI?si=FyN1TqcMN3uuBuOM.

2. Oh, "Kingdom Impact," https://youtu.be/RJrLZVxKBPY?si=g6wP1MFQZ9qR7QhE.

Unknown Movements

While a social movement is a sustained campaign that is loosely organized to support a social goal, it can also be defined as a formal organization that takes the collective pursuit of social change as its primary goal.[3] A social movement is "a purposive and collective attempt of a number of people to change individuals or societal institutions and structures."[4] So, a social movement engages in the collective pursuit of social change by organizing people, ideas, and resources.

Social movements can be further described as having goals aimed at changing society and its members, as well as being organizations with an incentive structure in which purposive incentives predominate.[5] Given this definition, we can make the claim that all movements begin as unknown movements and, over time, grow into entities that are recognized nationally, regionally, continentally, or even globally.

Christianity as an Unknown Movement

Christianity began as an unknown movement, and we have the benefit of seeing its evolution through the records of the New Testament. When Jesus Christ began his ministry on earth, he cast his vision to twelve people from different walks of life and invited them to be his followers. This group became known as the Twelve – the core team that Jesus intentionally equipped over the three years of his ministry. As this ministry progressed, more people got drawn in as they witnessed or were direct beneficiaries of the teachings and miracles of Christ.

Jesus, the incarnate expression of God among us, began his ministry by proclaiming the arrival of this kingdom, recruiting and training his disciples so that they acquired revealed knowledge and skills necessary for the work of the Great Commission. When we analyze the practice of the disciples in the book of Acts, it is clear that they followed a line of service well learned from their Master: announcing the kingdom of God, proclaiming the need for repentance, and making disciples who were capable of generating other disciples.

This reality was so strong and powerful that even after the beginning of the great persecution that arose against the church at the time of Stephen's death, and despite the apostles remaining in Jerusalem, the remaining disciples proclaimed the kingdom after fleeing Jerusalem and being scattered in other

---

3. Armstrong and Bartley, "Social Movement Organizations," 4448.
4. Zald and Ash, "Social Movement Organizations," 329.
5. Zald and Ash, 329.

areas (Acts 8:1–4). Their unity and their ministerial service were so well articulated and consolidated that it appeared that they had one soul and one heart. During his time on earth, thousands were recorded to have followed Jesus; after his ascension, the numbers multiplied exponentially, and the reach of Christianity became global.

Many other movements have been initiated over time, birthed by various causes, including concern, discontent, and frustration over particular spiritual, political, economic, social, technological, environmental, or legal problems. The initiators of such movements were either individuals or collective groups, but as the movements grew, so did the need for sustainable leadership.

Identifying Leaders

Scripture includes examples of leaders who intentionally selected their protégés, as was the case with Elijah and Elisha (1 Kgs 19:19). Elisha was busy tending to his business when Elijah threw his cloak over his shoulders – a proposition and invitation to Elisha to follow him. We see Moses and Joshua in a similar relationship. Exodus 17:8–16 describes how Moses first sought out Joshua and commanded him to lead an army and fight the Amalekites, while Moses stood at a vantage point and interceded for his success.

Before his ascension, Jesus Christ entrusted his disciples with the task of fulfilling the Great Commission. This being the goal of his ministry, we see the prayerful intentionality and careful consideration that Jesus took in selecting the twelve disciples who would be leaders of the Christian movement. His chosen group was diverse in profession, income, and education. Since it is the Lord who sees the heart and the true motives of human beings (1 Sam 16:7), the process of identifying leaders should be undertaken prayerfully.

Who Is a Leader?

While it is tempting to extend the title of leadership to many, we must acknowledge that every movement has leaders and followers. Not all are leaders, neither are all followers.

> A story is told of a group of children who were playing a war game and getting ready to attack an enemy camp. They gave themselves very high-sounding titles, including Chief Commanding Officer, Field Marshal General, Major General, Lieutenant General, Lieutenant, Major, etc. There was no soldier among them without

a title. The tragedy struck when the enemy descended upon them; there was no one to fight back. Everyone falsely assumed that his title entitled him as a leader to give command to a junior officer until the most junior officer has no one to execute the command. Too many cooks spoil the broth.[6]

Real leaders are in short supply and, since Christian leadership has always required superhuman strength and faith, are constantly sought after. J. Oswald Sanders ponders on this phenomenon: "Why is our need for leaders so great and candidates for leadership so few? Every generation faces the stringent demands of spiritual leadership and welcomes the few who come forward to serve."[7]

Men and women who made a difference in their generation solved their generation's problems. By doing so, they left indelible footprints on the sands of time.[8] Christian leaders should seek to be of service rather than dominate, encourage and inspire respect rather than exploit others, and reflect, pray, and act on the call of Christ to be servants first.[9] Thus, a consideration of leadership must pay attention to the position that the leader holds, the person that the leader is, and the process in which the leader is selected.[10]

Selecting a Leader

When King Saul sinned by disobeying God's command to destroy Amalek completely, the Lord rejected him as king. Thereafter, the Lord instructed Samuel, "How long will you grieve over Saul, since I have rejected him from being king over Israel? Fill your horn with oil, and go. I will send you to Jesse the Bethlehemite, *for I have provided for myself a king* among his sons" (1 Sam 16:1 ESV, emphasis added). We see God actively involved in the leadership selection process. The Lord provides leaders whose role as leaders is to serve his will.

Samuel met seven of the sons of Jesse and, in his judgment, it seemed that Eliab was surely going to be the Lord's anointed (1 Sam 16:6). However, God spoke to Samuel, saying, "Do not look on his appearance or on the height of his stature, because I have rejected him. *For the LORD sees not as man sees: man*

---

6. Adeyemo, *Africa's Enigma*, 65.
7. Sanders, *Spiritual Leadership*, 18.
8. Adeyemo, *Africa's Enigma*, 21.
9. D'Souza, *Leadership*, 12.
10. Ford, *Transforming Leadership*, 26.

looks on the outward appearance, but the LORD *looks on the heart"* (1 Sam 16:7 ESV). In identifying and selecting leaders for unknown movements, we can easily make evaluations based on human standards and be biased by what we see. We may be drawn to individuals because of how they present themselves. Many a time, we can be caught in the moment and exclaim, like Samuel, that surely the Lord's anointed is before us! Let us not fall into the trap of relying on outward appearances; instead, let us look to the Lord, who sees the heart.

Leaders across generations have exhibited five basic attributes: charisma, character, competence, confidence, and courage. All these qualities derive from one common source – an act of grace, popularly known as anointing.[11] For every leadership assignment God gives, he pours himself and his strength into the life of the candidate, resulting in a profoundly transformative experience. No cultural or social historical indicator – including gender, age, tribe, or class status – is grounds for discrimination in leadership that is founded on God's anointing. Dr. Adeyemo describes how anointed leaders see potential, see the power of God, see bearings, see blessings in disguise, see the supernatural, see the invisible, see things as they could be, see opportunities, and see a new beginning.[12] Unknown movements need anointed leaders.

Attributes of a Leader

No universal list of specifications, characteristics, or competencies of leaders exists. However, through research, there have emerged multiple theories of leadership that can guide us in describing the ideal way of identifying leaders within unknown movements.

A Spirit-Led Life

It is important that a Christian leader exhibits the fruit of the Holy Spirit. A Spirit-led person will display love, joy, peace, patience, kindness, goodness, faithfulness, gentleness, and self-control (Gal 5:22–23). Such transformational traits guide leaders' engagement with themselves and their community. Love, which heads the list, is critical since a leader's heart and motives are displayed through how they love God, themselves, and others. Dr. Sanders sheds light on the last fruit, self-control, which he terms a discipline.[13] Discipline undergirds

---

11. Adeyemo, *Africa's Enigma*, 21.
12. Adeyemo, 32.
13. Sanders, *Spiritual Leadership*, 52.

all the other traits because before conquering the world, we must first conquer the self. A leader practises self-denial, discipline, and self-restraint. If a leader demonstrates strong self-discipline, others will sense this and usually cooperate with the expectations placed on them.

Visionary

The Lord reminds us that without vision, people perish (Prov 29:18). Thus, a key trait of a leader is the insight to see beyond the present and cast a compelling vision. Those who have powerfully and permanently influenced their generation have been "seers" – people who have seen more and further than others – and also persons of faith – for faith is vision.[14] Leaders can see more widely and fully than others – they see far horizons. Dr. Adeyemo elaborates on this, explaining that faith-driven vision comes with an incredible ability to see into the past (hindsight), see penetratingly into the present (insight), and see into the future (foresight).[15]

Wisdom

Wise leadership is spoken about throughout Scripture. King Solomon, when given the opportunity by the Lord to ask for anything, proceeded to ask for an understanding heart so that he could govern well and know the difference between right and wrong. His request pleased God, and King Solomon received a wise and understanding heart (1 Kgs 3:5, 9–12). Throughout Solomon's leadership, we see how this wisdom was exercised in handling different issues. King Solomon learned how to persuade others through wisdom. Similarly, unknown movements will need leaders who can engage wisely with people, processes, and strategies. Dr. Sanders explains this as the need to have leaders rightly apply knowledge in moral and spiritual matters, handling dilemmas, and negotiating complex relationships.[16] Leadership by influence is one that is open to other people's viewpoints, creates democratic space for mavericks, forces the leader to listen to and learn from others, makes the leader vulnerable, and enriches the leader's store of collective wisdom.[17]

---

14. Sanders, 55.
15. Adeyemo, *Africa's Enigma*, 32.
16. Sanders, *Spiritual Leadership*, 57.
17. Adeyemo, *Africa's Enigma*, 36.

Transformational

Transformational leaders play a critical role in shaping the destination of movements, making the movements personal, and creating a sense of belonging. At the heart of transformational leadership is change. Leaders change teams or organizations by creating, communicating, and modelling a vision and inspiring others to strive for it.[18] Transformational leadership's fundamental focus is to engage in a process that serves to change and transform others, and leaders commit themselves to developing others to their fullest potential. Transformative leadership increases follower motivation by fulfilling the higher needs of followers, appealing to moral ideals, and empowering followers. These leaders make their followers feel trust, admiration, loyalty, and respect towards the leader and motivate them to do more than they originally expected to do.[19] In essence, a transformative leader can generate enthusiasm and commitment from their followers towards the greater good.

Capacity Building

Training and equipping leaders is a delicate task. Any gift that is exercised without the disciplines of training, denial, and pressure cannot function at its best. The issue, therefore, is not whether leaders are born or made. Nature and nurture work together to develop effective leaders.[20]

The apostle Paul viewed this process of equipping as one of entrusting to reliable people who would be competent to teach others (2 Tim 2:2). In essence, we see this as a multigenerational process of discipleship that began with Paul, was passed on to Timothy, then to those who were reliable and faithful, and, thereafter, to others. This demonstrates that capacity building of leaders is not an end in itself but one that has a ripple effect through generations.

Leader-Making Using a Discipleship Model

Over the years, the leadership development niche has been commercialized, with programmes being mainstreamed in educational institutions and developed for broad consumption. However, Dr. Sanders argues that

---

18. David Kirimi et al. *Transformational Corporate Leadership*, 37.
19. Yukl, *Leadership in Organizations*, 253.
20. Adeyemo, *Africa's Enigma*, 68.

leadership training cannot be done on a mass scale. It requires patience, careful instruction, and prayerful, personal guidance over a considerable period of time. Disciples are not manufactured wholesale. They are produced one by one, because someone has taken the pains to discipline, to instruct and enlighten, to nurture and train one that is younger. When a person is really marked out for leadership, God will see that that person receives the necessary disciplines for effective service.[21]

The long-term goal of Christian discipleship is to reach others so that they can reach still more people. The entire life of a disciple is structured according to God's will. Jesus is their Lord and the only ruler of all areas of their life. Thus, we consider these three tenets to be fundamental in the capacity building of leaders of unknown movements: being with Christ, living for Christ, and, finally, leading like Christ.

Being with Christ

Effective leadership starts on the inside and is a heart issue. Leadership is first a spiritual matter of the heart. Scripture records that "Jesus went up on a mountainside and called to him those he wanted, and they came to him. He appointed twelve that *they might be with him and that he might send them out*" (Mark 3:13–14, emphasis added). Christian leadership requires that significant time be spent with the Lord. The leader must learn to do everything that Jesus has commanded and to convey the truth by words and example.[22] When Jesus called Simon Peter and Andrew, he said, "Follow me, and I will make you fishers of men" (Matt 4:19 ESV). This call had an objective – "I will make you fishers of men" – and a condition had to be fulfilled – "Follow me" – to achieve that objective. Thus, we see that the prerequisite for the work that God has called us to do as leaders is that we spend time with the Lord.

Living for Christ

It requires brutal honesty to uncover and correct the subtleties of the heart and the veils of justification we place over self-serving motives. Equipping leaders in unknown movements includes helping them to learn the full counsel of God that can guide them holistically. Christian leadership is a gift that is purpose-

---

21. Sanders, *Spiritual Leadership*, 150.
22. Salvador, *Princípios Elementares*, 66.

driven and requires training, denial, and commitment.[23] Equally important is Jesus's insistence that disciples must deny themselves, take up the cross, and renounce everything and everyone – including their own lives – in order to follow him (Mark 8:34–38; Luke 9:23; 14:25–33). The apostle Paul captures the essence of sacrificial lives unto the Lord: "Therefore, I urge you, brothers and sisters, in view of God's mercy, to offer your bodies as a living sacrifice, holy and pleasing to God – this is your true and proper worship" (Rom 12:1).

Christian leaders are called to put their lives in order by applying Jesus's teachings to all areas of life, which results in the disciple's character being transformed and their conduct being changed.[24] Capacity-building programmes for leaders should equip them to develop the attributes that Dr. Adeyemo says should be nurtured within Christian leaders:[25]

- Strive to be like Christ always.
- Seek to be filled with the Holy Spirit daily.
- Search the Bible for guiding principles for decision-making.
- Submit personal opinion to collective wisdom.
- Serve with diligence rather than wait to be served.
- Set up policies, systems and structures drawn from the kingdom principles.
- Steer the "vessel" to the promised land.

Leading Like Christ

Leading like Jesus is more than a theory; it is about changing how you lead others and committing to change your behaviour to be more like Jesus.[26] The disciples whom Jesus called each brought life experiences and skills to their new task, but they did not have practical knowledge of how to fulfil this new role. Christ called the disciples, trained them, and then sent them out.

> After spending three years under the leadership of Jesus, the disciples were transformed from untrained novices to fully equipped, inspired, and spiritually grounded leaders able to fulfill the Great Commission to go to all nations with the good news. How did Jesus accomplish the transition from call to commission? It entailed a perfect execution of a familiar process

---

23. Adeyemo, *Africa's Enigma*, 41.
24. Salvador, *Princípios Elementares*, 66.
25. Adeyemo, *Africa's Enigma*, 72.
26. Blanchard and Hodges, *Lead Like Jesus*, 119.

by a leader personally committed to accomplishing a goal through the growth and development of those who follow . . . Having presumably been guided through four normal stages of learning a new task – from *novice* (someone just starting out) to *apprentice* (someone in training) to *journeyman* (someone capable of working independently) and finally *master/teacher* (someone highly skilled and able to teach others) . . . Jesus brought to His season of leadership a clear understanding of the journey from dependence to independence.[27]

Leaders of unknown movements need to be guided through the learning process, from novice – where they receive basic information – to apprenticeship – where they receive assurance and correction in the training – to journeyman – where they receive appreciation, encouragement, and inspiration – and, finally, masters or teachers – where they are given the opportunity, challenge, and blessing to pass on what they know to the next generation of learners. This, then, is the process that the apostle Paul must have had in mind when he reminded Timothy to "entrust" the teachings to reliable people (2 Tim 2:2).

Conclusion

If we wish to identify and develop the capacity of leaders who are at the service of the kingdom, we must take into consideration that ever since the beginning of humanity, God has been working continuously to establish a kingdom according to the perfect standards of his own heart. We need to intentionally seek and rely on God in the process of identifying, selecting, equipping, and commissioning leaders for unknown movements.

Bibliography

Adeyemo, Tokunboh. *Africa's Enigma and Leadership Solutions*. Nairobi: WordAlive, 2009.
Armstrong, Elizabeth A., and Tim Bartley. "Social Movement Organizations." In *The Blackwell Encyclopedia of Sociology*, edited by George Ritzer, 4448–51. Oxford: Blackwell, 2007. https://doi.org/10.1002/9781405165518.wbeoss158.
Blanchard, Ken, and Phil Hodges. *Lead Like Jesus*. Nashville: W Publishing Group, 2005.
D'Souza, Anthony. *Leadership*. Nairobi: Paulines Publications Africa, 1994.

---

27. Blanchard and Hodges, 125–26.

Ford, Leighton. *Transforming Leadership*. Downers Grove: InterVarsity Press, 1991.
Kirimi, David, and A. Kirimi Barine. *Transformational Corporate Leadership*. Wake Forest: Integrity Publishers Incorporated, 2012.
Mordomo, João. "A Call to Startups to Start Making Disciples." *Lausanne Movement*, 17 July 2019. YouTube video. https://youtu.be/goMt57CE2kI?si=FyN1TqcMN3uuBuOM.
Oh, Michael. "Kingdom Impact in Every Sphere of Society." *Lausanne Movement*, 27 June 2019. YouTube video. https://youtu.be/RJrLZVxKBPY?si=g6wP1MFQZ9qR7QhE.
Salvador, Igreja em. *Princípios Elementares*. São Paulo: Acesso Tecnologia, 2013.
Sanders, Oswald J. *Spiritual Leadership*. Chicago: Moody, 1994.
Yukl, Gary. *Leadership in Organizations*. Saddle River: Prentice Hall, 2002.
Zald, Mayer N., and Roberta Ash. "Social Movement Organizations: Growth, Decay, and Change." *Social Forces* 44, no. 3 (1996): 327–41.

26

Resilience: Longevity and Preventing Burnout

John and Denise Lewis

Introduction

This short chapter seeks to address some of the issues pertaining to burnout in pastoral ministry and the practices and disciplines necessary for successful longevity in ministry.

Burnout is a key term used within leadership spaces, and its importance in Christian ministry is no exception. Burnout presents a unique challenge within ministerial leadership as it not only impacts the individual leader but is known to leave churches failing to find their footing when pastors succumb to pressures of the ministry.

Pastoral Burnout

The concept of burnout originated with Freudenberger, who proposed that the central thesis of the burnout concept is its development in the social context of work life.[1] The concept has since been extended to include all professions, occupational groups, and education.[2]

The term "burnout" is used to describe the physical and emotional tiredness that occurs because of engaging in strenuous tasks or activities over

---

1. Schaufeli, Maslach, and Marek, "Professional Burnout . . . ," 1–2.
2. Maslach, Schaufeli, and Leiter, "Job Burnout," 397–422.

an extended period.³ Based on this definition, Christian ministry burnout brings about similar symptoms of mental and physical exhaustion, along with an inability to perform duties effectively.

Burnout is defined as a psychological syndrome that is developed in response to chronic stress, which may be environmental, interpersonal, or a combination of these variables.⁴ The dimensions of psychological burnout, as identified within the Maslach Burnout Inventory – General Survey for Students or MBI-GS (S) – a psychological assessment, are emotional exhaustion, depersonalization, and a diminished sense of accomplishment.⁵

The theoretical underpinning of this study is Maslach and Jackson's three-factor structure of burnout, where the three factors are emotional exhaustion, depersonalization, and reduced personal accomplishment.⁶ Emotional exhaustion is an indicator of job stress, which creates a sense of being under pressure and the results are in the depletion of emotional resources.⁷ Depersonalization is a detached and cynical response to colleagues or others in the work environment.⁸ The final component, reduced personal accomplishment, is noted as a decline in competence and productivity in response to the situation.⁹

Pastors and leaders who do not maintain a balance between work and rest become candidates for burnout in ministry. Several researchers have found consistent results regarding why pastors prematurely leave the ministry. Chandler, who explored a few of the causes that led to pastoral failure in ministry, posits that physical and emotional stressors and burnout are key factors that prevent people from fulfilling their ministerial vocation.¹⁰ Elkington identifies individualized spirituality, postmodernism, and secularism as three

---

3. Merriam-Webster, "burnout," 2022. https://www.merriam-webster.com/dictionary/burnout.

4. Maslach, Schaufeli, and Leiter, "Job Burnout," 99–113.

5. See https://www.mindgarden.com/313-mbi-general-survey-for-students.

6. Maslach, Schaufeli, and Leiter, "Job Burnout," 397–422.

7. Maslach and Jackson, "Measurement of Experienced Burnout," 99–113; Maslach and Rostami, "The Psychometric Characteristics of Maslach Burnout Inventory Student Survey: Among Students Of Isfahan University," 15.

8. Maslach and Jackson, "Measurement of Experienced Burnout," 99–113; Schaufeli, Maslach, and Marek, 22.

9. Enoch et al., "Association Of Medical Student Burnout . . . ," 173–81; Maslach and Jackson, "Measurement of Experienced Burnout," 99–113; Rostami et al., "The Psychometric Characteristics of Maslach Burnout Inventory Student Survey . . . ," 15.

10. Chandler, "Pastoral Burnout," 273–87.

main reasons why pastors and leaders leave the ministry.[11] Additionally, McCormick observes that there is a correlation between a leader's self-confidence and successful leadership.[12] The experiences of trauma, experiences of failure, unmet needs, and financial pressures adversely impact the quality of leadership and, consequently, increase stress that leads to exhaustion and burnout.[13]

Analysing the pastors' job description, activities, demands, and expectations related to the pastoral roles leads to the conclusion that pastors will be predisposed to chronic stress and burnout.[14] Chandler believed that the multiplicity of activities pastors often had to carry out was a possible cause of burnout and notes that burnout "advances across three dimensions: emotional exhaustion, depersonalization, and reduced accomplishment."[15] Therefore, pastors who are inundated with numerous tasks are likely to become drained, thereby being left vulnerable to the adverse effects of burnout on their physical, social, and spiritual well-being. Meek et al. also note that because of the exhaustion and stress that often accompanies ministry, it takes resiliency to endure the race and finish well. Pastors who suffer from burnout are more likely to experience feelings of hopelessness and a desire to give up ministry – if only to regain their sense of self. Pastors who choose to stay in ministry despite suffering from burnout may fail to lead effectively and may fall into ungodly habits as a coping mechanism. It takes resiliency to endure the race and finish well.[16]

In order to finish well in ministry, we must guard our hearts against two key temptations: overwork and moral infidelity. Immorality is one of the main reasons leaders fail. Edmonson focuses our attention on the issue of managing temptations:

> Managing temptations is where the rubber meets the road in the life of a follower of Christ because spiritual maturity and responsibility only lead to a ramping up of the enemy's attacks. The enemy has one goal: take every Christ-follower out or do what he can to keep them down, away from becoming self-aware,

---
11. Elkington, "Adversity in Pastoral Leadership," 6.
12. McCormick, "Self-Efficacy," 22–33.
13. Popphan, "Dark Side of Leadership," 15; Meek et al., "Maintaining Personal Resiliency," 30.
14. Demerouti et al., "The job-demands-resources model of burnout," 499–512.
15. Chandler, "Pastoral Burnout," 273.
16. Meek et al., "Maintaining Personal Resiliency . . . ," 339–47.

because that is the place where every Christ-follower is in grave danger of leadership failure.[17]

Ministerial Burnout

Pastoral burnout and other stressors are leading causes of pastors failing to achieve longevity and prematurely leaving the ministry. Doolittle notes that

> burnout has an important impact upon the professional satisfaction of clergy. Identifying protective behaviours that may prevent against burnout is important for the long-term emotional health of individual clergy as well as the wider church.[18]

The issue of ministry burnout has not been sufficiently addressed – hence the exit of many pastors from ministry. The unrealistic expectations placed upon pastors and leaders can debilitate their physical, emotional, and mental health, thereby affecting their ability to function. Otey concurs:

> Pastors minister to people who are often emotionally demanding and who have unrealistic expectations of how the pastor should interact with them. For example, pastors often listen to complaints individuals may have about how the church is run, and pastors are expected to actively listen, convey concern, and do so with great tact and diplomacy – even with chronic complainers.[19]

Factors Enabling Longevity in Ministry
God's Call on a Person

Most pastors and leaders who have undoubtedly received a call to ministry finish well. McKenna et al., Joynt, and Strunk, Milacci, and Zabloski, who researched the significance of the call to ministry, emphasize that a call to ministry is beyond oneself.[20]

Engelbrecht draws our attention to the fact that the call provides a sense of identity and positively impacts our longevity in ministry. This call will be

---

17. Edmonson, "Folleadership," 39.
18. Doolittle, "Impact of Behaviors," 88–95.
19. Otey, "Emotional and Spiritual Dimensions," 4.
20. McKenna et al., "A Qualitative Study of Transcendent Calling," 294–303; Joynt, "Exodus of Clergy," 4; and J. Strunk, F. Milacci, and J. Zabloski, "The Convergence of Ministry, Tenure, and Efficacy," 537–50.

sustained, first and foremost, by our relationship with the God who gave the call. This relationship is modelled for us by the Trinity, which so eloquently reflects the "wholeness of God." This is the Triune God who is in relationship first with himself, in harmony with the Son and the Holy Spirit. This model is a relationship of harmony working with and for each other, not in hierarchy but, rather, working with and for each other out of love for each other and for the glory of the whole.[21] Thus, the work of the Trinity enables the fulfilment of our calling. It cannot be overemphasized that the call of God upon our lives is a holy calling that is empowered by the Holy Spirit of God for the glory of God.

Spiritual Disciplines

Spiritual disciplines – properly practised – are the cornerstones for finishing well in ministry. Morton emphasizes that

> spiritual practices enhance and deepen relationships. It [service and effective ministry] is also deepened through living in unbroken community with the body of Christ. For effective leadership, Scripture teaches that intimacy resulting from holiness enables revelation through prayer, Scripture, solitude, communion with the body, and other spiritual practices. Only then can stewards understand sufficiently his world, his plan, timing, and method and the role he calls them to play.[22]

Those who habitually practise the spiritual disciplines of prayer, solitude, intercession, fasting, accountability, fidelity, and so on are more likely to succeed at finishing well in ministry. I will describe these disciplines in detail below.

Prayer

Prayer is the medium by which we can have access to God. In answer to prayer, God changes us and empowers us to change circumstances.

Melton says,

> I believe that an aspect of prayer that is often neglected is the art of listening to God, sitting before him in an attitude of waiting, and a willingness to hear what he might have to say, particularly with a heart open to being changed in his presence.[23]

---

21. Engelbrecht, "Vocations," 67.
22. Morton, "Spiritual Practices," 57.
23. Melton, "Spiritual Formation," 49.

Listening to the voice of God is fast becoming a lost art. We are inundated with information overloads that can easily distract us from hearing the voice of God. Melton also notes:

> People prioritize their time based on the value placed on each thing chosen to do. If one desires the kind of change in character that I have described here, one will prioritize the time to be in God's presence, to listen to his voice, and be willing to obey.[24]

We make time for the things that we prioritize, and this same principle applies to prayer. When we commit to times of prayer, we listen to the voice of God and, hopefully, obey. The importance of this discipline cannot be overemphasized in the lives of pastors who preach and teach on the importance of prayer.

Pastors and leaders should embrace this privilege of praying so that they may experience answers to their prayers and the prayers of their congregants. Morton reflects, "Prayer decides all matters in the sense that through listening in prayer (and other spiritual practices) the already decided will of God is discerned. Christian leaders always must be in prayer as they live daily and fight life's given battles."[25] Ultimately, God is the one who responds to our prayers and helps us to be victorious in our struggles.

Solitude

Solitude is essential to our spiritual formation because it allows us to quiet our hearts before God and experience a sense of his presence. Solitude enables us to engage in an intimate encounter with God. Bailey remarks,

> The silence of solitude should not imply laziness or inactivity. Solitude should always beget active listening. Sensitivity to the movement of the Spirit is central to solitude. By disrupting the daily habits that distract the believer, space is created for God to speak. To overlook God's divine revelation would be to miss the point of solitude altogether.[26]

God is more desirous to meet with us than we are inclined to be in solitude with him. He delights when we come before him, seeking his strength and guidance for our lives. When we allow our calendars to drown out these

---

24. Melton, 52.
25. Morton, "Spiritual Practices," 73.
26. Bailey, "Biblical Spiritual Disciplines," 83.

important times of solitude in our lives and allow the busyness of ministry to consume us, this leads to barrenness and spiritual bankruptcy. Even in ministry, we can find ourselves working *for* God but not *with* God.

Intercession

Intercession is an aspect of prayer, but it involves praying specifically on behalf of others rather than for ourselves. As pastors carry the weight of their churches, they are burdened with the various needs of their members and the church. They are called upon to intercede on behalf of families in crisis, students with challenges at school, marriages in conflict, and the bereaved and also to handle a multitude of prayer requests. Intercession happens when pastors realize that God is their ultimate resource and that, therefore, they no longer have to carry the load of these legitimate concerns alone but can bring all these petitions before God.

Clements-Jewery posits that

> the act of intercession thus reinforces the personal nature of the universe. As an instance of faith active in love, prayer both makes certain possibilities greater and strengthens the likelihood of divine response, so that those who pray may have every confidence that their prayers will make a difference to the world, through the God who both influences and is influenced by the creation.[27]

Jesus Christ intercedes on our behalf by taking our petitions before our heavenly Father and responding to our petitions by his Spirit.

Fasting

Lengyel provides a historical backdrop to fasting. He notes:

> Fasting was a common practice among eighteenth-century New England Puritans. It was customary to observe regular fast-days, as both a spiritual discipline and a response to perceived divine judgment. Congregations and communities would gather and petition God for help, embracing fasting as a means to exercise control over the appetites of the flesh. These passions, when left unchecked, could hinder a faithful believer from being effectively heard in prayer. Fasting was the ultimate ascetic discipline,

---

27. Clements-Jewery, "Intercessory Prayer," 106.

holding obvious appeal for a community that prided itself on its unmitigated pursuit of God.[28]

There was a determined desire and passion for God in the practise of this Christian discipline among these believers. They viewed this exercise as a means to live victoriously over sin in their lives. Unfortunately, this practice is fast disappearing from the church today.

Piper notes:

> Under the Spirit's leading, Jesus prepared himself for this testing by fasting. "Jesus was led up by the Spirit into the wilderness to be tempted by the devil. And after fasting forty days . . ." the Spirit of God willed that the Son of God be tested on his way into the ministry, and he willed that Jesus triumph in this testing through fasting. It must not go unnoticed that Jesus triumphed over the great enemy of his soul and our salvation through fasting.[29]

Piper goes on to say,

> The root of Christian fasting is the hunger of homesickness for God. I mean that we will do anything and go without anything if, by any means, we might protect ourselves from the deadening effects of innocent delights and preserve the sweet longings of our homesickness for God. Not just food, but anything.[30]

Accountability

Accountability, which requires a person to be transparent before another person, is sometimes seen as a negative quality. I believe that the question of trust and confidentiality are issues in an accountability relationship. Unless both parties share and respect these values, it becomes difficult to pursue an accountability relationship. Nevertheless, those who do have an accountability partner feel secure in their ministry and continue to serve faithfully and successfully.

Lynn and Ramsey acknowledge that "being accountable" first means being accountable to the God who gives us life and redeems us in grace.[31] Ephesians sheds light on this type of accountability. "Offering and sacrifice" (Eph 5:2) is not what we offer one another but what we offer God. Here, "wisdom" is

---

28. Lengyel, "Recovering the Disciplines," 23.
29. Piper, "Hunger for God," 54.
30. Piper, 19.
31. Lynn and Ramsey, "What Is Accountability?," https://mministry.org/what-is-accountability/.

oriented towards discerning together what God is saying to us rather than relying on our best "conventional wisdom." "Reverence for Christ" points to us offering our reverence wholeheartedly to God and allowing that reverence to shape how we then turn to one another in accountability. Neither our lives nor any church board can exist without the grace of God (2 Cor 8:7). The knowledge of God's grace orients us to freely give ourselves to one another and offer one another – even those who oppose us – the same grace we ourselves are experiencing as made known to us in Jesus Christ.[32]

As highlighted by Lynn and Ramsey, the collaborative wisdom of accountability partners is referenced in Scripture. It is when we respond in obedience to these biblical mandates that our lives can be meaningful and fruitful over the long haul.

Fidelity

Aponte states,

> Fidelity must be a conscious choice you make – one that can encourage the emotional creativity to be able to get along for that many years. This requires the relational competencies including, self-awareness, conscious empathy, and kindness. Fidelity is a choice that you must negotiate regularly to protect your most intimate bond while you both continue to grow as individuals.[33]

Aponte also admonishes:

> Each of you must take the time to reflect on your own thoughts and feelings about sexual fidelity in your marriage. Examine your implicit view of sexual monogamy. This is likely to be influenced by your own family background, religious beliefs, traditional sex roles, personal moral values, and personal insecurities.[34]

It must be noted that the demands on a couple in ministry can often cause strain in the marital relationship. If a couple in ministry is not vigilant about keeping their marriage safe and protected from intrusions, they are vulnerable to infidelity.

---

32. Lynn and Ramsey.
33. Aponte, "Choosing Fidelity," 3.
34. Aponte, para 11.

Sanford emphasizes that

> marital fidelity is a daily commitment to seek the best for your spouse and family. Marital fidelity is strengthened when you affirm your spouse, listen to your spouse, and seek to meet his or her needs. It is also strengthened when you set healthy boundaries for your media consumption and for your relationships outside of the home.[35]

Every couple must institute safeguards for their marriage. We must manage our time appropriately so that we are not consumed by our preoccupation with social media.

Rest or Sabbath

Pastors are held to a higher standard when it comes to "practising what we preach." Unless we are personally refreshed by the work of the Holy Spirit in our lives and work as pastors, we ourselves become spiritually empty and cannot function out of a life of resourcefulness. Hence the need for rest and recreation in a physical sense but also in the spiritual arena of our lives. Kraft points out:

> In the relentless busyness of modern life, we have lost the rhythm between action and rest. There is a universal refrain: I am so busy. As it all piles endlessly upon itself, the whole experience of being alive begins to melt into one enormous obligation. Sabbath time is a revolutionary challenge to the violence of overwork. Many of us, in our desperate drive to be successful and care for our many responsibilities, feel terrible guilt when we take time to rest.[36]

Seemingly, rest evades us. As pastors and leaders, we are highly motivated and have the tendency to go on working longer hours than the average person. Therefore, we must make a deliberate decision to take time to rest and recuperate, especially after an intense period of ministry. Kraft makes a further observation:

> I believe that most leaders travel too fast and attempt to do too much. If priorities protect my purpose and passion, then pacing prolongs it. Someone said, "I am running on fumes and don't know where the next gas station is." That's the thought in Psalm

---

35. Sanford, "Maintaining Marital Fidelity," 3.
36. Kraft, *Leaders Who Last*, 66–67.

139:3: "You chart the path ahead of me and tell me where to stop and rest. Every moment, you know where I am" (TLB).[37]

God designed us for the Sabbath; and when we ignore his laws, we often pay in the form of severe consequences such as ill health, depression, and burnout. Bailey reminds us:

> Trust in God's provision is usually relegated to isolated moments of unusual need when personal abilities and resources are insufficient to solve the problem at hand. Implementing a Sabbath frees the believer from the misplaced expectation that he is responsible for his future, placing God squarely in command.[38]

We forfeit rest and Sabbath when we become anxious about how we are going to meet our needs. Therefore, we overwork ourselves and refuse to trust in God to provide for us.

Authentic Leadership

Pastors and other Christian leaders who seek to be authentic and without pretence in their leadership are more likely to have longevity in their ministries. Walumbwa et al. define authentic leadership as "an exhibited pattern of leader behaviour where openness and clarity in the leader's behaviour is demonstrated through the sharing of all necessary information, the accepting of other's inputs, and the disclosing of the leader's personal values, motives, and sentiments."[39] When our actions and behaviours are compatible with our words, we become authentic before our followers.

Puls, Ludden, and Freemyer, having examined the correlation between authentic leadership and long-term effectiveness in ministry, conclude that apart from authenticity, one cannot be truly effective and achieve longevity in ministry.[40]

This is indeed a grave call for authenticity in leaders in all vocations of life, and this is particularly true when it comes to pastoral leadership. Since we receive our mandate to lead from God, we are held to a higher standard of accountability as ministers of God. George suggests that

---

37. Kraft, 67.
38. Bailey, "Biblical Spiritual Disciplines," 99.
39. Walumbwa et al., "Authentic Leadership," 89–126.
40. Puls, Ludden, and Freemyer, "Authentic Leadership," 55–75.

to become authentic, each of us must develop our own leadership style, consistent with our personality and character. Unfortunately, the pressures of an organization push us to adhere to its normative style. But if we conform to a style that is not consistent with who we are, we will never become authentic leaders.[41]

Finishing the Race

The apostle Paul asserts, "I have fought the good fight, I have finished the race, I have kept the faith" (2 Tim 4:7). The prerequisites for finishing well include an intimate relationship with God, an insatiable appetite for learning, demonstration of a Christlike character, and a fulfilled sense of purpose. According to Ong, all effective leaders who stay the course and end the race of life and ministry well display a growing awareness of their sense of life's purpose and destiny, progressively accomplishing the things God has laid out for them and staying and finishing the course.[42]

Conclusion

Pastors who fail to practise accountability, have no support system, and fail to dedicate themselves to prayer, studying God's word, and honing their spiritual disciplines and Christian values are more prone to experiencing exhaustion and burnout. In order to achieve successful longevity pastors must be dedicated to the study of God's word, prayer, the work of the Holy Spirit, integrity, accountability, humility, compassion, regular retreats, and affirmation of the call of God.

Bibliography

Aponte, C. "Choosing Fidelity in Your Marriage." *Psychology Today*, 23 October 2019. https://www.psychologytoday.com/us/blog/marriage-equals/201910/choosing-fidelity-in-your-marriage.

Bailey, K. M. "A Phenomenological Study of How Biblical Spiritual Disciplines Influence Women's Character and Leadership Practices in Christian Faith-Based Institutions in Higher Education in North America." PhD diss., Pepperdine University, 2017.

---

41. George, *Authentic Leadership*, 13.
42. Ong, "Finishing Well in Ministry: Lessons from Paul," 6.

Brazeau, C., R. Schroeder, S. Rovi, and L. Boyd (2010). "Relationships between Medical Student Burnout, Empathy and Professionalism Climate." *Academic Medicine* 85: 33–36. https://doi.org/10.1097/ACM.0b013e3181ed4c47.

Chandler, D. J. "Pastoral Burnout and the Impact of Personal Spiritual Renewal, Rest-Taking, and Support System Practices." *Pastoral Psychology* 58, no. 3 (2009): 273–87. http://dx.doi.org/10.1007/s11089-008-0184-4.

Doolittle, B. R. "The Impact of Behaviors upon Burnout among Parish-Based Clergy." *Journal of Religion and Health* 49, no. 1 (2010): 88–95. https://doi.org/10.1007/s10943-008-9217-7.

Edmonson, J. L. "Folleadership: The Priority and Practice of Following Christ in Order to Maintain Integrity in Ministry." PhD diss., Bakke Graduate University, 2010.

Elkington, R. "Adversity in Pastoral Leadership: Are Pastors Leaving the Ministry in Record Numbers, and If So, Why?" *Verbum et Ecclesia* 34, no. 1 (2013): Art. #821, 13 pages.

Engelbrecht, T. "Vocations and the Church." PhD diss., Bakke Graduate University, 2019.

Enoch L., J. T. Chibnall, D. L.Schindler et al. "Association Of Medical Student Burnout With Residency Specialty Choice." *Medical Education* 47, no. 2 (2013): 173–81.

George, B. *Authentic Leadership: Rediscovering the Secrets to Creating Lasting Value*. Hoboken: Jossey-Bass, 2003.

Joynt, S. "Exodus of Clergy: Responding to, Reinterpreting or Relinquishing the Call." *Verbum et Ecclesia* 38, no. 1 (2017).

Kraft, D. *Leaders Who Last*. Wheaton: Crossway, 2010.

Lengyel, T. G. "Recovering the Disciplines: A Comparative Study on the Spiritual Disciplines as Expressed in the Lives, Teaching and Ministry of Jonathan Edwards, Charles Finney and Richard Foster." PhD diss., Duke Divinity School, 2018.

Lynn, E., and M. Ramsey. "What Is Accountability?" *The Ministry Collaborative*, 28 January 2021. https://mministry.org/what-is-accountability/.

Maslach, C., and S. E. Jackson. "The Measurement of Experienced Burnout." *Journal of Organizational Behavior* 2 (1981): 99–113.

Maslach, C., W. B. Schaufeli, and M. P. Leiter. "Job Burnout." *Annual Review of Psychology* 52, no. 1 (2001): 397–422.

McCormick, M. J. "Self-Efficacy and Leadership Effectiveness: Applying Social Cognitive Theory to Leadership." *Journal of Leadership Studies* 8, no. 1 (2001): 22–33.

McKenna, R. B., J. Matson, D. M. Haney, O. Becker, M. J. Hickory, D. L. Ecker, and T. N. Boyd. "Calling, the Caller, and Being Called: A Qualitative Study of Transcendent Calling." *Journal of Psychology and Christianity* 34, no. 4 (2015): 294–303.

Meek, K. R., M. R. McMinn, C. M. Brower, T. D. Burnett, B. W. McRay, M. L. Ramey, D. W. Swanson, and D. D. Villa. "Maintaining Personal Resiliency: Lessons Learned from Evangelical Protestant Clergy." *Journal of Psychology and Theology* 31, no. 4 (2003): 339–47.

Melton, J. "Spiritual Formation for the Transformational Leader." Master's diss., Bakke Graduate University, 2009.

Morton, J. "Spiritual Practices and Effective Christian Leadership." PhD diss., Bakke Graduate University, 2015.

Otey, A. "The Emotional and Spiritual Dimensions of Being a Pastor: Authenticity and Identity." PhD diss., Texas A&M University, 2010.

Piper, J. *A Hunger for God: Desiring God through Fasting and Prayer.* Wheaton: Crossway, 1997.

Popphan, J. H. "Overcoming the Dark Side of Leadership: How to Become an Effective Leader by Confronting Potential Failures." *Air and Space Power Journal* 33, no. 4 (2019): 96–98.

Puls, T. R., L. L. Ludden, and J. Freemyer. "Authentic Leadership and Its Relationship to Ministerial Effectiveness." *Journal of Applied Christian Leadership* 8, no. 1 (2014): 55–75.

Rostami, Z., M. R. Abedi, W. B. Schaufeli S. A. Ahmadi, and A. H. Sadeghi. "The Psychometric Characteristics of Maslach Burnout Inventory Student Survey: Among Students of Isfahan University." *Zahedan Journal of Research in Medical Science* 2013: 29–32.

Sanders, John. "Review of P. Clements-Jewery: Intercessory Prayer: Modern Theology, Biblical Teaching and Philosophical Thought." *Religious Studies Review* 32, no. 2 (2006): 106. https://doi.org/10.1111/j.1748-0922.2006.00060_2.x.

Sanford, D. "Maintaining Marital Fidelity." *Focus on the Family*, 1 January 2004. https://www.focusonthefamily.com/marriage/maintaining-marital-fidelity/.

Schaufeli, W. B., C. Maslach, and T. Marek (Eds.). *Professional Burnout: Recent Developments in Theory and Research.* Taylor & Francis, 1993.

Strunk, J., F. Milacci, and J. Zabloski. "The Convergence of Ministry, Tenure, and Efficacy: Beyond Speculation toward a New Theory of Pastoral Efficacy." *Pastoral Psychology* 66, no. 4 (2017): 537–50.

Walumbwa, F. O., B. J. Avolio, W. L. Gardner, T. S. Wernsing, and S. J. Peterson. "Authentic Leadership: Development and Validation of a Theory-Based Measure." *Journal of Management* 34, no. 1 (2008): 89–126. https://doi.org/10.1177/0149206307308913.

Zabloski, J., and F. Milacci "Gifted Dropouts: Phenomenological Case Studies of Rural Gifted Students." *Journal of Ethnographic & Qualitative Research*, vol. 6 no. 3 (2012): 175–90.

27

Building Organizational Capacity

Nadim Costa and Sam Metcalf

> As it was in the Beginning. Two Structures of God's Redemptive Mission.[1]
>
> Robert Blinco
> President Emeritus, Frontiers

In August 1973, at the All-Asia Mission Consultation in Seoul, missiologist Ralph Winter delivered an address entitled "The Two Structures of God's Redemptive Mission." His words, profound in that moment fifty years ago, have stood the test of time and experience in describing the biblical, historical, and missiological structures necessary for the health and expansion of the Christian movement. Winter's address was a poignant demonstration of the well-known adage that the great Christian revolutions come not by the discovery of something that was not known before, but that they happen when someone takes radically something that was always there.

We maintain that any consideration of organizational structures for mission – together with the corresponding leadership necessary for such mission – that does not understand and embrace this fundamental structural paradigm will fall short of God's missional purposes and designs. Missional vision without the appropriate missional structures is not a vision but a dream that will likely languish unfulfilled. Case study after case study in a broad array of cultures and contexts over the past five decades have proven this to be true. When Winter's *modalities* (the church in its local, parish, or diocesan form) relates in a synergistic and healthy manner with *sodalities* (the church

---

[1]. Byline regularly used in Dr. Robert Blinco's blog, *Lighthouse & Flint*. https://robertblincoe.blog.

in its sent, missionary, task-oriented form), the Christian movement has the potential to flourish. When either one dominates or controls the other, the Christian movement suffers. As Robert Blincoe, former President of Frontiers, succinctly observes, these structural distinctives always have been and always will be.[2]

Granted, Winter's technical terminology can make it difficult for people to get their arms around these important concepts. A recent book by Dr. Angie Ward proposes a new term for sodalities, labelling them "missional extensions."[3] Hopefully, that may catch on, but for our purposes in this chapter, we will use the original technical terms employed by Winter in his 1973 address and subsequent paper.

Historically, two of the major Christian traditions – Eastern Orthodoxy and Roman Catholicism – got it right and captured this fundamental structural dynamic. Unfortunately, the Protestants, in reaction to the Catholics, threw the baby out with the bathwater during the Reformation, denying the validity of the Catholic missionary and monastic orders. This structural blindness was one of the great shortcomings of the Reformation, and it took almost three centuries for correctives to be introduced. William Carey earned the title "Father of Modern Missions" because – with great difficulty – he, along with some others, reintroduced this structural necessity into the Protestant world.

However, throughout the centuries since Carey's time, Protestants too often have been handicapped with this inadequate and deficient ecclesiology born out of the Reformation. To this day, this deficiency continues to stymie effective missionary efforts. This tendency to deny the legitimacy of the sodality – which is sometimes labelled "the supremacy of the church local" – has consistently hindered the capacity of Protestant leaders and organizations to fulfill Christ's Great Commission.

All the leadership development strategies and leadership theories in the world will ultimately fall short without an ecclesiology that places equal value on both the church local (modalities) *and* the church mobile or the church sent (sodalities). This structural imperative is foundational to the Church of the future as it engages with a world in increasing chaos and disruption.

---

2. Blinco.
3. Angie Ward, *The Whole Church for the Whole World*.

What We Know[4]

We know that modalities are
- designed to conserve fruit and new ground;
- inclusive;
- a place where pastors and teachers thrive;
- structured primarily for nurture and care;
- multigenerational;
- made up of "first-decision" people (trust Jesus and belong) who are difficult to discipline;
- effective – and responsible – for near-neighbour evangelism;
- occasionally able to multiply in an near-neighbor context, most often when a local church plants another local church;
- able to last for five generations in their average life cycle; and
- designed to build, establish, and preserve.

We know that sodalities are
- task-oriented, mobile, and flexible;
- adept at taking new ground;
- designed to cross-cultural, linguistic, social, and geographic barriers;
- made up of ministry specialists, where apostolic leaders thrive;
- narrow in focus;
- often transdenominational and multidenominational;
- made up of "second-decision" people, who are not only committed to Christ (first decision) but who share a second vocational commitment to others and organisations of specific calling,[5] such as Catholic orders and Protestant missionary societies, where discipline is more easily exercised.
- able to have extended generational life cycles and are more easily renewed; and
- inherently entrepreneurial and nimble.

---

4. For a more in-depth treatment of the structural realities of modalities and sodalities, see Metcalf, *Beyond the Local Church*. For a more academic treatment, see Blincoe, *New Social Contract*.

5. See Ralph Winter's *Two Structures of God's Redemptive Mission* for a more detailed explanation of this reality.

Leadership Implications

- Effective leaders in modalities and sodalities are not easily interchangeable.
- Effective leadership development does not ensure fruitfulness unless those leaders are positioned in structures where they can flourish.
- To thrive in either a modality or a sodality, those who lead must know their own giftedness and know in which structure they best fit.
- Leaders must be able to operate and minister *in their proper lane* – that is, where role and giftedness are well aligned.
- In reality, many personnel conflicts are, at their core, structural deficiencies that paralyze good people and waste valuable human resources.
- Without identifying and developing leaders (positioned in the appropriate structures), movements[6] of the gospel inevitably flounder and may even implode.

Organizational Implications

- Whenever and wherever there are genuine "movements" of the gospel – not just church planting or evangelism – there are *always* sodality people and often sodalic organizations in the mix.
- Whether in revivals, awakenings, people movements, or in contemporary church planting movements (CPMs) or disciple making movements (DMMs), throughout every era of the broader Christian movement, sodalic people have played critical entrepreneurial roles.
- In movements, sodality people act as catalysts, as "spark plugs" to ignite and launch such movements. They are *always* present but not always obvious.
- Modalities – local congregations and parishes – rarely reproduce or multiply. They are not designed by God to do so. They are primarily conservation and nurture structures. When multiplication does take place, it is normally in near-neighbour contexts and rarely cross linguistic, cultural, social, or geographic barriers.

---

6. By "movements" we mean, when the good news of Jesus spreads contagiously through a network of social relationships whereby many people become committed followers of Jesus and groups of these disciples rapidly multiply. Such movements have the potential to radically impact whole towns, cities, and nations.

- Historically, spirituality and spiritual vitality have flowed from the sodalities into the modalities.
- The mechanisms of discipline are different in each structure because of the sociological distinction between first- and second-decision people.
- For the overall Christian movement to thrive, there must be mutual understanding and appreciation of the strengths and capabilities of each of these God-designed structures.

A Case Study

Together, we have been privileged to participate in and observe an unprecedented move of God that is sweeping the Levant, North Africa, and migrant populations in Europe. During the past three decades, more people in these regions have decided to become followers of Jesus than during the preceding six hundred years. This move of God is astonishing and remarkable, something that both of us never thought we would witness in our lifetimes.

The sodalic organization that Nadim leads – NEO Leaders – has been at the forefront of this unprecedented harvest in twenty-nine nations. In early 2023, NEO reported that the number of individuals who had participated in Discovery Bible Studies (DBS) during the past decade had passed the one-million mark, with such participation taking place in over fifty thousand such groups.[7] NEO Leaders has quietly mobilized over two hundred full-time missionaries in these regions and works with over eight thousand bi-vocational volunteers.

In each and every setting in these scores of nations and dozens of cultures and subcultures – with their wide variety of socioeconomic and linguistic distinctives – these realities of modality and sodality relationships have been proven true over and over again.

What We Have Experienced

In the initial stages of the gospel movements in these regions, both labour and leaders for these movements came from modalities. These were usually

---

7. There are many other metrics that could be cited – for example, the estimated number of people who have decided to follow Jesus, the number of groups that multiply, how many times they have multiplied, and the corresponding results that permeate the social settings of each.

discontented apostolic pioneers, who had been frustrated in local church settings, and were "outward focused" and longing for more.

These pioneers were then placed directly into the harvest, developing relationships with people far from God using a simple Discovery Bible Study (known as DBS in the world of missions) as the primary tool of engagement.

Initially, the greatest opposition and criticism of these nascent movements came from pastors and leaders of existing churches and institutions. These leaders felt threatened for a variety of reasons, mainly because these sodalic pioneers were reaching people whom these pastors had feared and had never dreamed would be responsive to the good news. There was some professional jealousy. There was also the fear that these DBS groups would veer off into heresy and that ordinary people could not read and obey the Bible so easily. And these critics were pastoring churches that were rarely open or hospitable to new followers of Jesus.

As a sodality, we worked hard, from the beginning, not to ignore or dishonour the local church in word, deed, or thoughts. After about year five, when these movements began to take off and the results became recognizable, there was a softening in the pastors' attitudes of suspicion and opposition. Since the harvest was undeniable, they began to ask how their churches and their people could avail themselves of such ministry processes and growth.

Gradually, partnerships began to emerge, based on mutual respect and understanding of the unique characteristics and contribution of each ministry structure. When people began to follow Jesus, some were absorbed into existing churches for a variety of reasons. But overall, existing churches did not tend to be hospitable to an influx of "outsiders."

Consequently, the DBS groups most often evolved into new church expressions. This is understandable since DBS groups, properly created, have the essential functions of a healthy local church embedded in them from the very beginning, even before participants embrace Jesus and decide to follow him.

As these gospel movements gained traction and groups multiplied, there was a distinct shift in the source of leadership. We saw leaders begin to emerge and multiply *from* the harvest. It was overwhelmingly true that these leaders were not developed in classrooms but, rather, non-formally and relationally through on-site mentoring and apprenticeship. Training was just-in-time, and transformation took place by the quality and intensity of life-on-life exposure.

Faithfulness and fruitfulness were the guiding qualifications for identifying, choosing, and stewarding these emerging leaders.

In the regions where the NEO works, institutional religion plays an oversized role in everyday life. Religious affiliation is listed on identity cards, and matters such as where one lives, how one votes, and which courts one is able to access are all determined by religion. And the religious bodies that have "official" recognition are usually the long-standing traditional churches. Out of sheer necessity, mission, NGO, relief and development, and educational sodalities are compelled to relate, in one way or another, to these official church organizations for covering, protection, and legitimacy. So, the synergy and interdependency between sodalities and modalities in the region are, to some degree, forced because of these legalities. Such interdependency may not always be healthy, but it is necessary.

The effective synergy and partnerships that have begun to grow between these sodalities and modalities exhibit the following characteristics:

- One or more visionary pastors, unthreatened by apostolic people and sodalic organizations, often stepped forward to cooperate.
- These pastors invited collaboration. They longed to see their own people mobilized to effectively reach people who were far from God.
- These pastors were not afraid of outcomes that were more "kingdom" than "my local congregation." They accepted the fact that the fruit may not all flow into their pews and that new expressions of the church would emerge.
- Such cooperation was rarely a programme or a congregation-wide effort.
- In each congregation, this involved identifying a small cadre of appropriately gifted and called people who were open to receive training and responsive to accountability.
- Nadim and his leaders have been adamant that these leaders, drawn from their respective congregations, must be overseen by him and his team. Consequently, they could choose and dismiss leaders as they saw fit.
- Those chosen were often outside the existing leadership structures of the local congregation. Just because someone was an "elder" or held an institutional leadership role did not mean that they were qualified for this ministry initiative. Wholly different criteria were used for leadership selection.
- In some situations, demographics played a distinct role in this recruitment process. While respecting the positions of older generations in these cultural settings, responding specifically to the

tsunami of youth meant recruiting those who were able to relate effectively to this group.
- Nadim and his teams simultaneously and consistently served the broader constituency of the local congregations, providing training events and other outside stimulus that could add value to pastors and their flocks.
- Resisting pressures to produce quick results, Nadim adopted a "go slow to go fast" approach.
- Building a solid leadership foundation was essential to accommodate the exponential growth that was to occur in succeeding years.

In the Final Analysis

Nadim is fond of saying that in these regions of the world, we are "just chasing God and what he is doing" and we are always playing "catch up." We find that such movements of the good news are uncontrollable. They are messy. They are vivid, real-life examples of how the Spirit blows wherever he pleases (John 3:8).

So, does this mean that God does not bless or work apart from these structural dynamics? Obviously, not. God can do whatever he pleases. But working through these heaven-designed structural paradigms – which have been illuminated biblically, demonstrated historically, and tested missiologically – aligns us more intentionally with God's plans and purposes. Our chances of effectiveness grow exponentially. We cannot help but believe that it gives God great pleasure to see us "getting it" in relation to what partnership with him and with each other really means and can accomplish.

We would be remiss if we did not reflect on the deeply spiritual and supernatural dimension of these structural and leadership realities. All the structures can be in place and all the leadership training delivered, but the wisdom of Psalm 127:1 – "Unless the Lord builds the house, the builders labour in vain" – remains true at all times and in every situation. Even when we, in our fallen humanity, fail to get things right, it is astonishing how accommodating and forgiving the Triune God can be as he brings eternal results and even beauty out of our inadequacies.

We are also acutely aware that these remarkable outcomes are a direct result of the decades of prevailing prayer that have been poured out for these regions and these people groups. The cause and effect are clear. We can safely say that where these gospel movements are occurring today – and, we would argue, have occurred throughout history – the manifest presence of the Holy Spirit is overwhelming and obvious. The supernatural breaks into the natural, and there are signs and wonders not unlike in the book of Acts – physical healing, dealing with the demonic, angelic visitations, dreams and visions, and so on. The supernatural is normalized. Expected. Embraced.

What this means, in the final analysis, is that organizational health and capacity and the development of effective leadership for the *Missio Dei* is essentially a deeply spiritual undertaking. It is the grand work of the Spirit of God in the present age.

May the Lord of the harvest give us eyes to see how we should go about reaping the harvest and a deeper understanding of the structures that he has so graciously designed for that divine undertaking.

Bibliography

Blincoe, Robert Alan. *A New Social Contract Relating Missions Societies to Ecclesiastical Structures*. Pasadena: William Carey, 2012.

Metcalf, Sam. *Beyond the Local Church: How Apostolic Movements Can Change the World*. Downers Grove: InterVarsity Press, 2016.

28

Looking to the Future: Lausanne 4/Seoul 2024[1]

Joseph W. Handley and David W. Bennett

The stage is being set for an unprecedented convergence of faith, mission, and leadership as we prepare to gather in South Korea for the Fourth Lausanne Congress on World Evangelization, also known as Seoul 2024. The Fourth Lausanne Congress is far more than just an event. It is a multi-year process, engaging leaders around the globe via listening calls, regional gatherings, and an ongoing virtual platform. It is poised to be a beacon of hope for a world that is hungry for unity, collaboration, and impactful leadership in global mission.

Unveiling the Vision

In 2023, the Lausanne Movement – a movement that is steeped in history as a vanguard for global mission – was stirred anew by an announcement by Michael Oh, its global executive director. From the Incheon campus of the Onnuri Community Church, Oh's words came ringing across continents, resonating with the pulse of thousands of key influencers. The stage was being set to mark a pivotal moment as South Korea, together with Japanese and other Asian Lausanne leaders, prepared to host the fiftieth anniversary celebration of Lausanne's inception.

---

1. This article was adapted from several key documents in preparation for the Lausanne 4/Seoul Congress:
   https://lausanne.org/l4/global-listening/the-evangelical-church-interacting-between-the-global-and-the-local.
   https://lausanne.org/about/blog/why-seoul-2024.

> Lausanne 4 is a multi-year, global, polycentric process facilitated by the platform of Lausanne, towards catalytic collaboration of the global church, for the discipling of all nations and the shaping of the world in 2050.
>
> Michael Oh

Lausanne 4: A Journey of Listening, Gathering, and Action

Behind the scenes, a multi-year, global initiative, Lausanne 4 (L4), had already been unfolding. This was not a single event but a process. This was not just about the Congress itself but about a journey – a rhythm of listening, gathering, and taking action. The L4 journey, encapsulated in ongoing cycles of engagement and reflection, was aimed at catalyzing collaboration across the global church. Its focus was clear: to disciple nations and shape the world by 2050.

Listening groups were formed within issue networks and regions to learn about the critical gaps we face in world evangelization today. Twelve regional meetings were held with evangelical leaders from each region, and a further twenty-four meetings – comprising twenty-three issue networks and the Younger Leaders Generation (YLGen) network – were also held. These meetings, held virtually, took place between September 2020 and July 2021, a time when churches and organizations were heavily impacted by the COVID-19 pandemic.

Each group interacted with the same five questions:

- What are the most significant gaps or remaining opportunities toward the fulfilment of the Great Commission?
- What promising breakthroughs or innovations do you see that can accelerate the fulfilment of the Great Commission?
- In what areas is greater collaboration most critical in order to see the fulfilment of the Great Commission?
- Where is further research needed?
- To whom else should we be listening as part of this process?

Throughout 2023, regional meetings were held all over the world preparing for L4, exploring the issues identified in the listening calls and highlighting the key gaps that needed to be addressed. In addition, interviews were conducted with researchers and specialists across the globe to identify trends and issues that would be especially important for the church to address in the decade ahead. A *State of the Great Commission* report was released, written by nearly 150 authors selected from across all twelve Lausanne regions, focusing on thirty-nine challenges and opportunities impacting all regions and all sectors of the church, parachurch and mission organizations, the workplace, and society at large.

From these thirty-nine issues, twenty-five were selected for special focus during Seoul 2024. The number twenty-five represented the number of large breakout spaces available at the Seoul 2024 venue, and the twenty-five issues were chosen for their suitability for innovative design thinking leading to collaborative action. The following framework was used to determine the top twenty-five issues:

1. The issue is globally significant, not just regional.
2. The issue is dynamically shaping our world through 2050.
3. In general, the global church does not have many organizations focusing its efforts on the issue.
4. The issue is conducive to collaboration and design thinking.
5. The issue is a cross-disciplinary concern and would benefit from a variety of voices.

None of these twenty-five issues are single advocacy issues but, rather, complex challenges that require integrated reflection and action.

The Architecture of Seoul 2024

Seoul 2024 will not be confined within the walls of physical presence; instead, its reach will extend to a polycentric framework, beckoning the entire world into the process. The Congress is designed with inclusivity at its core – blending physical and virtual participation, inviting a diverse array of voices, with intentional representation from men and women of various age groups, regions, languages, and professional backgrounds.

Virtual Engagement: Extending the Reach

The virtual facet of Seoul 2024 stands as a gateway that bridges distances and breaks down barriers. Through this immersive experience, participants will not just be spectators but active contributors, fostering connections, sharing insights, and collectively brainstorming solutions. Both on-site and virtual participants are presently engaging in an eleven-month preparatory process of reading, viewing, and interaction around carefully curated pre-Congress content. During the week of Seoul 2024, virtual participants will have the opportunity to view the plenary sessions online and to engage in their own virtual table groups and collaborative sessions. In addition, an innovative satellite site initiative will expand the impact of the Congress even further, making it accessible to millions globally as they gather across thousands of sites to view and discuss selections from the plenary sessions.

Thus, even those who are not on-site in Seoul during the September 2024 gathering will have an important voice and will be able to contribute by participating in the virtual process. All these voices and ideas will be included as we seek to tackle these twenty-five areas together as a global church. And all who affirm *The Lausanne Covenant* and share the Lausanne spirit are invited to participate in the Collaborative Action Teams that are addressing these important issues of our day.

Collaborative Action: From Vision to Action

The heartbeat of Seoul 2024 is in catalyzing collaborative action. It is not just about listening to plenary presentations or even about discussing those presentations in table groups; rather, it is about rolling up our sleeves and delving into the twenty-five "gaps" in global mission – addressing challenges, crafting strategies, and committing to collaborative initiatives aimed at fulfilling the Great Commission.

These are the twenty-five gap issues that will be central to the innovation design and collaborative action sessions at Seoul 2024. Each issue will be supported by insights from the *State of the Great Commission* report and considered in terms of implications for the church, the parachurch and mission organizations, and various sectors of the workplace.

> REACHING PEOPLE | How Can Emerging Population Blocks Be Reached?
> 1. The Global Aging Population
> 2. The New Middle-Class
> 3. The Next Generation
> 4. Islam
> 5. Secularism
> 6. Least Reached People
>
> MINISTRY IN A DIGITAL AGE | What Is Ministry in a Digital Age?
> 7. Scripture in a Digital Age
> 8. Church Forms in a Digital Age

9. Discipleship in a Digital Age
10. Evangelism in a Digital Age

UNDERSTANDING HUMANNESS | What Does It Mean to Be Human?
11. AI and Transhumanism
12. Sexuality and Gender
13. Wholistic Health

POLYCENTRIC MISSIONS | What Is Polycentric Mission?
14. Polycentric Missions
15. Polycentric Resource Mobilization

MISSION & HOLINESS | How Can Spirituality and Holiness Define Missions?
16. Integrity and Anti-Corruption
17. Integrated Spirituality and Mission
18. Developing Leaders of Character

BEARING WITNESS WITHIN COMMUNITIES | What Is Community?
19. People on the Move
20. Urban Communities
21. Digital Communities
22. Ethnicism and Racism

SOCIETAL INTERACTION | What Is the Influence on Society?
23. Christianity, Radical Politics, and Religious Freedom
24. Caring for Creation and the Vulnerable
25. Societal Trust and Influence of Christianity

Of course these twenty-five issues do not represent all the gaps, challenges, or topics that bear on the fulfilment of the Great Commission in various regions of the world. But they represent topics where deeper reflection, better planning, and more concerted collaborative action is needed across the globe.

Post-Seoul: Nurturing the Flame

Lausanne is not just a one-off event; it is a spark, igniting a flame that burns beyond its closing. The post-Seoul phase, which will unfold as a strategic continuation, aims to nurture ideas, support initiatives, and sustain collaborative efforts, envisioning a sustainable strategy for mission beyond

2024. Additional regional and issue-focused gatherings will take place in 2025, and the next Lausanne Younger Leaders Gathering will be convened in 2026 – all with a view to responding to the challenges of our day and preparing for the mid-century mark of 2050, a generation from now.

The stage is set, the journey is being mapped out, and the torch of collaborative leadership will "pay it forward," igniting a flame that will illuminate the path towards a future where the vision of Lausanne – the gospel for every person, disciple-making churches for every people and place, Christlike leaders for every church and sector, and kingdom influence in every sphere of society – can be realized.

Through collaboration, we aim to build a transferable process to accelerate global mission. Through Spirit-filled and Spirit-guided conversation, fresh acts will arise. We are prayerfully seeking to mobilize and equip every on-site and virtual participant in the Congress to commit to collaborative action as part of a team – working together and taking wise action towards fulfilling the Great Commission alongside multiple people in the church, in parachurch organizations, and in the workplace to accomplish together what none of us could do alone.

Collaborative action is a process of reflective action to explain what is currently happening, discern what should be happening, prayerfully seek to close these "Great Commission gaps," and commit to a process of collaborative action through organic teams that will be consolidated post-Seoul 2024. We must move together to serve God's purposes by taking action as described below:

1. Prepare and train every Seoul 2024 participant with transferable tools and a collaborative design process to become reflective practitioners who work towards integrated solutions to key gaps in fulfilling the Great Commission.

2. Identify and form Collaborative Action Teams before, at, and beyond the Congress, with every participant positioned to commit to a collaborative missional process.

3. Accelerate global mission by helping intergenerational participants to move together in regions and Issue Networks or affinity groups, strengthening and yet mixing the silos of Lausanne's core structures.

This book is a key part of this process. Each chapter aligns within Lausanne's fourfold vision:

- The gospel for every person
- Disciple-making churches for every people and place
- Christlike leaders for every church and sector
- Kingdom influence in every sphere of society

The Leadership Development Issue Network identified each of these chapters (apart from the introductory section) as key components within this fourfold call. These are the primary gaps in the world today when it comes to developing leaders for the global church and mission. Our hope and plan is that each of them will complement these twenty-five issues through L4/Seoul 2024 and become Collaborative Action Teams post-Congress.

If you would like to participate in these teams to address any of these gaps, reach out to the co-catalysts and we will connect you with the relevant person.[2]

Bibliography

Bennett, David. "Why Seoul 2024?" *Lausanne Movement*, 1 September 2023. https://lausanne.org/about/blog/why-seoul-2024.

"The Evangelical Church Interacting between the Global and the Local." *Lausanne Movement*. https://lausanne.org/l4/global-listening/the-evangelical-church-interacting-between-the-global-and-the-local.

Ward, Angie. *The Whole Church for the Whole World*. Downers Grove: InterVarsity Press (prepublication form), 2024.

---

2. You can contact us here: https://lausanne.org/networks/issues/leadership-development.

Conclusion

A Pathway Forward

Joseph W. Handley, Gideon Para-Mallam, and Asia Williamson

Introduction

The Lausanne Movement, a significant force in global evangelicalism, has a rich history, many transformative moments, and an enduring impact. The first section of our book explores the origins, pivotal moments, key figures, and ongoing relevance of the Lausanne Movement, highlighting its contribution to leadership development, collaboration, diversity, and engagement in reaching the world for Christ. Divided into five sections, this book provides an in-depth analysis of the current realities for developing leaders, offering insights and key takeaways from each of the authors, who are outstanding mission leaders.

Four of the sections of this book come directly from the vision of the Lausanne Movement: "The gospel for every person, disciple-making churches for every people and place, Christlike leaders for every church and sector, and kingdom impact in every sphere of society."[1] And to fulfil this vision, we followed the Lausanne mission, "Connecting influencers and ideas for global mission."[2] Thus, the content of this book came directly from influencers in global mission who have connected and collaborated to focus on these four key focal points.

Section I: The Lausanne Movement

Our first section delves into the origins of the Lausanne Movement, tracing its roots to the convergence of various streams of mission and evangelicalism. Notably, this section highlights the influence of figures like William Carey,

---

1. https://lausanne.org/about.
2. https://kc4k.org/the-lausanne-movement-in-100-seconds-connecting-influencers-and-ideas-for-global-mission/.

who laid the groundwork for ecumenical mission conferences, including the Edinburgh 1910 World Missionary Conference. This conference played a vital role in inspiring the Lausanne Movement, emphasizing world evangelization. However, the true watershed moment occurred in 1974 at the Lausanne Congress on World Evangelization – commonly known as Lausanne '74. This event – with its diverse spectrum of evangelical participants and the creation of *The Lausanne Covenant* – united evangelicals worldwide and introduced new missiological paradigms. Despite challenges during the "Quiet Years," the Lausanne Movement was revitalized through the Cape Town 2010 Congress, bringing together a new generation of leaders and fostering collaboration among different groups within the Lausanne Movement. Today, *The Lausanne Covenant*, *The Manila Manifesto*, and *The Cape Town Commitment* are vital documents that influence and shape the course of mission endeavour.

Section II: The Gospel for Every Person

"The gospel for every person" emphasizes the universal reach of the mission of God. The Lausanne Movement is dedicated to spreading the gospel to every individual, regardless of their location, culture, or background. Our aim is to ensure that every person has the opportunity to hear and respond to the message of Jesus Christ.

Thus, our second section focuses on leadership development strategies for effectively spreading the gospel to unreached people and places. Our colleagues highlight the importance of leadership in reaching the unreached and address challenges for mission and the global church. They stress the importance of cultivating leaders with qualities such as a shepherd's heart, a servant attitude, and responsible stewardship, who are capable of engaging with diverse cultures and prioritizing the mission of spreading the gospel to the least reached of our world. Additionally, they explore the significance of nurturing and learning from new believers, adopting an incarnational ministry style and developing outward-looking leaders within the church. This section also examines the transformative impact of digital technology on global missions, emphasizing the need for a balance between digital outreach and incarnational ministry.

Section III: Disciple-Making Churches for Every People and Place

"Disciple-making churches for every people and place" underscores the importance of establishing and nurturing churches within every cultural and ethnic group worldwide. The vision is to inspire the creation of local Christian communities that effectively share the gospel and contribute positively to their respective cultural contexts.

With this in mind, our third section probes crucial themes of collaboration and innovation in mission. This section emphasizes that collaboration is paramount in fulfilling the Great Commission and advocates for effective cooperation between leaders, networks, and organizations. Our colleagues address silo thinking and the need for collaborative leadership, promoting fresh expressions of church, empowering women in ministry and leadership, and magnifying unheard voices. This section also explores the response to persecution and the need for faithfulness amid trials.

Section IV: Christlike Leaders for Every Church and Sector

"Christlike leaders for every church and sector" focuses on developing leaders who embody the character and ministry of Jesus Christ. This involves leadership development, spiritual and character formation, equipping for ministry, contextual leadership, multiplication of leaders, global collaboration, and diversity in leadership. These leaders play a pivotal role in the spiritual growth and health of the church.

Our fourth section thus explores the evolving landscape of global mission and the importance of inclusive leadership development. Our authors advocate for leadership development across all sectors of society, recognizing the changing global dynamics and the need to mobilize the whole church to fulfil the Great Commission. This section highlights the significant contributions of women in missions, emphasizes the need to listen to marginalized voices within the church, and underscores the importance of faithfulness in responding to contemporary challenges such as persecution.

Section V: Kingdom Impact in Every Sphere of Society

"Kingdom impact in every sphere of society" emphasizes the role of believers and churches in influencing all aspects of society. This vision calls for comprehensive engagement in areas such as social justice, ethics, cultural engagement, faith in the workplace, collaboration, prayer, cultural relevance, and transformational discipleship. It seeks to bring the values and principles of God's kingdom into every facet of life, promoting positive change and a redemptive impact in the world.

Our fifth section explores the multifaceted aspects of leadership development and engagement in the modern world. Our colleagues underscore the importance of leadership in both traditional ministry and the broader public sphere, advocating for a holistic approach to leadership that impacts all facets of life. They address the need to accelerate leadership development in the context of global missions, the identification and development of leaders within unknown movements, and the structural paradigm of modalities and sodalities in missions and leadership. This section also explores the impact of nationalism on politics, religion, and missions, urging leaders to navigate nationalism effectively while prioritizing global Christian unity.

The Future: Lausanne 4/Seoul 2024

The final chapter discusses the upcoming Fourth Lausanne Congress on World Evangelization, Seoul 2024, and its significance in the context of global faith, mission, and leadership. Seoul 2024 represents a multi-year process aimed at fostering unity, collaboration, and impactful leadership in global mission. This chapter outlines the Lausanne 4 journey of identifying key issues and sets the stage for addressing these issues through collaborative action during the Congress and beyond. It also emphasizes the importance of polycentrism and the virtual component in engaging a diverse range of voices and fostering connections. Ultimately, the goal is to accelerate global mission and fulfil the Great Commission by working together across various sectors.

Principles Learned about Global Mission Leadership

Effective mission leadership is essential for guiding individuals and communities towards spiritual growth, social transformation, and movements for Christ worldwide. Such leadership is rooted in a set of foundational principles that provide a solid framework for shaping leaders' character, values, and actions. In this book, we have explored these foundational principles and their significance in nurturing leaders who can make a positive impact on the world.

Leadership Foundations: At the core of effective mission leadership lies a set of principles that are grounded in biblical authority and kingdom-centred leadership. These principles emphasize the importance of aligning leadership values with God's word and his purposes. Leaders are called to prioritize a Christ-centred and mission-centric approach, embracing change as they learn from the past and draw inspiration from role models who have exemplified these principles in their lives. Moreover, leaders must possess a deep understanding of the fundamental concepts that drive their faith, ensuring clarity in their beliefs and actions. They should be adaptable and open to the changing dynamics of the world, and be able to use storytelling and biographies as tools for imparting wisdom and insight.

Leadership Values: Leadership values form the moral and ethical compass by which effective mission leaders navigate their lives and ministries. These values encompass a focus on spiritual maturity and the multiplication of leaders who empower others to succeed. Since authenticity and vulnerability are key, leaders must align their behaviours with their values to foster trust and credibility. Discipleship, which plays a crucial role in nurturing the next generation of leaders, must emphasize inclusivity and gender equality. Leaders must be unwavering in their faith, exhibiting faithfulness amid adversity and integrating their faith into all aspects of life. This integration bridges the sacred-secular divide and is a powerful example for others to follow.

Leadership Collaboration: Collaboration lies at the heart of effective mission leadership. Since leaders recognize that working in isolation limits their impact, they are intentional about seeking to collaborate and to avoid a silo mentality. They embrace flexibility and openness, focusing on the bigger picture and inspiring others through mentorship and support. Leaders build connections across generations and advocate for unity and solidarity within their communities. Empowering local leadership is a priority, and leaders understand the importance of developing leadership through relational and nonformal means. Prayerful leadership selection ensures that leaders are chosen with divine guidance, leading to a more effective and Spirit-filled leadership.

Spiritual Leadership: Spiritual leadership is characterized by servant-leadership, authenticity, and a commitment to spiritual disciplines. Leaders prioritize Christ, serving others, aligning their behaviours with their values, and demonstrating vulnerability. Spiritual disciplines – including prayer, solitude, intercession, and fasting – provide leaders with the spiritual nourishment they need to sustain their resilience. Accountability plays a crucial role in personal growth and development by holding leaders to high standards. Fidelity and marital integrity are emphasized to maintain personal integrity and effectiveness, while rest and Sabbath observance prevent burnout. Leaders are deeply rooted in their long-term purpose and calling, which provides the endurance needed to fulfil their ministry and leadership roles.

Leadership values, collaboration, spiritual leadership, and a Christ-centred life provide the solid foundation that underpins effective mission leadership. These principles guide leaders in their journey to become instruments of transformation and positive change, grounded in faith, values, and a commitment to serving others. By embracing these principles, leaders can inspire and empower those around them to pursue a deeper relationship with God, contribute to the betterment of society, and help fulfil the Great Commission. In doing so, they fulfil their divine calling and leave a lasting legacy of faith and transformation.

Conclusion

The Lausanne Movement stands as a beacon of global evangelization, rooted in history, shaped by pivotal moments, and committed to spreading the message of evangelism and social responsibility to the world. Its enduring legacy reflects its vital role in shaping global Christianity and its ongoing dedication to the Great Commission. The Lausanne Movement's impact extends beyond evangelism to encompass leadership development, collaboration, inclusivity, and engagement in Christian missions. Thus, our long-standing motto – "The Whole Gospel for the Whole World" – continues to be one of our rallying calls. Seoul 2024, the upcoming Congress, represents a continuation of this legacy and aims to address contemporary challenges and to empower leaders to fulfil the Great Commission in an ever-changing world.

We trust that this book will help to address many of the critical gaps in developing leaders for the Great Commission in the coming years. We hope that it will also serve as a catalyst to develop Collaborative Action Teams from the Seoul Congress to address these critical issues in the coming decades. If you would like to be involved in this endeavour, contact us at: https://lausanne.org/networks/issues/leadership-development.

We are accelerating mission together and are eager to see what God has in store for us through Seoul 2024 and beyond!

Contributor Biographies

Abigail Abok is a researcher and writer passionate about driving positive change, using writing to advocate for a more just and equitable world. As a team member of The Para-Mallam Peace Foundation in Nigeria, she works to advance the organization's objectives geared towards building sustainable peace.

Femi Adeleye is the Langham Preaching director for Africa. He is also the director of the Institute for Christian Impact, an initiative to nurture a new generation of leaders to impact Africa with kingdom values. Before this he served for three years as the director of church partnerships for World Vision International, focusing on enhancing World Vision's partnerships with churches around the world. Prior to joining World Vision, Femi worked for thirty-two years with the International Fellowship of Evangelical Students (IFES), as associate director for partnership and collaboration in his last years there.

Kiichi "Paul" Ariga is founding president of All Japan Revival Mission and global ambassador for A3/Japan. He is a renowned evangelist known for his exuberance, powerful testimony, and zeal for Christ. Formerly he was the president of Kansai Bible College, helping it to be one of the more fruitful pastor training centers in the country.

Ramez Atallah is senior advisor of the Bible Society of Egypt. He served on the first Lausanne Board from 1975 to 1994, then rejoined Lausanne in 2006 to chair the Program of the 2010 Cape Town Congress. He has BSc and MSW degrees from McGill University and an MDiv and DD from Gordon-Conwell Theological Seminary in Boston. He has been the general secretary of the Bible Society of Egypt (1990–2021), the Middle East and North Africa regional director for IFES (1980–1990), and the Quebec regional director for Inter-Varsity Canada.

Johnson Asare studied at Maranatha University College, Philippines Baptist Theological Seminary and Absury Seminary. He is the founder and executive director (emeritus) of Markaz Al Bishara (Centre of Good News), an NGO in Ghana that operates mission networks across Africa. He serves on several boards globally. He is an ordained minister with thirty-six years of experience in church planting, leadership development, community development, and business as mission practitioner.

Nana Yaw Offei Awuku is global director of Generations, Lausanne Movement, based in Ghana. Serving to connect influencers and ideas across generations to accelerate global mission. Nana was on staff with Scripture Union Ghana for over 20 years till 2017 and served on the senior management team as the director for field ministries.

David W. Bennett is a global associate director for the Lausanne Movement, providing strategic oversight to the global directors for Regions, Generations, Issue Networks, Collaboration, and Partnerships, having previously served as a youth worker, associate pastor, church planter, and as senior pastor of globally orientated churches in California, Oregon, and Massachusetts. He holds a BS from the Massachusetts Institute of Technology and MDiv, DMin, and PhD degrees from Fuller Theological Seminary.

Sarah Breuel is the founder and director of Revive Europe. Originally from Brazil and currently living in Rome, Sarah has worked for IFES for seventeen years in four national movements (Brazil, Canada, Norway, and Italy) and the European region for six years as evangelism training coordinator for IFES Europe. Included in Christianity Today's "33 under 33" list of leaders to watch, Sarah served as chair of the Lausanne Younger Leaders Gathering 2016. She has a business degree, an MDiv from Regent College, and serves globally in the Lausanne board of directors. Sarah is married to René. They have planted a vibrant church in Rome and have two boys, Pietro and Matteo.

Doug Birdsall is honorary chair for the Lausanne Movement, ambassador-at-large for A3 movement, serving on the board of directors for A3 and was president of A3 from 1991 to 2007. Prior to serving as Ambassador, Doug was the executive chairman for the Lausanne Movement.

Joshua Bogunjoko is a family physician, missionary, and past SIM international director. Prior to serving as a medical doctor, he was a leader in the evangelical student movement, the Nigeria Fellowship of Evangelical Students throughout his University days and was the National President of the Nigeria Christian Corpers Fellowship.

Eurico Buanaissa is general secretary of ABEMO.

Esther Chengo is the co-regional director for Lausanne Movement in English, Portuguese, and Spanish-speaking Africa. She is passionate about ministry, partnerships, and next-gen leadership.

Nadim Costa is from the Middle East and leads NEO Leaders, an agency committed to launching and multiplying movements of the gospel in the Levant, North Africa, and among migrant communities in Europe.

Jose L. Cruz is Spanish DMin coordinator at Dallas Theological Seminary and has served as a lead pastor in Central America, Latin America coordinator for a non-profit organization, cross-cultural church planter (Middle East, El Salvador, US), and seminary professor.

Brenda Darke promotes the inclusion of people with disabilities through written materials, teaching at the ESEPA seminary, collaborating with the Viva network for at risk children, mentoring, and through the Uno en Cristo (One in Christ) church-based support group for families.

C. J. Davison is head of strategic development at Union School of Theology in Wales to help take formal and non-formal theological education around the world. He serves with Lausanne Movement's younger leaders network, is the author of *Missional Friendships*, and writes at DelightinChrist.org.

Lars Dahle is professor of systematic theology (with a specialty in Christian apologetics) at NLA University College, Norway, and serves also as executive director of Damaris Norway. He was the lead editor of *The Lausanne Movement: A Range of Perspectives* (Regnum, 2014) and has been Lausanne catalyst for Media Engagement since 2013.

Prashan De Visser is Global Unites president and founder; a governing board member at Wesley College, Sri Lanka; council member at Colombo Theological Seminary; and a Colgate Rochester Crozer Divinity School visiting lecturer.

Jeyakaran Emmanuel co-founded the Powerhouse Churches in Chennai, India along with his wife Kavitha. He served with City to City India as national catalyst before coming on board recently with A3 as vice president for global ministry. He has a passion for networking across the body of Christ and has been involved with several networks including the GPro Commission, Movement Day, Chennai Transformation Network, and Asia CPX.

Kavitha Emmanuel is a social activist and pastor. She currently leads the Disruptive Women's network of Movement.org in South Asia. She also founded Women of Worth and the "Dark is Beautiful" campaign, which addresses the toxic effects of colourism. She has a doctorate in transformational leadership from the Bakke Graduate University.

Andrew Feng is director of global partnerships for Indigitous.org, an organization dedicated to driving innovation, developing the next generation, and fostering collaboration through Christian hackathons and cohort programmes. He provides strategic guidance to nonprofit organizations worldwide, leveraging his expertise in cultivating impactful partnerships.

Patrick Fung is global ambassador of OMF International (formerly the China Inland Mission). He formerly served as the general director of OMF International from 2005–2023, sharing the good news of Jesus Christ in all its fullness with East Asia's peoples. Patrick was formerly on the Lausanne Movement's international board and is currently the advisory team chair of Lausanne YLGen and the programme chair for the Fourth Lausanne Congress on World Evangelization.

Pearl Ganta is an accomplished independent filmmaker and global speaker, and has dedicated over two decades to media and missions, creating impactful content through her production company, Ur Vision Communications. She empowers the next generation through filmmaking training and advocates for women's leadership, community development, and child welfare, as a global catalyst with the Lausanne Movement and founder of the Apnao Foundation..

Joseph W. Handley has a PhD in intercultural studies from Fuller Theological Seminary, California, USA. He is the president and CEO of A3, a global network that accelerates church and marketplace leaders for mission movements. He serves as a global catalyst for leadership with the Lausanne Movement and as faculty for Fuller Seminary and the Oxford Centre for Mission Studies. He is the author of *Polycentric Mission Leadership* (Regnum, 2022).

Mary Ho is the international executive leader of All Nations, a global Christian missions organization with workers making disciples and church planting in over forty-five countries. She received her doctor of strategic leadership from Virginia Beach-based Regent University in 2016.

Jonah Jala is the global engagements lead for Indigitous. She is based in the Philippines and came to Christ when she was a freshman through a campus ministry. In our connected and digital world, Indigitous is a global movement taking the gospel to new people, new places, and new spaces. It means indigenous + digital and engages Christians to challenge what that means in their place and space then to champion it.

Rudolf Kabutz is a media research strategist at TWR Africa, specializing in future media perspectives and engaging media user communities. With a background in nuclear physics and strategic foresight, he supports global media collaboration to share the hope of the Gospel. He also acts as a catalyst for the Lausanne Media Engagement Network, promoting purposeful media engagement for societal transformation. His work empowers individuals to ask critical questions for exploring the future for action paradigm in the present.

Ken Katayama is a great commission influencer and an advocate for unreached people groups. He serves as the president and CEO of Crossover Global, which seeks to provide gospel access to unreached peoples of the world by planting multiplying churches. Ken resides in Columbia, South Carolina with his family.

Eraston Kighoma is the executive director of the Centre for Intercultural Missions and Research and also serves as a coordinator for the Democratic Republic of Congo with the Lausanne Movement's Creation Care Network. He teaches mission and intercultural studies in a variety of seminaries and universities. He is the author of *Church and Mission in the Context of War* (Langham Academic, 2021), for which he was awarded the first Research Prize for Intercultural Theology in 2022 by the German Association of Mission Studies. He is a co-author of "Living *the Gospel in Conflict Zones: God At Work in Eastern Congo*" (Lausanne Global Analysis, 2023).

Denise Lewis is a clinical psychologist. She has a BA from St. Georges University, Grenada, an MA from Jamaica Theological Seminary (1990), an MA (counseling/psychology) from Columbia International University (2001), and a PhD (clinical psychology) from Walden University (2020).

John Lewis is founder and director of The Grenada Institute for Theological Education. He holds a BA Jamaica Theological Seminary (1989), an MDiv Columbia International University (2000) and a DTL (doctor of transformational leadership) Bakke Graduate University (2023).

Laura B. Macias is director of missional engagement at Trinity United Presbyterian Church in Santa Ana, and a PhD candidate at Johnson University in Knoxville. She has served as a cross-cultural missionary with Mission Aviation Fellowship and an executive director with JOYA Scholars.

Idris Mammadov, from Azerbaijan, is a lawyer in civil law and has a Bachelor of Theology degree. He serves as executive vice president of Crossover Global and is the founder of the Alov church network.

Sam Metcalf led Novo, a North American based mission sending agency. Today, as president emeritus, he coordinates CoNext, a global partnership of like-minded sodalities committed to gospel movements.

Michael A. Ortiz is executive director of the International Council for Evangelical Theological Education and vice president for Global Ministries and professor of missiology and intercultural ministries, Dallas Theological Seminary. In 2015 he received his PhD from Seminario Teológico Centroamericano following his ThM from Dallas Theological Seminary in 2008.

Funmi J. Para-Mallam is professor of gender and development studies and senior fellow at the National Institute for Policy and Strategic Studies, Nigeria.

Gideon Para-Mallam is the president and CEO of The Gideon & Funmi Para-Mallam Peace Foundation, which advocates for the persecuted church. He is an ordained minister and has been involved in leadership with the International Fellowship of Evangelical Students and other organizations for over thirty years.

Jocabed Solano Miselis is directora de Memoria Indígena (director of Indigenous Memory) and a missionary at Unidos en Misión, and is from the Gunadule nation, an indigenous people group of Panama.

Evi Rodemann is a theologian and event manager from Germany who is passionate about encouraging and investing into younger leaders within the Lausanne Younger Leaders Initiative and through her organization LeadNow working across Europe. She currently serves as the congress event coordinator for the Fourth Congress and is finishing her PhD on long-lasting event impact.

Darío López is pastor of Iglesia de Dios del Peru, Lima, Peru (pastor with the Church of God of Peru in Lima, Peru), and has a PhD in theology from the Oxford Centre for Mission Studies and the Open University.

Janelle Stoops is co-director of Frontiers USA and has been involved in ministry among Muslims for the past twenty-five years. She served as a single woman and then wife and mother of young children in two pioneering locations. She is completing a master's in organizational leadership with a concentration in global leadership and communication and is passionate about seeing the gospel brought to the peoples and places with the least access.

Kohei Takeda is co-chair of Lausanne Movement Younger Leaders Generation for East Asia and Japan, and associate pastor for Japanese Language Ministries, Faith Bible Church, Seattle.

Peter Tarantal is an associate international director, OM global leadership team. Chair of the Majority World Christian Leaders Conversation, a group of leaders from Africa, Asia, Latin America and MENA, who serve as a think tank for the church and ministries in the Majority World.

Francis Tsui is an adjunct associate professor with the Institute of Faith & Global Engagement at the University of Hong Kong co-leading a Character Leadership Certificate Program for the undergraduates. Francis is currently on the global board of Galilean Movement; a member of the board of directors with A3 (formerly Asian Access); and a trustee with AsiaCMS. He was educated in multiple disciplines including history (MPhil and PhD), business administration (MBA), as well as intercultural leadership studies (MA and DMin).

Paul Turner is director of the Arrow Perú leadership programme and missionary with Latin Link in Peru working in the area of leadership development.

Asia Williamson has a DMin in global leadership from Asbury Theological Seminary, Kentucky, USA. She is co-founder of One Rock International and director of CWR Asia. She is a lecturer in leadership, apologetics and theology at Waverley Abbey and Westminster Theological Centre, UK, and has authored two biographies.

Mark Williamson is CEO of One Rock International, providing leadership training and coaching for Christians all over the world so they can start up or scale up mission projects. He also leads the Sanctuary Westminster missional community for young adults in central London and is the chair of Fresh Expressions UK.

Nick Wu is US director for Indigitous. His heart is to innovate new pathways for the next generation to collaborate with their digital and marketplace skills. He also has a passion for storytelling, producing and editing documentaries about global missions, and he is currently working on his MA in intercultural studies at Dallas Seminary.

Allen Yeh is formerly professor of intercultural studies and missiology at Biola University. He earned his BA from Yale, MDiv from Gordon-Conwell, MTh from Edinburgh, and DPhil from Oxford, and is the author of *Polycentric Missiology: 21st Century Mission from Everyone to Everywhere* (IVP, 2016), and co-editor (along with Tite Tienou, former dean of Trinity Evangelical Divinity School) of *Majority World Theologies: Theologizing from Africa, Asia, Latin America, and the Ends of the Earth* (William Carey, 2018).

Hwa Yung is bishop emeritus of the Methodist Church in Malaysia. Among his many roles, he has served as a pastor and bishop within the Methodist Church, and as principal of Malaysia Theological Seminary. He has also been involved with various international ministries, including as chair of the council of trustees for the Oxford Centre for Mission Studies, a member of the international board of the Lausanne Movement, and as President of IFES (2011–2019).

Langham Literature and its imprints are a ministry of Langham Partnership.

Langham Partnership is a global fellowship working in pursuit of the vision God entrusted to its founder John Stott –

to facilitate the growth of the church in maturity and Christ-likeness through raising the standards of biblical preaching and teaching.

Our vision is to see churches in the Majority World equipped for mission and growing to maturity in Christ through the ministry of pastors and leaders who believe, teach and live by the word of God.

Our mission is to strengthen the ministry of the word of God through:
- nurturing national movements for biblical preaching
- fostering the creation and distribution of evangelical literature
- enhancing evangelical theological education

especially in countries where churches are under-resourced.

Our ministry

Langham Preaching partners with national leaders to nurture indigenous biblical preaching movements for pastors and lay preachers all around the world. With the support of a team of trainers from many countries, a multi-level programme of seminars provides practical training, and is followed by a programme for training local facilitators. Local preachers' groups and national and regional networks ensure continuity and ongoing development, seeking to build vigorous movements committed to Bible exposition.

Langham Literature provides Majority World preachers, scholars and seminary libraries with evangelical books and electronic resources through publishing and distribution, grants and discounts. The programme also fosters the creation of indigenous evangelical books in many languages, through writer's grants, strengthening local evangelical publishing houses, and investment in major regional literature projects, such as one volume Bible commentaries like *The Africa Bible Commentary* and *The South Asia Bible Commentary*.

Langham Scholars provides financial support for evangelical doctoral students from the Majority World so that, when they return home, they may train pastors and other Christian leaders with sound, biblical and theological teaching. This programme equips those who equip others. Langham Scholars also works in partnership with Majority World seminaries in strengthening evangelical theological education. A growing number of Langham Scholars study in high quality doctoral programmes in the Majority World itself. As well as teaching the next generation of pastors, graduated Langham Scholars exercise significant influence through their writing and leadership.

To learn more about Langham Partnership and the work we do visit **langham.org**

www.ingramcontent.com/pod-product-compliance
Lightning Source LLC
Chambersburg PA
CBHW071954220426
43662CB00009B/1120